Great Thai Cooking

for my

American Friends

Creative Thai Dishes Made Easy

Yupa Holzner

Published by Royal House Publishing Co., Inc.
P.O. Box 5027
Beverly Hills, CA 90210
Printed in the United States of America
Library of Congress Catalog Card Number: 88-62141
ISBN: 0-930440-27-7

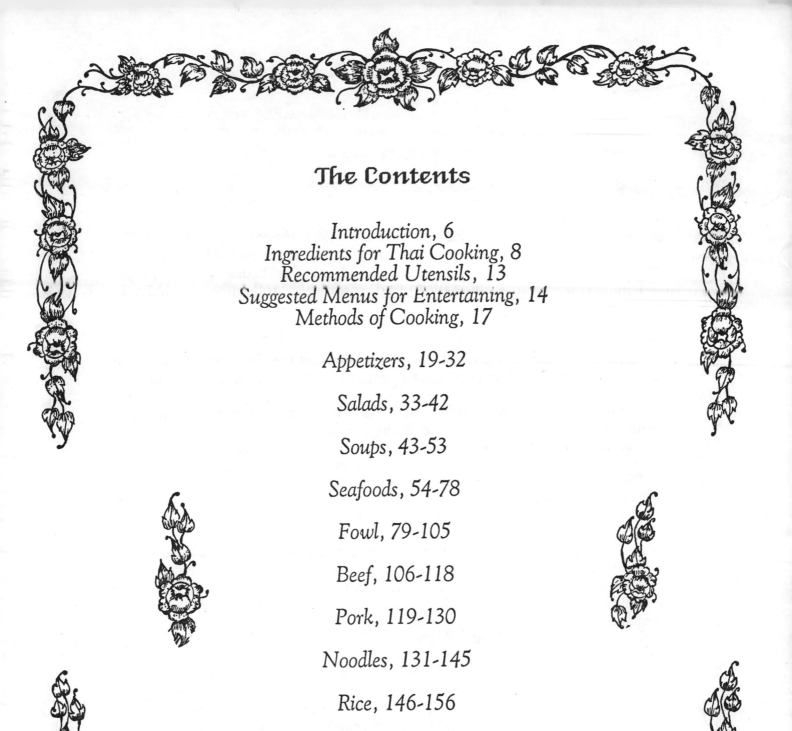

The Contents

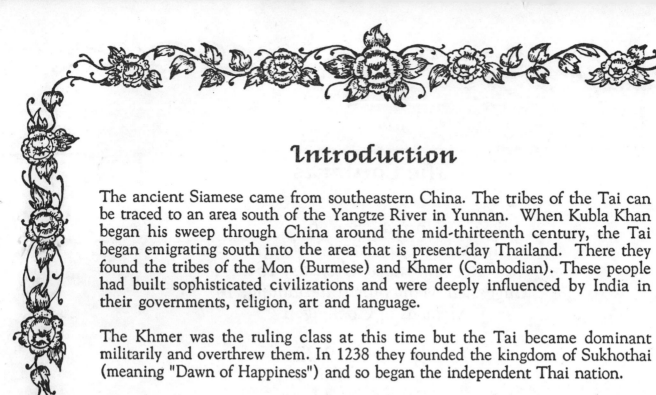

Introduction

The ancient Siamese came from southeastern China. The tribes of the Tai can be traced to an area south of the Yangtze River in Yunnan. When Kubla Khan began his sweep through China around the mid-thirteenth century, the Tai began emigrating south into the area that is present-day Thailand. There they found the tribes of the Mon (Burmese) and Khmer (Cambodian). These people had built sophisticated civilizations and were deeply influenced by India in their governments, religion, art and language.

The Khmer was the ruling class at this time but the Tai became dominant militarily and overthrew them. In 1238 they founded the kingdom of Sukhothai (meaning "Dawn of Happiness") and so began the independent Thai nation.

Sukhothai is a wonderful word to use in describing the origins of the country's varied and exciting cuisine. The foreign influences of Burma, Laos, India, China and Cambodia have enriched Thai cooking, but Thai food has its own character. Hot and spicy, sweet and sour, pungent and aromatic, Thai dishes titillate the palate with chili peppers, exotic curry mixtures and fragrant herbs and flavorings such as coriander (cilantro), lemon grass, mint, Laos root, tamarind and many you may not be familiar with.

Fruits and vegetables of the country are spectacular and bring exclamations of amazement from the newly-initiated. Durian, called the premier fruit in Thailand, and only grown on several provinces in the spring, is a truly incomparable experience in all its creamy, cheesy, almondy elegance. But prepare to have a clothespin for your nose, as the rind exudes a most unfortunate odor; never mind, it's worth it!

Vegetables, such as long green bean (Tuaphug Yoa), koa (Gratin) and cherry eggplant (Makeua Puong), eggplant, etc., are served raw and help to round out the flavors of a Thai meal. The Thai people like to have a representation of a number of different flavors to have good balance to the meal.

Barbecues are a very popular part of Thai cooking. Meats are marinated and spiced and roasted on skewers for the sate or roasted whole and served with intriguing sauces.

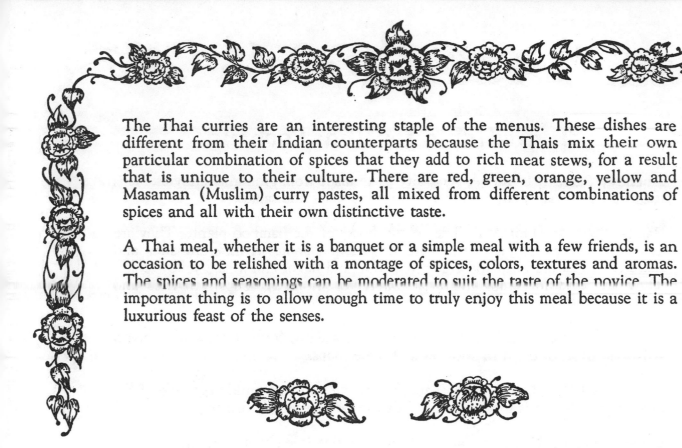

The Thai curries are an interesting staple of the menus. These dishes are different from their Indian counterparts because the Thais mix their own particular combination of spices that they add to rich meat stews, for a result that is unique to their culture. There are red, green, orange, yellow and Masaman (Muslim) curry pastes, all mixed from different combinations of spices and all with their own distinctive taste.

A Thai meal, whether it is a banquet or a simple meal with a few friends, is an occasion to be relished with a montage of spices, colors, textures and aromas. The spices and seasonings can be moderated to suit the taste of the novice. The important thing is to allow enough time to truly enjoy this meal because it is a luxurious feast of the senses.

About the Author

Yupa's love of her native cuisine began at an early age, preparing meals for her family. Born in the village of Phontong Roi-et (the Golden Hills), which is in the east of Thailand, she learned from her mother the preparation of the foods of her province and developed a keen interest in investigating and experimenting with Thai dishes.

Her family moved to Bangkok and she discovered different styles of Thai cooking involving different regional vegetables, spices and herbs. She learned of the many foreign influences that affect Thai cooking and has offered a varied and extensive collection of recipes, reflecting these influences, in her book to give the reader a true feeling of cooking and dining in Thailand.

Since coming to America, Yupa has taught Thai cooking for California State University in San Bernardino, California, Pierce College in Woodland Hills, California, The Learning Tree (an adult education center) and in her private cooking classes. She contributes regularly to newspapers and magazines such as Sunset.

Currently she is working on her latest cookbook and creating new recipes, with which she often delights her friends and business associates at her informal but sumptuous dinner parties at her home in Canyon Country, California.

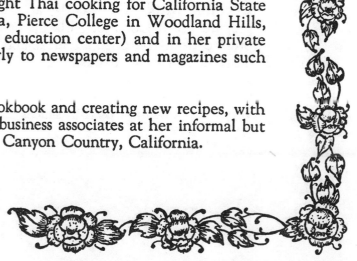

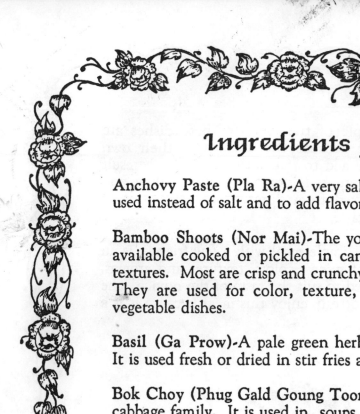

Ingredients for Thai Cooking

Anchovy Paste (Pla Ra)-A very salty paste made from ground anchovies. It is used instead of salt and to add flavor to some soups and salads.

Bamboo Shoots (Nor Mai)-The young shoots of the bamboo plant. They are available cooked or pickled in cans or jars and come in different sizes and textures. Most are crisp and crunchy with a mild flavor and a pale yellow color. They are used for color, texture, and flavor in many soups, stir-fries and vegetable dishes.

Basil (Ga Prow)-A pale green herb that has a light, fresh licorice-like flavor. It is used fresh or dried in stir fries and some soups.

Bok Choy (Phug Gald Goung Toong)-A white stemmed, mild vegetable of the cabbage family. It is used in soups, stir-fries and vegetable dishes.

Calrose Rice or Rice (Kao Jao)-A short-grain rice (see chapter on Rice).

Chantaboon Rice Sticks-A dried, clear noodle made from rice flour. They come in many different thicknesses and are used in Phat Thai and many other noodle dishes.

Chili Paste with Bean Oil (Nam Prik Pao)-A somewhat sweet, hot jam-like paste made from a combination of chiles. It is used to add spice and flavor to a large variety of dishes.

Chinese Broccoli (Ka Na)-A dark green vegetable that has a strong, almost bitter, flavor. Used in stir-fries, noodle and vegetable dishes. May be used in place of broccoli.

Cilantro (Chinese Parsley)-The leaves of the coriander plant look similar to parsley, but are not as curly. They have a strong, fresh coriander-like flavor and are used in a large variety of Oriental dishes.

Coconut Milk (Ga Tee')-Can be purchased in Thai markets. A recipe to prepare Fresh Coconut Milk appears in the Dessert chapter. Coconut milk is pressed from the coconut meat and is white and creamy. It is mostly used in desserts and curry dishes.

Crushed Red Chiles (Prik-Bod)-These dried, crushed chile pods and seeds are very hot. They are used in sauces and as a condiment to serve at the table.

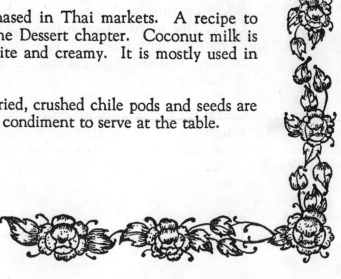

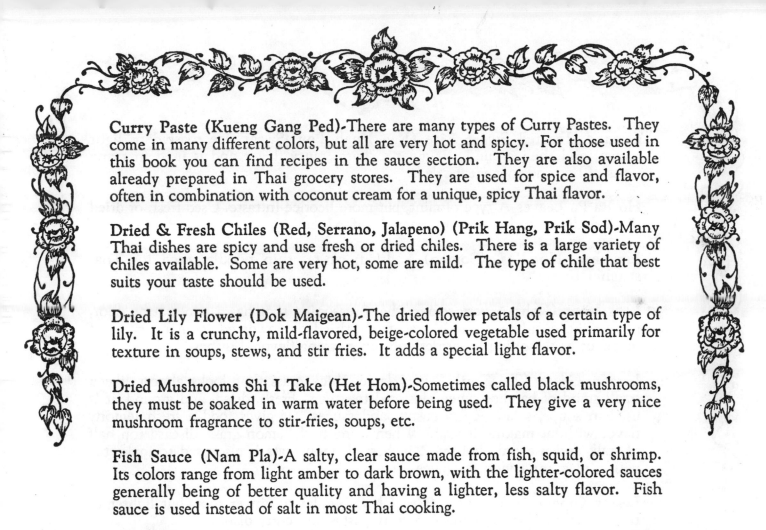

Curry Paste (Kueng Gang Ped)-There are many types of Curry Pastes. They come in many different colors, but all are very hot and spicy. For those used in this book you can find recipes in the sauce section. They are also available already prepared in Thai grocery stores. They are used for spice and flavor, often in combination with coconut cream for a unique, spicy Thai flavor.

Dried & Fresh Chiles (Red, Serrano, Jalapeno) (Prik Hang, Prik Sod)-Many Thai dishes are spicy and use fresh or dried chiles. There is a large variety of chiles available. Some are very hot, some are mild. The type of chile that best suits your taste should be used.

Dried Lily Flower (Dok Maigean)-The dried flower petals of a certain type of lily. It is a crunchy, mild-flavored, beige-colored vegetable used primarily for texture in soups, stews, and stir fries. It adds a special light flavor.

Dried Mushrooms Shi I Take (Het Hom)-Sometimes called black mushrooms, they must be soaked in warm water before being used. They give a very nice mushroom fragrance to stir-fries, soups, etc.

Fish Sauce (Nam Pla)-A salty, clear sauce made from fish, squid, or shrimp. Its colors range from light amber to dark brown, with the lighter-colored sauces generally being of better quality and having a lighter, less salty flavor. Fish sauce is used instead of salt in most Thai cooking.

Fresh Flat Rice Noodles (Guai Tiaw Sod)-A white, thick sheet of precooked noodle dough made from rice flour. They are cut into strips or chunks and used for stir fried noodle dishes and in some soups.

Fresh Mint Leaves (Saranea)-A green herb with wonderful minty aroma and taste. It gives a fresh minty flavor to stir-fries, soups, and hot and sour meat salads.

Fresh Yellow Egg Noodles (Ba Mee)-A fresh uncooked egg noodle made from wheat flour. It is used in a variety of vegetable and noodle dishes.

Ginger Root & Powdered (Keing)-The fresh tubers of the ginger plant are shaped like a hand with many fingers. They are light brown in color, and should be smooth and unwrinkled when fresh. Ginger root has a sharp, fresh flavor, and is a very popular Oriental seasoning, used fresh or ground in a large variety of dishes.

Ground Roasted Red Chiles (Prik Kuah Pon)-Dried serrano chiles roasted and then ground. Roasting the chile gives it a richer, fuller, almost nutty flavor. Ground roasted chile is very hot, and is used in a variety of hot and sour salads, soups, and some noodle dishes.

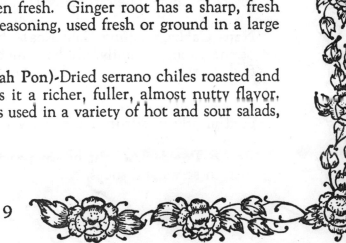

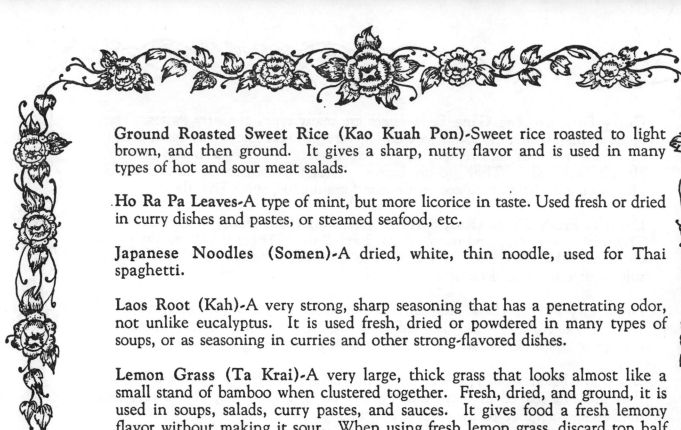

Ground Roasted Sweet Rice (Kao Kuah Pon)-Sweet rice roasted to light brown, and then ground. It gives a sharp, nutty flavor and is used in many types of hot and sour meat salads.

Ho Ra Pa Leaves-A type of mint, but more licorice in taste. Used fresh or dried in curry dishes and pastes, or steamed seafood, etc.

Japanese Noodles (Somen)-A dried, white, thin noodle, used for Thai spaghetti.

Laos Root (Kah)-A very strong, sharp seasoning that has a penetrating odor, not unlike eucalyptus. It is used fresh, dried or powdered in many types of soups, or as seasoning in curries and other strong-flavored dishes.

Lemon Grass (Ta Krai)-A very large, thick grass that looks almost like a small stand of bamboo when clustered together. Fresh, dried, and ground, it is used in soups, salads, curry pastes, and sauces. It gives food a fresh lemony flavor without making it sour. When using fresh lemon grass, discard top half of stalk and use only bottom 2 inches. Lemon grass is also used to make tea with a pleasant lemon fragrance.

Lesser Ginger or Rhizome (Gra Chai)-Similar to ginger root, but lighter in taste, it is used dried or fresh in curry pastes and curry dishes.

Maggi Seasoning-A strong dark brown sauce, similar in flavor to liquid bouillon concentrate.

Makrood Leaves and Rind-These small double leaves are shaped like a figure eight. They have a fresh fragrance much like lime. Makrood leaves have a slightly sour yet strong and pungent taste. They are used in soups. Thinly sliced leaves are used in all the different types of meat salads and curry pastes, etc.

Masaman Curry Paste-A roasted curry that is strong in flavor and very spicy.

Mung Bean Thread Noodles (Wun-Sen)-A clear, dried, thin noodle made from soy bean flour. Used in many Thai dishes.

Napa Cabbage (Phug Gald Koa)-This is a pale green, highly-bunched member of the cabbage family. It has crunchy thick leaves which are very light and fresh to the taste. It is used as a vegetable both steamed and raw.

Oyster Sauce (Nam Mun Hoi)-Thick sauce with a strong bouillon-like flavor, used mostly in stir-fry meat and vegetable dishes.

Pa Lo Powder-A light brown powder that is a mixture of many spices. It is used in stews and soups.

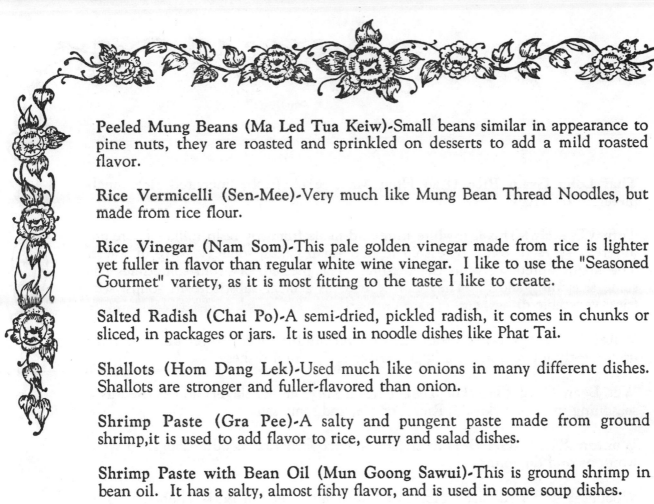

Peeled Mung Beans (Ma Led Tua Keiw)-Small beans similar in appearance to pine nuts, they are roasted and sprinkled on desserts to add a mild roasted flavor.

Rice Vermicelli (Sen-Mee)-Very much like Mung Bean Thread Noodles, but made from rice flour.

Rice Vinegar (Nam Som)-This pale golden vinegar made from rice is lighter yet fuller in flavor than regular white wine vinegar. I like to use the "Seasoned Gourmet" variety, as it is most fitting to the taste I like to create.

Salted Radish (Chai Po)-A semi-dried, pickled radish, it comes in chunks or sliced, in packages or jars. It is used in noodle dishes like Phat Tai.

Shallots (Hom Dang Lek)-Used much like onions in many different dishes. Shallots are stronger and fuller-flavored than onion.

Shrimp Paste (Gra Pee)-A salty and pungent paste made from ground shrimp, it is used to add flavor to rice, curry and salad dishes.

Shrimp Paste with Bean Oil (Mun Goong Sawui)-This is ground shrimp in bean oil. It has a salty, almost fishy flavor, and is used in some soup dishes.

Soy Bean Condiment (Tow Jiew Dom)-An Oriental seasoning of salted crushed soybean. Used instead of salt and to add flavor to stir-fried vegetables and steamed fish.

Soy Sauce, Light and Dark (Siew)-Light and dark soy sauce is used instead of salt and to add flavor to many Chinese-style dishes.

Spring Roll Skins (Paw Peea)-Flat, about 10 inches square, thin sheets of noodle dough. They are used to wrap Thai Egg Rolls and Spring Rolls.

Straw Mushrooms (Het Faing)-A mild-flavored Oriental mushroom widely available canned. They are used in a large variety of Oriental dishes. Canned button mushrooms can be used instead.

Sweet Rice (Sticky Rice) (Kao Niew)-Used as a finger food, and usually with barbecues. Also used in Papaya Salad.

Sweet Soy Sauce (Siew Khon Warn)-This thick, sweet, black soy sauce is used in some stir-fried noodle dishes.

Tamarind Sauce (Nam Makarm)-A tart juice made from the bean-like fruit of the Tamarind tree. It is used in many sweet and sour or hot and sour dishes. Lemon juice may be substituted.

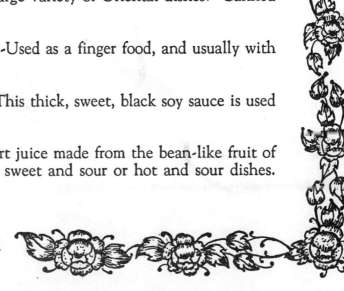

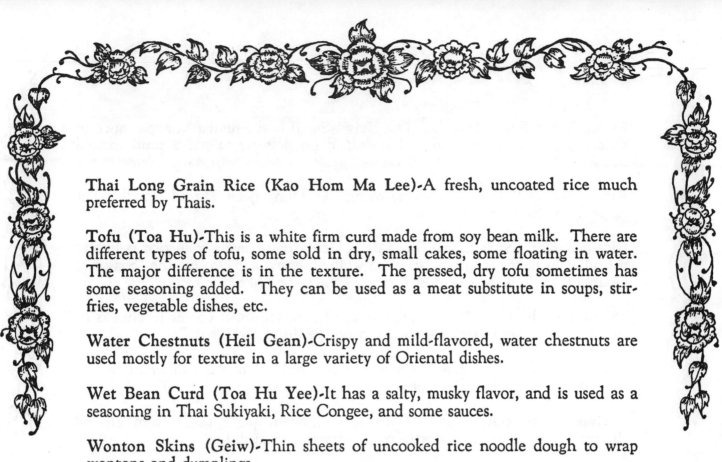

Thai Long Grain Rice (Kao Hom Ma Lee)-A fresh, uncoated rice much preferred by Thais.

Tofu (Toa Hu)-This is a white firm curd made from soy bean milk. There are different types of tofu, some sold in dry, small cakes, some floating in water. The major difference is in the texture. The pressed, dry tofu sometimes has some seasoning added. They can be used as a meat substitute in soups, stir-fries, vegetable dishes, etc.

Water Chestnuts (Heil Gean)-Crispy and mild-flavored, water chestnuts are used mostly for texture in a large variety of Oriental dishes.

Wet Bean Curd (Toa Hu Yee)-It has a salty, musky flavor, and is used as a seasoning in Thai Sukiyaki, Rice Congee, and some sauces.

Wonton Skins (Geiw)-Thin sheets of uncooked rice noodle dough to wrap wontons and dumplings.

Woodbear or Dried Black Fungus Mushrooms (Het Hu Nu)-When soaked in water, they expand to about 3 times their size. They have a crunchy texture and are used in soups and stir-fries, etc. Regular mushrooms may be substituted.

Yellow Bean Sauce (Tow Jiew Lueng)-Very similar in use to soy bean condiment, but more liquid.

Yellow Egg Noodles (Ba Mee)-Mostly used in noodle dishes.

(All these items may be purchased in most major supermarkets and in Oriental specialty markets.)

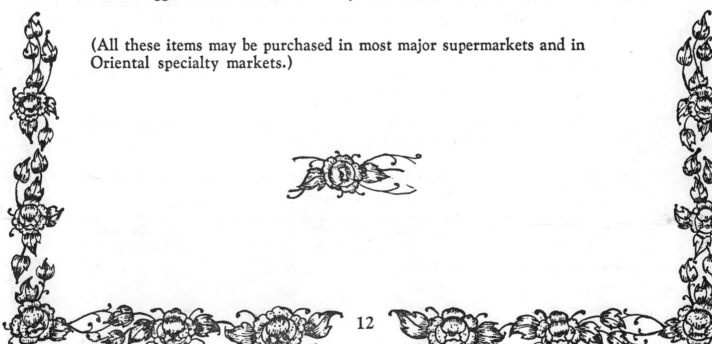

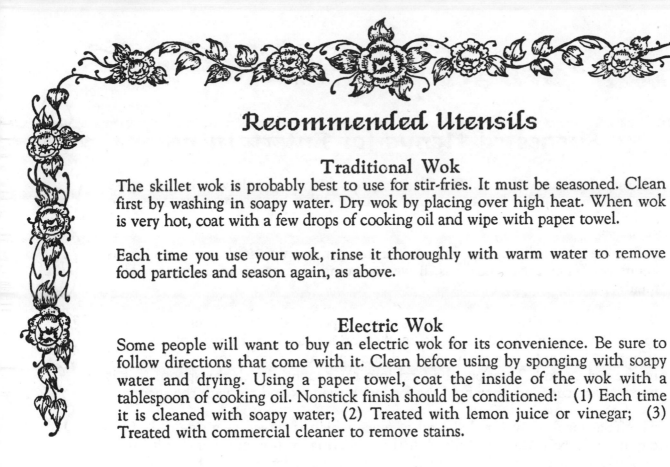

Recommended Utensils

Traditional Wok

The skillet wok is probably best to use for stir-fries. It must be seasoned. Clean first by washing in soapy water. Dry wok by placing over high heat. When wok is very hot, coat with a few drops of cooking oil and wipe with paper towel.

Each time you use your wok, rinse it thoroughly with warm water to remove food particles and season again, as above.

Electric Wok

Some people will want to buy an electric wok for its convenience. Be sure to follow directions that come with it. Clean before using by sponging with soapy water and drying. Using a paper towel, coat the inside of the wok with a tablespoon of cooking oil. Nonstick finish should be conditioned: (1) Each time it is cleaned with soapy water; (2) Treated with lemon juice or vinegar; (3) Treated with commercial cleaner to remove stains.

Cooking Tools

You will need certain tools for preparing the dishes. You should have wooden and smooth edge metal tools (spoons, ladels, skimmers, tongs and spatulas). Two long handled wooden spoons are suggested for stir frying. You will need a selection of knives for boning, chopping and slicing.

Steamers

It is a good idea to have a good steamer to cook fish, vegetables or sticky rice. There are a number of good steamers and electric steamers on the market and you will find them in any major department store, as well as Oriental specialty shops. You don't have to spend a lot of money to get a good one. Very basic ones work as well as the expensive ones.

Mortar and Pestle

If you want to have an authentic Thai kitchen, you will want to include a mortar and pestle. You may own a blender and/or food processor but a mortar and pestle is a very inexpensive tool to have for pounding garlic, chilis, ginger or ingredients for sauces.

The mortar will be a heavy earthenware receptacle and the pestle is carved out of wood. There are more expensive ones but, again, you don't have to pay an exorbitant price for one that works just as well as a more pretentious model.

Suggested Menus for Entertaining

"Sawadee" means welcome. The Thais are very friendly people who love to make you welcome in their homes and prepare a few dishes or a grand feast for you to savor and enjoy.

Before we get to the menus for entertaining, perhaps we should say a few words about the Thai eating customs, if we are going to prepare an authentic Thai meal.

The Thais do not eat with chopsticks as many people think. They use a fork and spoon. The fork is placed on the left and spoon is placed on the right of the plate. When eating, hold fork with left hand and push food into spoon, which is held in the right hand. They put the food into their mouths with the spoon. If it is necessary to cut food, they hold the food with the fork and cut with the spoon.

The Thai meal always includes a hot sauce which is served as a side dish. One day it could be fish sauce with chili slices floating on top, another day it might be anchovy or shrimp chili paste. This sauce is good for dipping the steamed or raw vegetables they serve with their meals.

Thai meals are not served in courses. Everything is served at one time, including soup, and all food is eaten at the same time. They usually put a serving of rice in the center of the plate and arrange small portions of each dish around it. They do not overlap their dishes so that the tastes blend. They like everything to give its true flavor, including the rice.

SAMPLE MENUS FOR FOUR

The Thais like to have at least three dishes at a meal to have the variety of flavors they like. This menu will give you the interesting assortment of flavors and textures that you want for a successful Thai dinner, and they can all be done very quickly when you are pressed for time.

Shrimp with Garlic
Beef, Chicken or Pork with Chili and Mint
Watercress with Soybeans
Saffron Rice

Shrimp Toast
Spinach Salad
Hot & Sour Combination Seafood Soup
Masman Curry Beef or Chicken
Plain Steamed Rice

❧ ❧ ❧

Spring Rolls
Crabmeat Salad
Broiled Cornish Game Hens in Herbal Butter
Garlic Noodles

❧ ❧ ❧

Pork, Beef or Chicken Sate
Cucumber Salad
Quick Roasted Beef
Ham Noodles

❧ ❧ ❧

Malay Salad
Chow Mein Soup
Roasted Chicken with Five Spice
Soy Sauce Noodles

❧ ❧ ❧

Hot & Sour Beef Salad
Crispy Chicken Wings
Thai Omelet
Bean Thread Noodles with Shredded Vegetables

❧ ❧ ❧

Hot & Sour Shrimp Soup
Cucumber Salad
Steamed Whole Chicken with Spicy Rice
Mandarin Noodles

❧ ❧ ❧

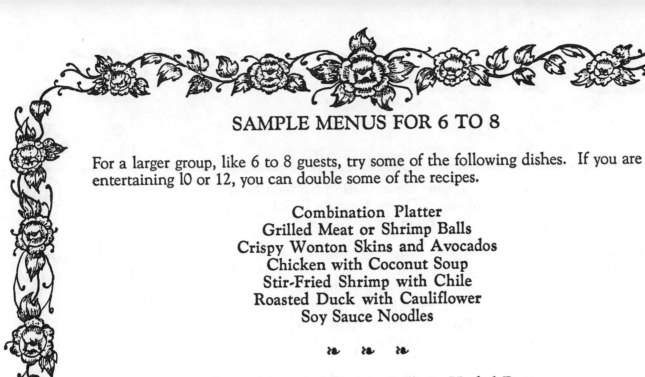

SAMPLE MENUS FOR 6 TO 8

For a larger group, like 6 to 8 guests, try some of the following dishes. If you are entertaining 10 or 12, you can double some of the recipes.

Combination Platter
Grilled Meat or Shrimp Balls
Crispy Wonton Skins and Avocados
Chicken with Coconut Soup
Stir-Fried Shrimp with Chile
Roasted Duck with Cauliflower
Soy Sauce Noodles

🦢 🦢 🦢

Barbecue Meat and Shrimp Balls in Herbal Butter
Wonton Soup
Cabbage Salad
Green Curry with Beef or Chicken
Stewed Duck or Chicken
Fried Rice with Corn

🦢 🦢 🦢

Thai Egg Rolls
Tofu Soup
Thai Kung Pao Chicken
Chicken or Shrimp with Broccoli
Fried Rice with Chicken and Pineapple
Mango with Sweet Rice

PARTY FOR 20

The Thais make a dinner party for 20 people a truly festive occasion with a whole cooked fish, platters of spicy barbecued chicken and perhaps trays of beautifully carved vegetables and fruit.

Sate (double recipe)
Fish Cakes
Hot and Sour Combination Soup (double recipe)
Sweet Crispy Noodles with Pork (double recipe)
Thai Barbecued Chicken Spicy (triple recipe)
Red Roast Pork (double recipe)
Beef Salad (triple recipe)
Deep Fried Whole Fish with Spicy Sauce (triple recipe)
Banana Nuggets (triple recipe)

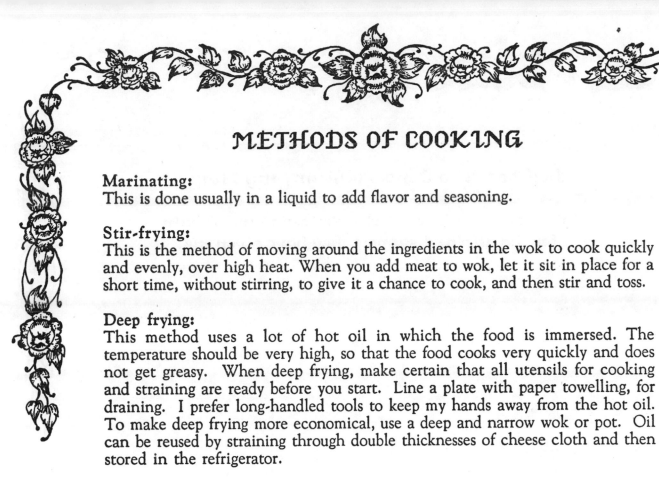

METHODS OF COOKING

Marinating:
This is done usually in a liquid to add flavor and seasoning.

Stir-frying:
This is the method of moving around the ingredients in the wok to cook quickly and evenly, over high heat. When you add meat to wok, let it sit in place for a short time, without stirring, to give it a chance to cook, and then stir and toss.

Deep frying:
This method uses a lot of hot oil in which the food is immersed. The temperature should be very high, so that the food cooks very quickly and does not get greasy. When deep frying, make certain that all utensils for cooking and straining are ready before you start. Line a plate with paper towelling, for draining. I prefer long-handled tools to keep my hands away from the hot oil. To make deep frying more economical, use a deep and narrow wok or pot. Oil can be reused by straining through double thicknesses of cheese cloth and then stored in the refrigerator.

Steaming:
Food is cooked over boiling water and not in it. The food is separated from water by means of a tray.

Baking & Roasting:
Foods that are cooked in an oven. This produces even cooking, without the use of fats.

Grilling:
Foods that are cooked on a grid over a fire, high heat, or coals. Foods cooked by this method are quickly browned on the outside and remain juicy on the inside. This is popular with Thais and used for their barbecues.

General Hints:
Prepare all ingredients and utensils ahead of time, and within close reach of the stove. Especially with stir-frying, there is little time to search for an ingredient or utensil.

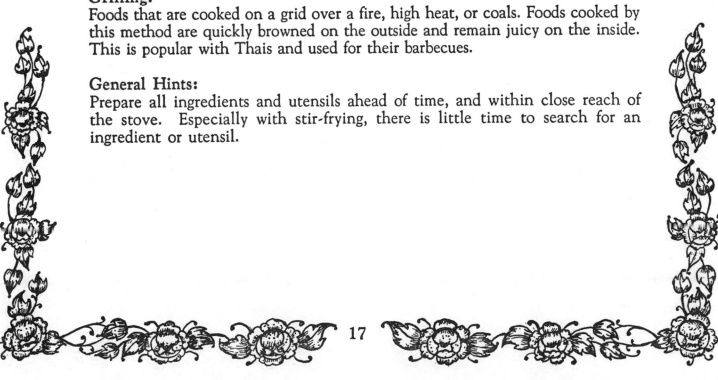

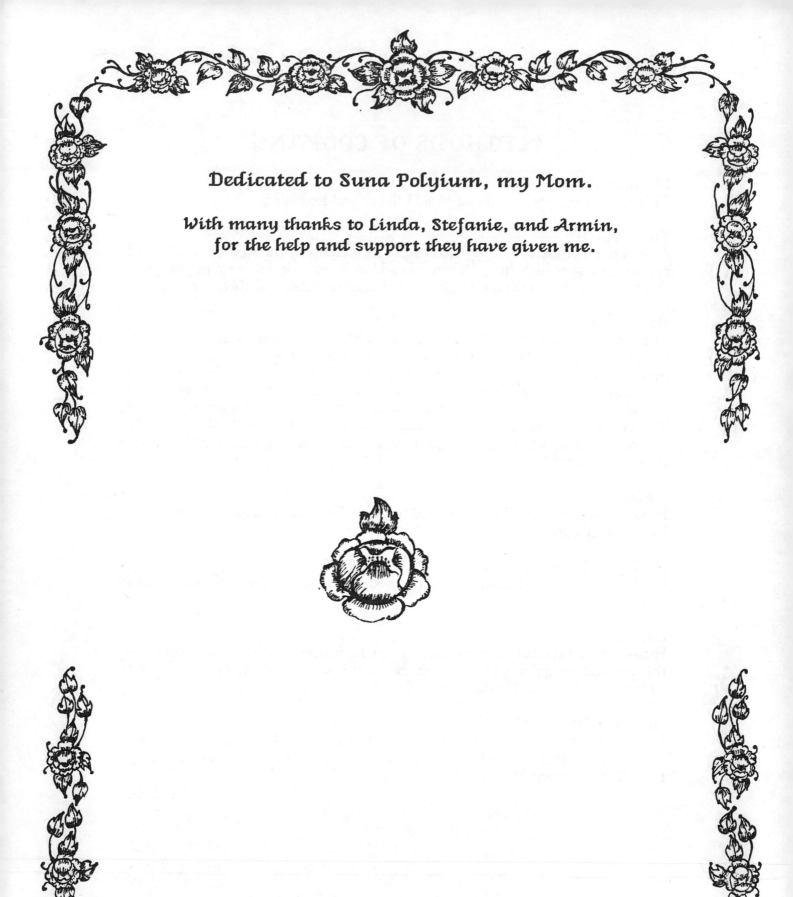

Dedicated to Suna Polyium, my Mom.

With many thanks to Linda, Stefanie, and Armin,
for the help and support they have given me.

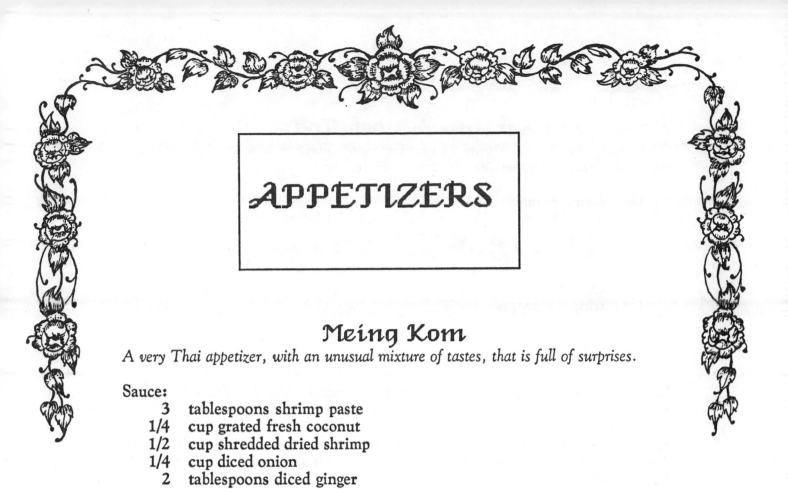

APPETIZERS

Meing Kom

A very Thai appetizer, with an unusual mixture of tastes, that is full of surprises.

Sauce:
3	tablespoons shrimp paste
1/4	cup grated fresh coconut
1/2	cup shredded dried shrimp
1/4	cup diced onion
2	tablespoons diced ginger

1 1/2	cups water
1	cup brown sugar
1/2	cup sugar
1 1/2	tablespoons fish sauce (nam pla)

Serve with:
1	small head butter or red leaf lettuce
2	thumb-size segments fresh ginger root, diced
1	lime, diced
1	small red onion, diced
2	cups grated, roasted coconut
1/2	cup peanuts
6	serrano chiles, sliced thin

In a mortar and pestle, grind together the first 5 sauce ingredients. Mix with 1 1/2 cups of water, add brown sugar, sugar and fish sauce. Transfer to 2 quart saucepan and simmer over low heat, until mixture turns into a soft paste. Do not overcook or sauce will be too hard. Remove from heat.

To serve, use one lettuce leaf, scoop 1 tablespoon of sauce mixture into the leaf. Put in a few pieces of fresh diced ginger root, diced lime, diced red onion, 1 tablespoon roasted grated coconut, several peanuts, 1 dried shrimp, and 1 slice serrano chili. Fold and eat.

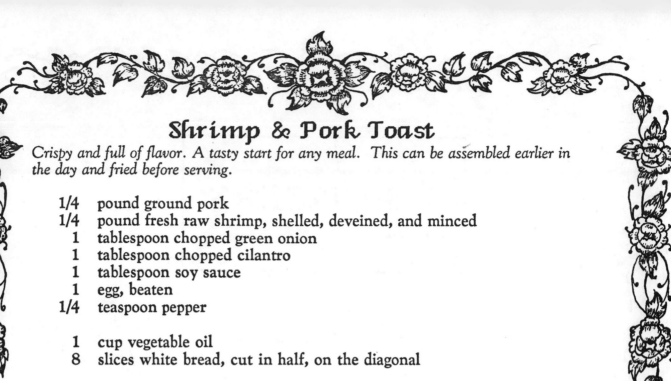

Shrimp & Pork Toast

Crispy and full of flavor. A tasty start for any meal. This can be assembled earlier in the day and fried before serving.

- 1/4   pound ground pork
- 1/4   pound fresh raw shrimp, shelled, deveined, and minced
- 1   tablespoon chopped green onion
- 1   tablespoon chopped cilantro
- 1   tablespoon soy sauce
- 1   egg, beaten
- 1/4   teaspoon pepper

- 1   cup vegetable oil
- 8   slices white bread, cut in half, on the diagonal

In medium bowl combine first 7 ingredients, stir to blend. Then spread 1 heaping tablespoon of the mixture over each bread triangle.

Heat oil in wok until sizzling hot. Fry 3 bread triangles at a time, until golden brown on both sides. Remove bread pieces from oil and drain on paper towel. Repeat with remaining triangles. Transfer to serving platter and serve with Pickled Chili and Cucumber Salad. Yields 4 to 6 servings.

Shrimp or Fish Cakes
(Taud Mun Pla)

Dipped in Sweet and Sour Sauce, these cakes are simply delicious. This can be prepared ahead of time and reheated in the microwave.

- 1   pound fresh ground shrimp or fresh ground fish.
  Available in Oriental markets, or grind your own.
- 1/2   cup finely chopped string beans
- 1/2   cup tapioca flour
- 1   tablespoon Red Curry Paste
- 1/2   tablespoon fish sauce (nam pla)
- 1   tablespoon chopped cilantro
- 1   stem green onion, chopped (green and white part)
- 1/8   teaspoon pepper
- 4   fresh makrood leaves, sliced thin (optional)
- 1   cup vegetable oil

In medium bowl, combine first 9 ingredients, mix well. Form into 18 patties, 1/4-inch thick. Heat oil in wok until sizzling hot. Fry 3 to 4 patties at a time, until golden brown on both sides. Remove patties from oil and drain on paper towel. Repeat with remaining patties. Transfer to serving platter and serve with Cucumber Salad and Sweet and Sour Sauce. Yields 3 to 4 servings.

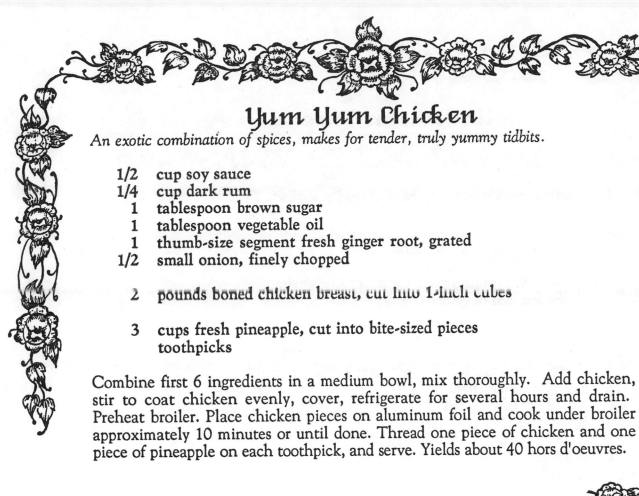

Yum Yum Chicken

An exotic combination of spices, makes for tender, truly yummy tidbits.

1/2	cup soy sauce
1/4	cup dark rum
1	tablespoon brown sugar
1	tablespoon vegetable oil
1	thumb-size segment fresh ginger root, grated
1/2	small onion, finely chopped
2	pounds boned chicken breast, cut into 1-inch cubes
3	cups fresh pineapple, cut into bite-sized pieces
	toothpicks

Combine first 6 ingredients in a medium bowl, mix thoroughly. Add chicken, stir to coat chicken evenly, cover, refrigerate for several hours and drain. Preheat broiler. Place chicken pieces on aluminum foil and cook under broiler approximately 10 minutes or until done. Thread one piece of chicken and one piece of pineapple on each toothpick, and serve. Yields about 40 hors d'oeuvres.

BBQ Pork Sate, Chicken or Beef

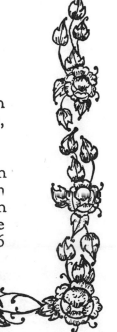

(Moo, Gai or Nuah Sate)

Already a tasty dish, when dipped in the peanut sauce, it is exceptional.

	wooden skewers
2	pounds lean pork (chicken or beef) cut into 2" long, thin strips
1	14-ounce can coconut milk
3	cloves garlic, crushed
2	tablespoons fish sauce (nam pla)
1	tablespoon coriander
1 1/2	tablespoons curry powder
1	teaspoon ginger powder
1/4	teaspoon pepper

Soak wooden skewers in water at least 1/2 hour. Remove just before using. In large bowl combine all ingredients, cover and refrigerate for 1 hour or more, turning several times.

Drain pork (chicken or beef), reserve marinade. Thread a few pieces of meat on the top half of each skewer, repeat with remaining meat. Grill over medium coals, until light brown, about 4 minutes. Turn and grill, until light brown on both sides, about 3 more minutes, brushing with reserved marinade while grilling. Served with Peanut Sauce, Cucumber Salad and toast. Yields 6 servings.

Yum Bean Thread
(Yum Wun Sen)
Hot and spicy, a dish to stimulate the appetite. Can be prepared 2 to 3 hours ahead.

- 4   2-ounce packages mung bean thread noodles
- 4   medium dried black fungus (wood ear) mushrooms

- 1   head butter or red leaf lettuce

- 1   pound lean ground pork (or small raw shrimp, shelled and deveined)
- 6   cups boiling water

- 1/2 cup fresh lime juice
- 2   thumb-size segments fresh ginger root, slivered
- 1/2 cup fish sauce (nam pla)
- 1/4 cup chopped cilantro
- 1/4 cup chopped green onion
- 1   tablespoon ground roasted red chili
- 1   small red onion, sliced very thin
- 2   stems fresh lemon grass, sliced very thin (use bottom 2" of stem)
- cilantro for garnish

Soak bean threads in hot water for 10 minutes, drain and cut into 2" lengths. Set aside. Soak mushrooms in hot water for 30 minutes. Drain, remove stems and slice thin. Set aside. Wash lettuce and separate leafs. Arrange on serving plate to create a lettuce bed. Set aside.

Place ground pork or shrimp in a large bowl. Add boiling water and mix well. Let stand for 1 minute, drain. Add bean threads, mushrooms, and the next 8 ingredients, stir to blend and serve on bed of lettuce. Garnish with cilantro. Yields 4 to 6 servings.

Grilled Meat or Shrimp Balls

This recipe is good for party fare. Just double or triple the recipe as needed. Let the guests grill their own just for fun.

- 5   wooden skewers, soaked in water at least 1/2 hour
- 1   package meat or shrimp balls (about 10 balls). (Can be purchased at Thai grocery stores.)
- 10 button mushrooms
- Sweet and Sour Sauce (see Basics)

Remove skewers from water just before using. Skewer meat, or shrimp balls and mushrooms, alternating 2 and 2. Brush with Sweet and Sour Sauce on all sides and grill over medium coals, turning and brushing with sauce occasionally, until done, about 3 minutes. Serves 2.

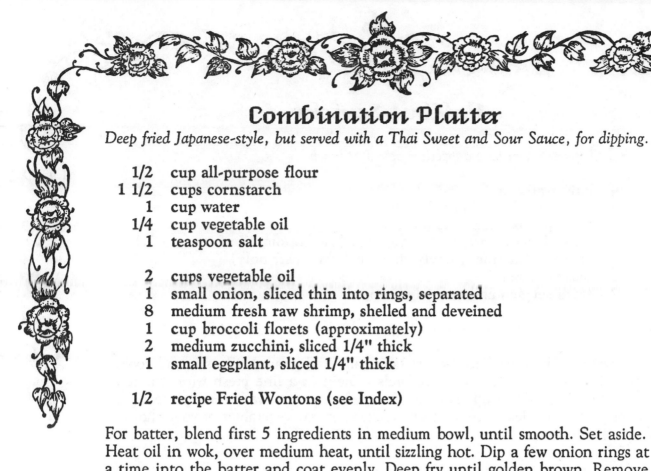

Combination Platter

Deep fried Japanese-style, but served with a Thai Sweet and Sour Sauce, for dipping.

- 1/2 cup all-purpose flour
- 1 1/2 cups cornstarch
- 1 cup water
- 1/4 cup vegetable oil
- 1 teaspoon salt

- 2 cups vegetable oil
- 1 small onion, sliced thin into rings, separated
- 8 medium fresh raw shrimp, shelled and deveined
- 1 cup broccoli florets (approximately)
- 2 medium zucchini, sliced 1/4" thick
- 1 small eggplant, sliced 1/4" thick

- 1/2 recipe Fried Wontons (see Index)

For batter, blend first 5 ingredients in medium bowl, until smooth. Set aside. Heat oil in wok, over medium heat, until sizzling hot. Dip a few onion rings at a time into the batter and coat evenly. Deep fry until golden brown. Remove from oil and drain on paper towel. Repeat with remaining onion, shrimp, broccoli, zucchini, and eggplant. Then fry a few wonton at a time, until golden brown and crisp. Drain on paper towel and repeat with remaining wonton. Arrange on serving platter. Serve with Sweet and Sour Sauce. Yields 4 servings.

Zucchini filled with Crab Meat

Fresh and light, zucchini never tasted so good. This can be prepared earlier in the day and stored in the refrigerator.

- 3 ounces cooked crab meat
- 1 clove garlic, pureed
- 1 tablespoon finely chopped onion
- 1/4 cup mayonnaise
- 1/2 tablespoon mustard
- 1/8 teaspoon salt
- 1/8 teaspoon pepper

- 2 medium zucchini, cut into 1/2-inch slices. Scoop out half the center, to create a cup

In a small bowl, combine first 7 ingredients, mix together thoroughly. Spoon 1 heaping teaspoon of mixture into each zucchini cup. Place on serving plate and serve. Yields 24 appetizers.

Halibut Seviche
(Thai Sewichi)
Tangy and spicy, it can be an appetizer or a light lunch.

- 4 cups water
- 1 pound fresh halibut fillets, ground
- 3 tablespoons fresh lime juice
- 2 stems lemon grass, sliced very thin (use bottom 2" of stems only)
- 3 stems green onion, finely chopped (white part only)
- 1 teaspoon salt
- 2 fresh serrano chiles, finely chopped

- 1 leaf iceberg lettuce or cabbage

Bring water to boil, in 2 to 3-quart saucepan. Add ground fish, stir and cook, until fish turns white, about 10 seconds. Drain in a fine mesh wire strainer. Add lime juice, toss. Add the rest of ingredients, mix well, then place onto lettuce or cabbage leave. Serve with crackers, or raw vegetables of your choice. Yields 4 servings.

BBQ Meat & Shrimp Balls in Herbal Butter
These can be assembled well ahead of time. At outdoor parties, I sometimes have my guests grill their own. It can be a lot of fun.

- 1 tablespoon chile paste with bean oil (nam prig pao)
- 2 ounces Herbal Butter (see chapter on Basics)
- 12 6" wooden skewers, soaked in water for at least 1/2 hour (remove just before using)

- 1 8-ounce package meat balls
- 1 8-ounce package shrimp balls*
- 1 green apple, peeled, cored, and cut into 12 equal pieces

In 1-quart saucepan, combine chile paste, and Herbal Butter. Place over low heat to melt, stir to blend. Set aside.

Skewer 2 meat balls and 2 shrimp balls on each skewer, add 1 apple piece on each end. Grill over medium hot coals, until light brown, about 6 minutes. Brush often with butter mixture while grilling. Remove to platter and serve. Yields 12 skewers.

Note: -*There are about 24 small balls in each package. and they can be purchased at Thai grocery stores.

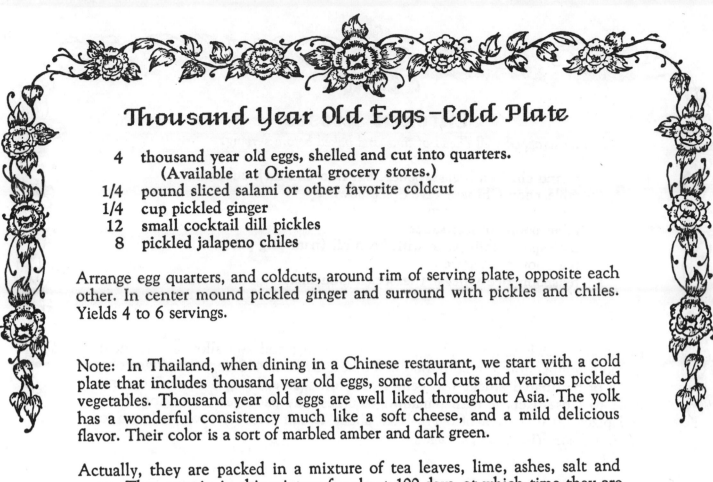

Thousand Year Old Eggs–Cold Plate

4   thousand year old eggs, shelled and cut into quarters.
     (Available at Oriental grocery stores.)
1/4 pound sliced salami or other favorite coldcut
1/4 cup pickled ginger
12   small cocktail dill pickles
8   pickled jalapeno chiles

Arrange egg quarters, and coldcuts, around rim of serving plate, opposite each other. In center mound pickled ginger and surround with pickles and chiles. Yields 4 to 6 servings.

Note: In Thailand, when dining in a Chinese restaurant, we start with a cold plate that includes thousand year old eggs, some cold cuts and various pickled vegetables. Thousand year old eggs are well liked throughout Asia. The yolk has a wonderful consistency much like a soft cheese, and a mild delicious flavor. Their color is a sort of marbled amber and dark green.

Actually, they are packed in a mixture of tea leaves, lime, ashes, salt and water. They remain in this mixture for about 100 days, at which time they are of a very firm texture and do not require any cooking. They are delicious. If you haven't tried thousand year old eggs you haven't really eaten Chinese food.

Thai Tartar

A spicy but pleasant way, to wake up the tastebuds. For a snack or a main course.

1   pound very lean ground beef
1/2 teaspoon salt

2   tablespoons fresh lime juice
2   tablespoons fish sauce (nam pla)
3   tablespoons minced shallots
1   tablespoon ground roasted chile
1/4 cup finely chopped cilantro or green onion
1/4 cup ground roasted sweet rice (from Thai markets)
6   fresh makrood leaves, sliced very thin

1   leaf iceberg lettuce or cabbage

In medium bowl, mix ground beef with salt, refrigerate for 1/2 hour. Add the rest of ingredients, mix well. Place tartar onto lettuce or cabbage leave and serve with crackers or raw vegetables of your choice. Yields 6 servings.

Chicken Kisses

These can be wrapped well ahead of time and baked before serving.

1	pound chicken breast, boned, cut into 1x1-inch cubes
1/4	tablespoon Chinese Five Spice powder
1	tablespoon dry sherry
2	tablespoons oyster sauce
1/2	tablespoon chili paste with bean oil (nam prig pao)
1	teaspoon corn starch
1	teaspoon rice vinegar (Seasoned Gourmet)
20	squares of tinfoil, 5x5-inches

In medium bowl, combine all ingredients, Stir to blend and allow to marinate at room temperature for 20 minutes. Preheat oven to 450-degrees. Place one piece of marinated chicken in center of a foil square, bring 4 corners up and twist to close. Repeat with remaining squares. Lay packages on baking sheet and place on first shelf of oven. Bake about 15 minutes. Remove packages to serving plate. Yields 20 packages.

Pork Dumplings
(Pork Shu Mei)

This is one of the many dumpling dishes that make up the very traditional Chinese Dim Sum lunch.

3/4	pound ground pork
1/2	cup water chestnut, chopped
1/4	pound fresh raw shrimp, shelled, deveined, and minced
1	teaspoon salt
1	teaspoon soy sauce
1	teaspoon sugar
1	teaspoon ground ginger
2	stems green onion, finely chopped (white and green parts)
1	8-ounce package round wonton skins, about 25 sheets
2	tablespoons shredded carrots

In medium bowl combine first 8 ingredients, stir to blend. Allow to rest at room temperature, for about 10 minutes. Scoop 1 tablespoon of meat mixture into center of each wonton skin, gather up sides and pleat around top, leaving top open. Top with a few shredded carrot pieces.

Add 5 cups of water to steamer, bring to boil over high heat. Place wonton onto steamer rack, do not crowd. Steam 10 to 15 minutes or until dumplings are tender. Remove to serving platter, serve hot. Dip with soy sauce, mustard and catsup, as you wish. Yields 25 dumplings.

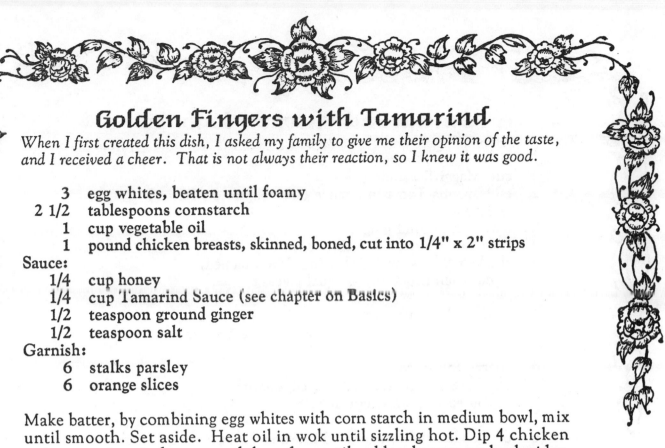

Golden Fingers with Tamarind

When I first created this dish, I asked my family to give me their opinion of the taste, and I received a cheer. That is not always their reaction, so I knew it was good.

3	egg whites, beaten until foamy
2 1/2	tablespoons cornstarch
1	cup vegetable oil
1	pound chicken breasts, skinned, boned, cut into 1/4" x 2" strips

Sauce:
1/4	cup honey
1/4	cup Tamarind Sauce (see chapter on Basics)
1/2	teaspoon ground ginger
1/2	teaspoon salt

Garnish:
6	stalks parsley
6	orange slices

Make batter, by combining egg whites with corn starch in medium bowl, mix until smooth. Set aside. Heat oil in wok until sizzling hot. Dip 4 chicken strips at a time in batter, and deep fry, until golden brown on both sides, approximately 1 minute. Remove strips from oil and drain on paper towel, repeat with remaining strips. Transfer chicken to serving plate. Set aside.

Remove all but 1 tablespoon oil from wok. Keep wok over medium heat. Add ingredients for sauce, stir and cook about 3 minutes, or until sauce thickens. Pour sauce over chicken. Garnish with parsley and orange slices. Serve at once. Yields 4 servings.

Cucumber Salad

1	medium cucumber
1/2	small red onion, chopped
1/4	teaspoon salt
1/2	cup rice vinegar (seasoned gourmet)

Garnish:
2	tablespoons coarse ground roasted peanuts
1	tablespoon cilantro leaves (without stalks)
1	fresh red serrano chili*

Quarter cucumber lengthwise and remove seeds, slice very thin. Then mix with red onion, salt and vinegar. Place in serving bowl, garnish with ground peanuts, cilantro and top with a Chili Flower.

Note: -* To decorate with a Chili Flower, leave stem attached to chile, slice into pod lengthwise to create four or five petals. Fold back petals and put on top of salad.

Tamarind Chicken Kabobs

The combination of spices and Tamarind Sauce gives this dish a tangy, fresh flavor.

- 1/4 cup Maggi Seasoning
- 2 tablespoons Tamarind Sauce (see chapter on Basics)
- 1 tablespoon brown sugar
- 1 teaspoon ground ginger
- 1 teaspoon ground fresh chile paste
- 4 chicken thighs, boned, leaving skin attached, cut each thigh into 4 equal pieces

- 1 green bell pepper, cored and cut into 8 wedges, then cut each wedge in half, to make 16 pieces

- 16 cherry tomatoes
- 2 small green apples, cored, peeled, quartered, and each quarter cut in half

- 16 6" wooden skewers, soaked in water for at least 1/2 hour (remove just before using)

In medium bowl combine first 6 ingredients, marinate about 1/2 hour at room temperature. Drain, reserve marinade. On each skewer thread one piece of bell pepper, chicken, tomato, and apple. Grill over medium hot coals, until chicken is done, about 10 minutes, turning and basting often with marinade. Yields 16 skewers.

Stuffed Mushroom Caps

This is one of my favorite appetizers...and one of our guest's favorites, too. It is easy to prepare.

- 1/4 cup walnuts, finely minced
- 1/4 pound fresh raw shrimp, shelled, deveined and minced
- 2 tablespoons finely chopped parsley
- 1/4 teaspoon salt

- 12 fresh large mushrooms caps
- 2 ounces Herbal Butter (see chapter on Basics), melted

Preheat oven to 350 degrees. In medium bowl combine first 4 ingredients, stir to blend. Stuff 1 teaspoon of mixture into each mushroom cap. Place mushroom onto baking sheet, brush mushrooms with Herbal Butter and spoon remaining butter over mushrooms. Place on middle shelf of oven and bake for about 15 minutes. Yields 12 pieces.

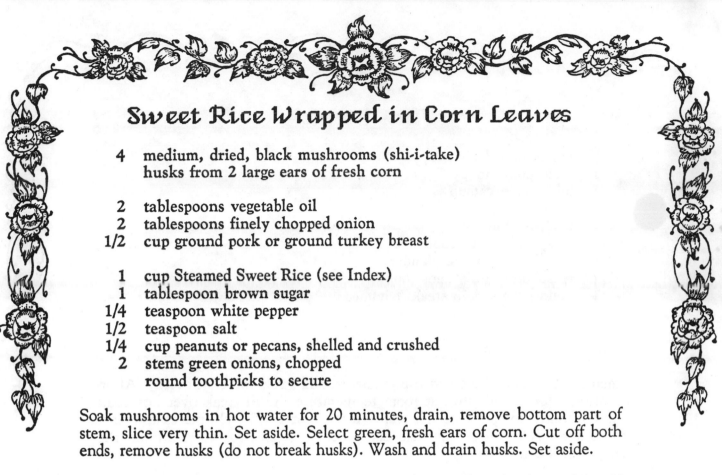

Sweet Rice Wrapped in Corn Leaves

4	medium, dried, black mushrooms (shi-i-take)
	husks from 2 large ears of fresh corn
2	tablespoons vegetable oil
2	tablespoons finely chopped onion
1/2	cup ground pork or ground turkey breast
1	cup Steamed Sweet Rice (see Index)
1	tablespoon brown sugar
1/4	teaspoon white pepper
1/2	teaspoon salt
1/4	cup peanuts or pecans, shelled and crushed
2	stems green onions, chopped
	round toothpicks to secure

Soak mushrooms in hot water for 20 minutes, drain, remove bottom part of stem, slice very thin. Set aside. Select green, fresh ears of corn. Cut off both ends, remove husks (do not break husks). Wash and drain husks. Set aside.

Set wok over high heat for 1 minute. Add oil and coat sides of wok evenly. Add onion and fry until light brown. Add mushrooms, and ground pork or turkey, stir and cook, until meat is partially done, about 1 minute. Add remaining ingredients, stir to blend. Remove from heat immediately.

Scoop 2 tablespoons of rice mixture into center of a corn husk. Bring sides up and fold over, secure with toothpicks (make sure the package is tight). Repeat with remaining packages. Set aside.

Pour 5 cups of water into steamer and bring to boil over high heat. Place packages onto steamer rack and steam for 40 minutes. Remove packages from steamer, and serve. (Rice should be eaten from husks) Yields about 15 packages.

Note: You may not enjoy wrapping the rice with corn husks. So, to shortcut, you may add 1/2 cup of water to rice mixture. Simmer in 2-quart covered saucepan for about 5 minutes. Remove from heat and fluff with fork. Serve as a sidedish, instead of Steamed Rice, with any meal.

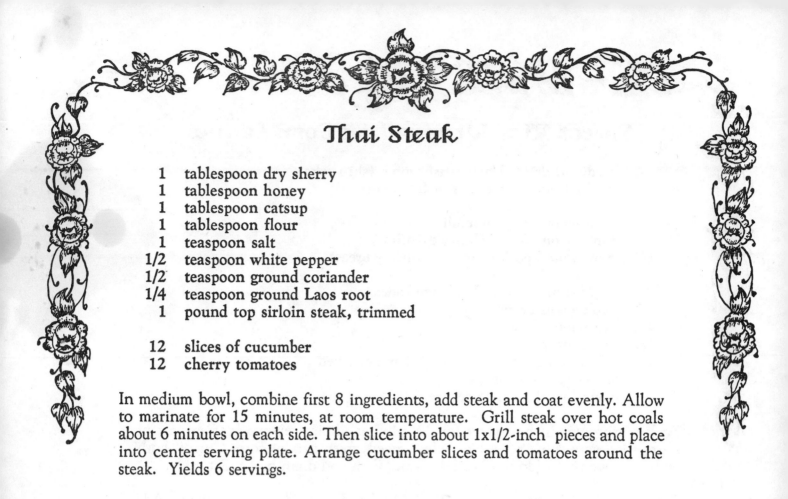

Thai Steak

1	tablespoon dry sherry
1	tablespoon honey
1	tablespoon catsup
1	tablespoon flour
1	teaspoon salt
1/2	teaspoon white pepper
1/2	teaspoon ground coriander
1/4	teaspoon ground Laos root
1	pound top sirloin steak, trimmed
12	slices of cucumber
12	cherry tomatoes

In medium bowl, combine first 8 ingredients, add steak and coat evenly. Allow to marinate for 15 minutes, at room temperature. Grill steak over hot coals about 6 minutes on each side. Then slice into about 1x1/2-inch pieces and place into center serving plate. Arrange cucumber slices and tomatoes around the steak. Yields 6 servings.

Shrimp Chips with Bean Dip

1	cup vegetable oil
1	3 1/2-ounce package shrimp chips*

For dip:
1/2	cup Bean Sauce (Nam Prig Dang)

Heat oil in wok, over high heat, until sizzling hot. Deep fry a few shrimp chips at a time, until golden brown on both sides. Drain on a paper towel. Repeat with remaining chips. Do not put too many chips into oil at once, as they will triple in size. Chips should puff immediately, if not, the oil is not hot enough. One 3 1/2 ounce bag of chips will yield as much as a medium-sized bag of potato chips. Serve with Bean Sauce for dipping.

Note: -*Shrimp chips are uncooked, shrimp-flavored crackers, available in Thai grocery stores. These are good for parties or snacks. You can fry them a day ahead and store them in plastic bags.

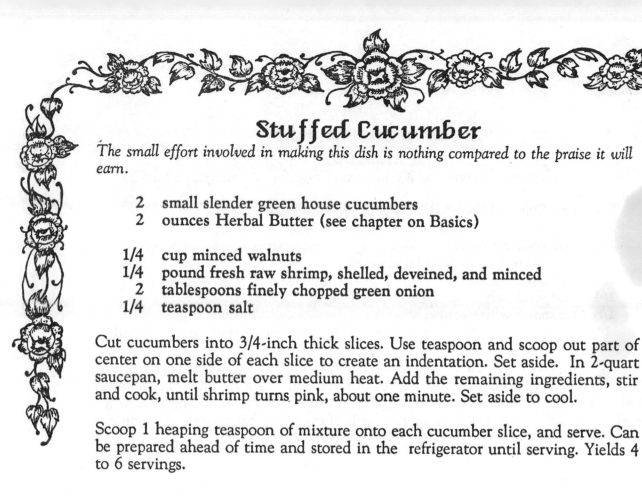

Stuffed Cucumber

The small effort involved in making this dish is nothing compared to the praise it will earn.

- 2 small slender green house cucumbers
- 2 ounces Herbal Butter (see chapter on Basics)

- 1/4 cup minced walnuts
- 1/4 pound fresh raw shrimp, shelled, deveined, and minced
- 2 tablespoons finely chopped green onion
- 1/4 teaspoon salt

Cut cucumbers into 3/4-inch thick slices. Use teaspoon and scoop out part of center on one side of each slice to create an indentation. Set aside. In 2-quart saucepan, melt butter over medium heat. Add the remaining ingredients, stir and cook, until shrimp turns pink, about one minute. Set aside to cool.

Scoop 1 heaping teaspoon of mixture onto each cucumber slice, and serve. Can be prepared ahead of time and stored in the refrigerator until serving. Yields 4 to 6 servings.

Fried Shrimp
(Goong Grob)

- 2 egg yolks
- 1 tablespoon dry sherry
- 1/4 teaspoon salt
- 1 teaspoon corn starch
- 1 pinch cloves
- 1/8 teaspoon white pepper

- 1 cup vegetable oil
- 1/2 pound medium fresh raw shrimp, shelled, and deveined, leaving tails attached

In medium bowl, combine the first 6 ingredients and mix until smooth. Set aside. Heat oil in wok until sizzling hot. Dip 3 to 4 shrimp at a time into batter and deep fry until golden brown on both sides, approximately 2 minutes. Remove shrimp from wok and drain on paper towel. Repeat with remaining shrimp and serve. Yields 2 servings.

Baked Sweet Rice

(Easan Ob)

These rice packets are different and a welcomed change for my family and friends.

1	cup Steamed Sweet Rice (see chapter on Rice)
1/4	pound fresh raw shrimp, shelled, deveined, and minced
1/4	cup coconut milk
1/4	cup roasted cashew nuts, crushed
1	tablespoon sugar
1/4	teaspoon salt
1/8	teaspoon white pepper
14	pieces of tinfoil 4x4-inch square, lightly coated with vegetable oil

In medium bowl combine first 7 ingredients, stir to blend. Scoop 1 1/2 tablespoons of rice mixture into center of a foil square, bring up 4 corners and twist to close. Repeat with remaining rice mixture. Set aside. Preheat oven to 400 degrees. Place packages on middle shelf of oven and bake about 25 minutes. Transfer to serving plate. Yields 14 packages.

Shrimp Stick

This dish is a must for shrimp lovers and also serves well as a main course.

1/4	cup Herbal Butter (see chapter on Basics)
1	tablespoon Tamarind Sauce (see chapter on Basics)
1/8	teaspoon salt
8	medium fresh raw shrimp, shelled, deveined, leaving tails attached
8	6-inch wooden skewers soaked in water at least 1/2 hour (remove just before using)

In 1-quart saucepan, melt Herbal Butter over low heat. Add Tamarind Sauce, and salt, stir to blend. Set aside. Skewer 1 shrimp lengthwise on the top half of each skewer, brush with melted Herbal Butter mixture.

Preheat oven to 500-degrees. Arrange shrimp skewers on baking sheet, place on middle shelf in oven, and bake about 5 minutes, or until shrimps turn pink. Brush shrimp, during the last minute of cooking time, with Herbal Butter. Remove skewers from heat and serve with sliced tomatoes or strawberries. Yields 4 servings.

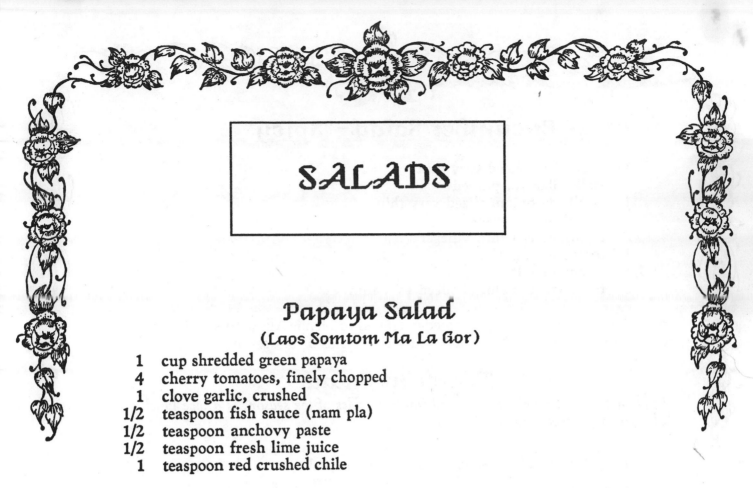

SALADS

Papaya Salad
(Laos Somtom Ma La Gor)

1   cup shredded green papaya
4   cherry tomatoes, finely chopped
1   clove garlic, crushed
1/2 teaspoon fish sauce (nam pla)
1/2 teaspoon anchovy paste
1/2 teaspoon fresh lime juice
1   teaspoon red crushed chile

To shred papaya, peel and cut into quarters and remove seeds. Use largest holes on shredder. Press down hard with papaya quarters and shred with long, even strokes, to get long, firm strips. Combine all ingredients in small bowl and knead together by hand. Serve with Steamed Rice and lettuce. Yields 1 or 2 servings.

Papaya Salad (Thai Somtom):
Add to Laos Somtom:
   1/4 tablespoon coarse ground roasted peanuts
   1/4 tablespoon shredded dried shrimp
   1/4 teaspoon sugar

Note:-To make somtom in the original Thai way, use mortar and pestle. Pound garlic and chile together to fine paste. Add the rest of ingredients and pound together, until well mixed.
     -You may substitute carrots for green papaya. It tastes very similar and is just as good.

Cucumber Salad

1   cucumber, sliced very thin
4   tablespoons seasoned rice vinegar

In medium bowl, toss sliced cucumber together with seasoned rice vinegar. Allow to stand at room temperature for about 15 minutes and serve. Yields 3 to 4 servings.

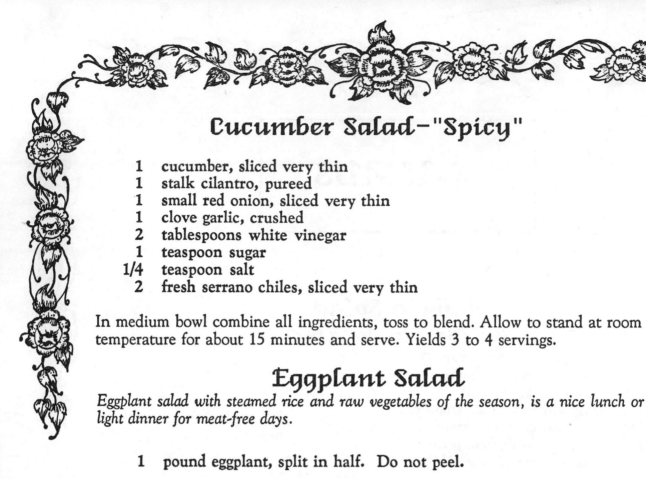

Cucumber Salad—"Spicy"

1   cucumber, sliced very thin
1   stalk cilantro, pureed
1   small red onion, sliced very thin
1   clove garlic, crushed
2   tablespoons white vinegar
1   teaspoon sugar
1/4 teaspoon salt
2   fresh serrano chiles, sliced very thin

In medium bowl combine all ingredients, toss to blend. Allow to stand at room temperature for about 15 minutes and serve. Yields 3 to 4 servings.

Eggplant Salad

Eggplant salad with steamed rice and raw vegetables of the season, is a nice lunch or light dinner for meat-free days.

1   pound eggplant, split in half. Do not peel.

1   tablespoon Maggi Seasoning
1/2 teaspoon ground roasted chile
2   stems green onions, finely chopped (white and green parts)
2   stalks cilantro, finely chopped
10 fresh mint leaves
2   cloves garlic, crushed

Bake eggplant in 500-degree oven until soft, then chop fine. With a fork, mash all ingredients including eggplant, in a small bowl, until well mixed. Serve with steamed rice and lettuce. Yields 2 servings.

Cabbage Salad with Ginger & Chiles
(Kim Chi)

2   pounds napa cabbage, cut leaves in half
5   cloves garlic, pureed
1   thumb-size segment fresh ginger root, grated
1   tablespoon crushed red chile
1/2 tablespoon sugar
4   tablespoons roasted sesame seeds, crushed
1   tablespoon salt

Combine all ingredients in large bowl and mix well. Pack into 1-quart storage jar. Refrigerate for 2 to 3 days and serve. Keeps well refrigerated for 2 weeks. Yields 6 servings.

Malay Salad

This salad with its Malaysian influence, is a refreshing treat on the buffet table.

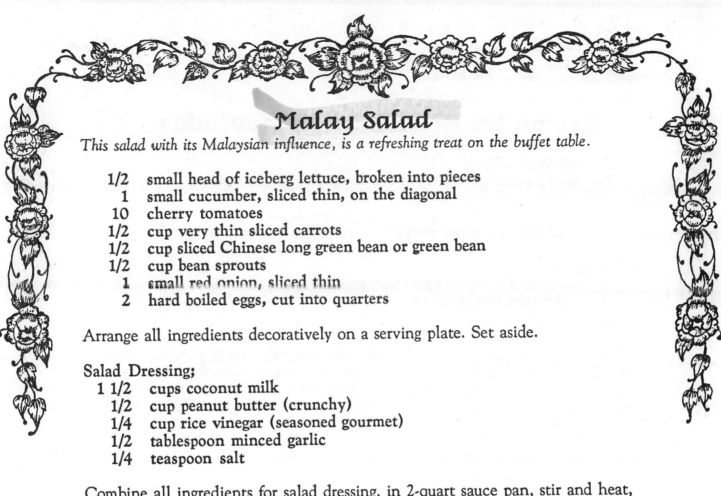

1/2	small head of iceberg lettuce, broken into pieces
1	small cucumber, sliced thin, on the diagonal
10	cherry tomatoes
1/2	cup very thin sliced carrots
1/2	cup sliced Chinese long green bean or green bean
1/2	cup bean sprouts
1	small red onion, sliced thin
2	hard boiled eggs, cut into quarters

Arrange all ingredients decoratively on a serving plate. Set aside.

Salad Dressing;

1 1/2	cups coconut milk
1/2	cup peanut butter (crunchy)
1/4	cup rice vinegar (seasoned gourmet)
1/2	tablespoon minced garlic
1/4	teaspoon salt

Combine all ingredients for salad dressing, in 2-quart sauce pan, stir and heat, until ingredients blend together, do not boil. Remove from heat. Allow dressing to cool. Serve salad, with dressing on the side. Yields 4 servings.

Tuna Rambuton Salad

Rambuton is a tropical fruit from Thailand. Even canned, it is sweet and crunchy and blends very nicely with the tuna in this salad.

1	6 1/2-ounce can chunk light tuna in spring water, drained
8	radishes, sliced
1	20-ounce can rambuton, drained, reserving juice
2	medium tomatoes, sliced
1/2	cup finely chopped green onion

Dressing:

1/4	cup white vinegar
1/2	teaspoon salt
1/4	teaspoon white pepper
	reserved juice from rambuton

Arrange tuna, radishes, rambutons and tomatoes in center of plate, top with green onions. Set aside. Combine all ingredients for dressing, mix well, pour over salad, and serve. Yields 4 servings.

Crispy Wontons Skins & Avocados

1/2	cup vegetable oil
10	square wontons skins, cut into long 1/4" wide strips
1	large avocado, cut into 1/4" wedges
4	stems green onions, sliced thin, on the diagonal (white and green parts)

Dressing;
3	tablespoons rice vinegar (seasoned gourmet)
1	tablespoon brown sugar
1/2	teaspoon salt

Add oil to wok and place over medium heat for 2 minutes. Drop a small piece of wonton skin into oil, if the piece rises to the top immediately, the oil is ready. Drop in a few wonton strips at a time, and deep fry until golden brown. Remove wonton and drain on paper towel. Repeat with remaining strips. Place wonton strips, avocado, and green onions into serving bowl. Set aside.

Mix all ingredients for dressing until smooth, and pour over salad, toss. Serve at once. Yields 2 servings.

Note:-Never throw away left over wonton skins. They are great deep fried, and mixed with left over chicken, or as a crispy addition to any salad.

Bamboo Salad

1	24-ounce jar shredded bamboo shoots with bai yanang drained, reserve marinade, separate bamboo shoots
1	tablespoon all-purpose flour
2	tablespoons roasted sesame seeds, crushed
1	teaspoon ground laos root
1	teaspoon ground roasted chiles
1/4	cup finely chopped green onion
3	stalks cilantro, chopped

In 2-quart sauce pan, sprinkle shredded bamboo shoots with flour, stir in reserved marinade. Stir and cook over high heat about 2 minutes or until sauce thickens. Remove from heat, add the rest of the ingredients and mix well. Serve with lettuce, cabbage, or any raw vegetable of your choice. Yields 2 servings.

Note: Bai-yanang is a green plant leaf, used in Thailand as a seasoning. Also included in the marinade is salt, so no additional salt is needed.

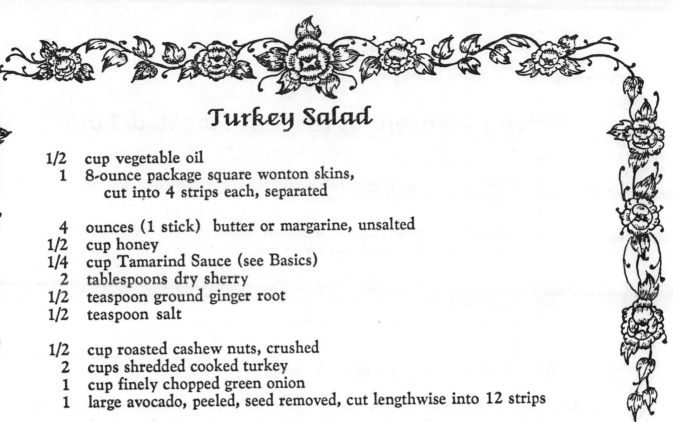

Turkey Salad

1/2 cup vegetable oil
1   8-ounce package square wonton skins,
      cut into 4 strips each, separated

4   ounces (1 stick) butter or margarine, unsalted
1/2 cup honey
1/4 cup Tamarind Sauce (see Basics)
2   tablespoons dry sherry
1/2 teaspoon ground ginger root
1/2 teaspoon salt

1/2 cup roasted cashew nuts, crushed
2   cups shredded cooked turkey
1   cup finely chopped green onion
1   large avocado, peeled, seed removed, cut lengthwise into 12 strips

Add oil to wok and place over high heat for 2 minutes. Drop small piece of wonton skin into the oil. When wonton skin rises to the top quickly, the oil is hot and ready. Deep fry small amount of wonton skins at a time until golden brown on both sides. Remove onto paper towel to drain, set aside. Repeat with remaining wonton skins.

In 2-quart saucepan, melt butter over medium heat. Add the next 5 ingredients, stir and cook, until ingredients are heated. Set aside and allow this dressing to cool, to about lukewarm. In salad bowl place fried wonton skins, the next 3 ingredients, and dressing, toss together and garnish with avocado. Yields 4 servings.

Greenhouse Cucumber & Orange Salad

1   small green house cucumber, sliced thin
2   navel oranges, peeled, separated into segments

Dressing:
3   tablespoons rice vinegar (seasoned gourmet)
1/2 teaspoon salt
1   tablespoon sugar
1/2 tablespoon dry sherry
1   teaspoon roasted sesame seeds

Arrange cucumber slices around the outside of a serving plate. Place orange segments in the center. Set aside. Mix all dressing ingredients, until smooth, pour over cucumber, and orange slices, serve. Yields 2 servings.

Crispy Wontons with Red Roasted Pork

- 1/2 cup vegetable oil
- 1 8-ounce package square wonton skins, cut into 4 strips each, separated
- 1 cup sliced Red Roasted Pork (see chapter on Pork)
- 2 tablespoons roasted sesame seeds, crushed
- 1/2 small iceberg lettuce, broken into pieces

Dressing;
- 1/4 cup water
- 1/2 cup Tamarind Sauce (see Basics)
- 1/2 cup sugar
- 2 teaspoons salt
- 1/2 teaspoon coarse ground black pepper

Add oil to wok and place over medium heat for 2 minute. Drop small piece of wonton into the oil. When the wonton skin rises to the top quickly, the oil is ready. Drop a few wonton skins at a time into the oil and deep fry until golden brown on both sides. Remove wonton and drain on paper towel. Repeat with remaining wonton skins.

Place wonton skins, and the next 3 ingredients into serving bowl. Set aside. Mix all ingredients for dressing, until smooth, pour over salad, toss and serve. Yields 4 to 6 servings.

Red Roasted Pork Salad with Plum Sauce

- 1 cup thin sliced radishes
- 4 hard boiled eggs, cut into quarters
- 1 medium greenhouse cucumber, sliced thin
- 2 cups thin-sliced Red Roasted Pork (see chapter on Pork)

Plum Sauce:
- 3 tablespoons plum sauce
- 1 tablespoon rice vinegar (seasoned gourmet)
- 3 tablespoons soy sauce
- 1 tablespoon honey
- 1/2 teaspoon coarse ground black pepper
- 1/4 teaspoon ground fresh chile paste

On serving plate, arrange radishes, and hard boiled eggs in center. Surround with green house cucumber and top with Red Roasted Pork. Set aside. Mix sauce ingredients together until smooth. Pour over salad and serve. Yields 4 servings.

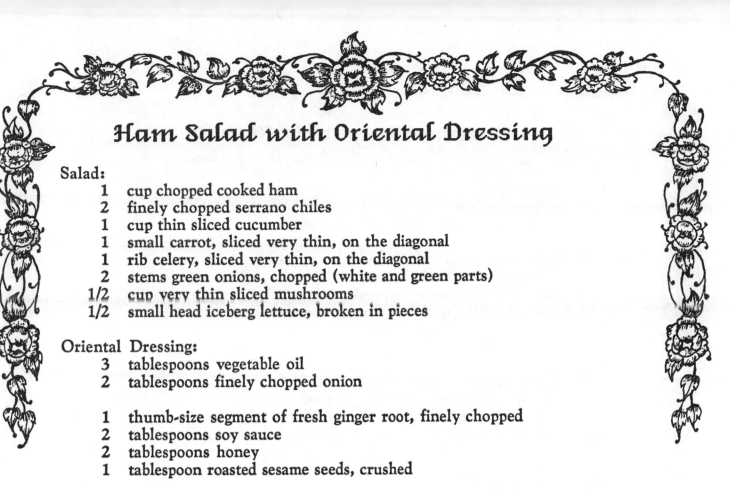

Ham Salad with Oriental Dressing

Salad:
- 1   cup chopped cooked ham
- 2   finely chopped serrano chiles
- 1   cup thin sliced cucumber
- 1   small carrot, sliced very thin, on the diagonal
- 1   rib celery, sliced very thin, on the diagonal
- 2   stems green onions, chopped (white and green parts)
- 1/2 cup very thin sliced mushrooms
- 1/2 small head iceberg lettuce, broken in pieces

Oriental Dressing:
- 3   tablespoons vegetable oil
- 2   tablespoons finely chopped onion

- 1   thumb-size segment of fresh ginger root, finely chopped
- 2   tablespoons soy sauce
- 2   tablespoons honey
- 1   tablespoon roasted sesame seeds, crushed

- juice of 2 limes
- 1   tablespoon sesame oil

Arrange salad ingredients decoratively on serving plate, set aside. Place 2-quart sauce pan over medium heat, for 1 minute. Add vegetable oil and coat pan evenly. Add onion, and ginger, cook until fragrant. Add the next 4 dressing ingredients, cook for 1 minute. Remove from heat, add lime juice, and sesame oil, stir to blend. Allow to cool, then pour over salad and serve. Yields 4 servings.

Watercress Salad

- 3   cups water
- 1   bunch watercress, coarsely chopped, about 3 cups

- 1   tablespoon dried shredded shrimp
- 1/4 small red onion, sliced very thin
- 1   tablespoon rice vinegar (seasoned gourmet)
- 1/2 tablespoon fish sauce (nam pla)

Boil 3 cups of water in 3-quart sauce pan, over high heat. Add watercress, cover, cook until watercress is limp, about 1 minute. Drain, place watercress in medium bowl. Add the rest of ingredients, mix well and serve. Yields 2 servings.

Steamed Vegetable Salad

This salad is elegant and surprisingly flavorful. Perfect for a light lunch.

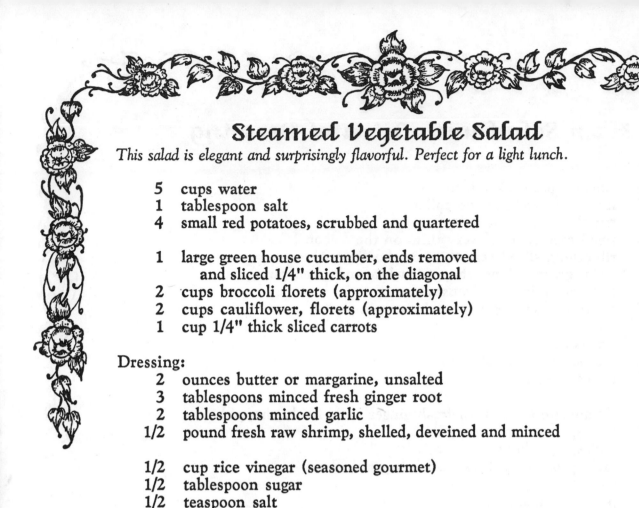

5 cups water
1 tablespoon salt
4 small red potatoes, scrubbed and quartered

1 large green house cucumber, ends removed
     and sliced 1/4" thick, on the diagonal
2 cups broccoli florets (approximately)
2 cups cauliflower, florets (approximately)
1 cup 1/4" thick sliced carrots

Dressing:
2 ounces butter or margarine, unsalted
3 tablespoons minced fresh ginger root
2 tablespoons minced garlic
1/2 pound fresh raw shrimp, shelled, deveined and minced

1/2 cup rice vinegar (seasoned gourmet)
1/2 tablespoon sugar
1/2 teaspoon salt
1/2 teaspoon white pepper

In vegetable steamer, bring water and salt to boil, over high heat. Add potatoes, cover, and steam about 15 minutes. Add the next 4 ingredients, cover and steam about 5 minutes or until vegetables are as tender as desired. Remove from heat and arrange cucumber around outside of a serving plate. Then arrange potatoes, and the rest of the steamed vegetables in center. Set aside.

In 1-quart saucepan, melt butter or margarine, over medium heat. Stir in ginger, and garlic, cook until fragrant. Add shrimp, stir, then add the remaining ingredients. Stir and cook, until shrimp is done, about 1 minute. Pour over vegetables and serve. Yields 4 servings.

Cabbage Salad—"Spicy"

1 cup very thin sliced red cabbage
1 cup very thin sliced white cabbage
2 cloves garlic, minced
1 tablespoon fresh lime juice
1 tablespoon fish sauce
2 tablespoons dried shredded shrimp
1/4 teaspoon crushed red chile

In medium bowl, toss together all ingredients. Mix well and serve. Yields 2 to 3 servings.

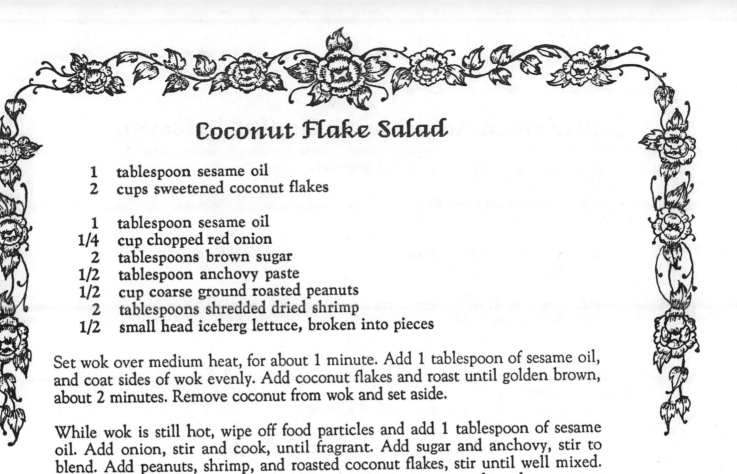

Coconut Flake Salad

1 tablespoon sesame oil
2 cups sweetened coconut flakes

1 tablespoon sesame oil
1/4 cup chopped red onion
2 tablespoons brown sugar
1/2 tablespoon anchovy paste
1/2 cup coarse ground roasted peanuts
2 tablespoons shredded dried shrimp
1/2 small head iceberg lettuce, broken into pieces

Set wok over medium heat, for about 1 minute. Add 1 tablespoon of sesame oil, and coat sides of wok evenly. Add coconut flakes and roast until golden brown, about 2 minutes. Remove coconut from wok and set aside.

While wok is still hot, wipe off food particles and add 1 tablespoon of sesame oil. Add onion, stir and cook, until fragrant. Add sugar and anchovy, stir to blend. Add peanuts, shrimp, and roasted coconut flakes, stir until well mixed. Set aside and allow to cool. Arrange lettuce on serving plate, lay coconut mixture on top and serve. Yields 4 to 6 servings.

Note: -Sesame oil is very delicate, so use great care not to burn it. Peanut oil may be substituted.

Spinach Salad

1 bunch spinach, sliced
1/2 cup sliced mushrooms
1/2 cup sliced radishes
1/2 pound bacon, chopped
2 tablespoons minced fresh ginger root
1/4 cup finely chopped onion
1/4 pound fresh raw shrimp, shelled, deveined and minced

1 beef flavored bouillon cube, dissolved in 3 tablespoons of hot water
1/2 teaspoon salt
2 tablespoons Tamarind Sauce (see Basics)

Decoratively arrange spinach, mushrooms, and radishes on serving plate. Set aside. Set 2-quart saucepan over high heat for 1 minute. Add bacon and fry, until light brown. Remove bacon and set aside. Remove all, but 2 tablespoons of bacon grease from saucepan. Keep saucepan over high heat, add ginger, and onion, cook until fragrant. Add shrimp, stir and cook, until shrimp turns pink, about 1/2 minute. Add remaining ingredients, stir to blend and set aside to cool. When cool, pour over salad, top with crispy bacon and serve. Yields 4 servings.

Crabmeat Salad with Shallot Dressing

1/4   cup rice vinegar (seasoned gourmet)
1/2   teaspoon salt
1   cup cooked crab meat
1/4   cup thin sliced shallots
2   tablespoons very thin-sliced fresh lemon grass (use bottom 2")
1/4   teaspoon white pepper
1   tomato, sliced thin

1/2   small head of iceberg lettuce (broken into pieces)
1/2   bell pepper, cut into rings
1/2   small red onion, cut into rings

In medium bowl, combine the first 7 ingredients, mix well. Set aside. Arrange lettuce on serving plate, top with bell pepper, and onion rings. Spoon crab mixture over salad, and serve. Yields 2 servings.

Hot Cucumber Salad
(Somtom Tang)
One of my Mom's old recipes. I still serve it often to my own family.

1   medium cucumber, sliced thin
1   small tomato, finely chopped
2   stems green onions, chopped (white and green parts)
1   clove garlic, crushed
1   tablespoon fish sauce (nam pla)
1   tablespoon chopped cilantro
1/4   teaspoon red crushed chile

Combine all ingredients in small bowl, mix well and serve. Yields 2 to 3 servings.

Sardine Salad

1   15-ounce can sardines in tomato sauce
1   small red onion, sliced very thin
1/4   cup chopped cilantro
1   tablespoon fish sauce (nam pla)
3   tablespoons fresh lime juice
2   fresh serrano chiles, finely chopped
8   leaves of lettuce

In medium bowl, toss the first 6 ingredients together. Arrange lettuce leaves on serving plate. Spoon sardine mixture into center. Yields 2 to 3 servings.

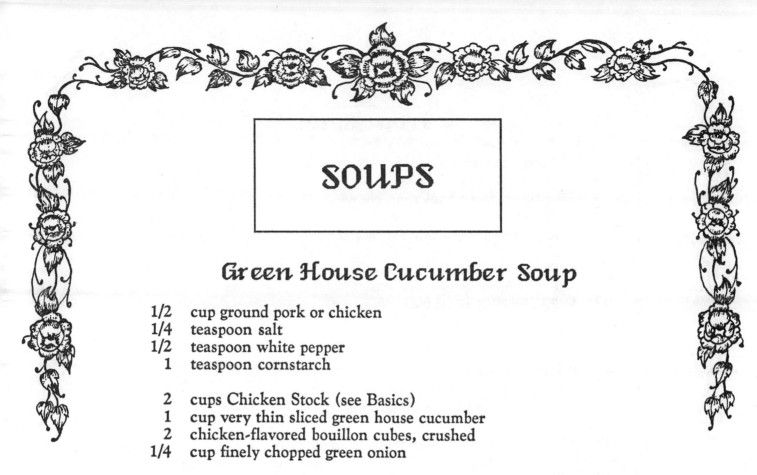

SOUPS

Green House Cucumber Soup

1/2	cup ground pork or chicken
1/4	teaspoon salt
1/2	teaspoon white pepper
1	teaspoon cornstarch
2	cups Chicken Stock (see Basics)
1	cup very thin sliced green house cucumber
2	chicken-flavored bouillon cubes, crushed
1/4	cup finely chopped green onion

Mix ground pork, or chicken with salt, pepper, and cornstarch, then roll into 8 balls. In 3-quart saucepan, bring chicken stock to boil, over high heat. Add meat balls, allow to boil, until meat is done, about 2 minutes. Add the rest of ingredients and bring to boil. Remove from heat and serve. Yields 2 servings.

Oyster Mushroom Soup
(Tom Kah Het)

2	cups Chicken Stock (see Basics)
3	tablespoons fish sauce (nam pla)
6	slices dried or fresh Laos roots, diced
1	8-ounce package fresh oyster mushrooms or 15-ounce can oyster mushrooms, drained
6	fresh makrood leaves or 1 bunch fresh basil
2	red serrano chiles, crushed (optional)
2	stems green onion, cut into 1/2" pieces (white and green parts)
3	stalks cilantro, cut into 1/2" pieces
2	tablespoons fresh lime juice

Combine chicken stock, fish sauce and Laos roots, in 3-quart covered saucepan. Bring to boil over high heat. Add chicken, and mushrooms, cover, and allow to boil until chicken is done, about 5 minutes. Remove from heat and add the remaining ingredients. Stir to blend and serve immediately. Yields 4 servings.

Trout Soup

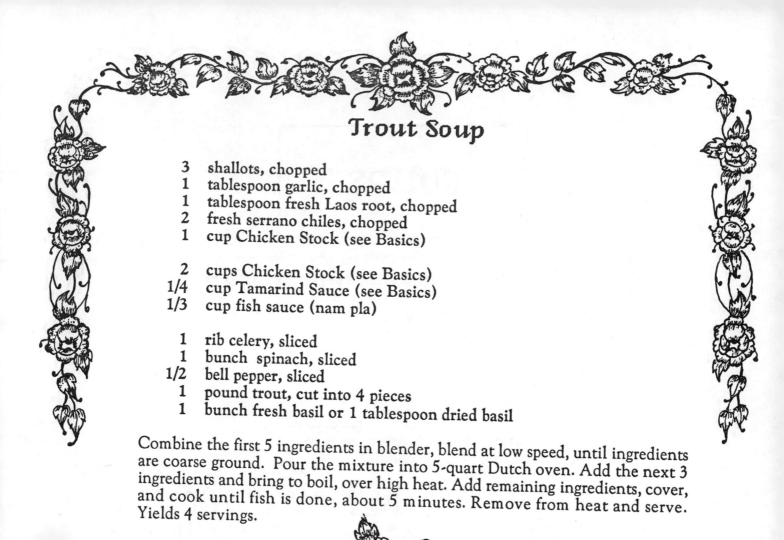

3 shallots, chopped
1 tablespoon garlic, chopped
1 tablespoon fresh Laos root, chopped
2 fresh serrano chiles, chopped
1 cup Chicken Stock (see Basics)

2 cups Chicken Stock (see Basics)
1/4 cup Tamarind Sauce (see Basics)
1/3 cup fish sauce (nam pla)

1 rib celery, sliced
1 bunch spinach, sliced
1/2 bell pepper, sliced
1 pound trout, cut into 4 pieces
1 bunch fresh basil or 1 tablespoon dried basil

Combine the first 5 ingredients in blender, blend at low speed, until ingredients are coarse ground. Pour the mixture into 5-quart Dutch oven. Add the next 3 ingredients and bring to boil, over high heat. Add remaining ingredients, cover, and cook until fish is done, about 5 minutes. Remove from heat and serve. Yields 4 servings.

Stuffed Rambuton Soup

This semi-sweet soup is typical of Bangkok-style food. It is often served with the meal, instead of prior to the meal.

1/4 pound ground pork or chicken
1/4 pound fresh raw shrimp, shelled, deveined, and minced
1/2 teaspoon white pepper
1 tablespoon minced garlic
1 tablespoon minced fresh ginger root

1 20-ounce can rambuton, drained, reserve juice
2 cups Chicken Stock (see Basics)
1 teaspoon salt
1/4 cup shredded carrots

Combine the first 5 ingredients, mix well. Stuff 1/2 tablespoon of the mixture inside each rambuton. Set aside. In 5-quart Dutch oven, bring chicken stock to boil, over high heat. Add stuffed rambutons, and the rest of ingredients, including reserved juice. Cover, and cook about 5 minutes. Remove from heat and serve. Yields 4 servings.

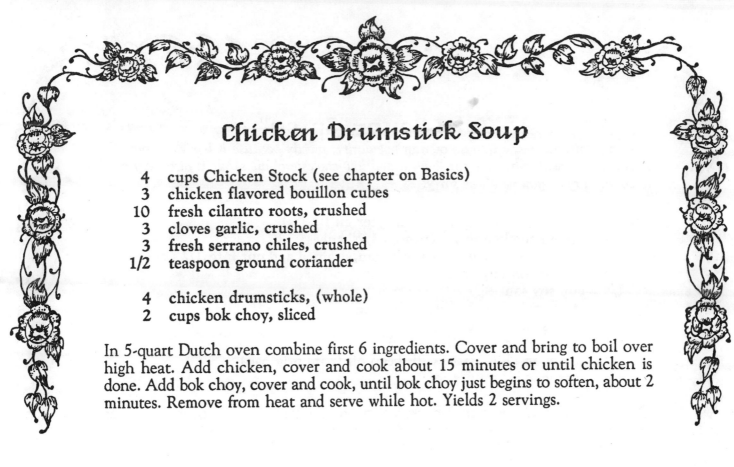

Chicken Drumstick Soup

    4   cups Chicken Stock (see chapter on Basics)
    3   chicken flavored bouillon cubes
   10   fresh cilantro roots, crushed
    3   cloves garlic, crushed
    3   fresh serrano chiles, crushed
  1/2   teaspoon ground coriander

    4   chicken drumsticks, (whole)
    2   cups bok choy, sliced

In 5-quart Dutch oven combine first 6 ingredients. Cover and bring to boil over high heat. Add chicken, cover and cook about 15 minutes or until chicken is done. Add bok choy, cover and cook, until bok choy just begins to soften, about 2 minutes. Remove from heat and serve while hot. Yields 2 servings.

Wonton Soup

(Geiw Nam)

    1   pound ground pork or chicken
    3   stems green onions, finely chopped (white and green parts)
  1/4   cup finely chopped cilantro
    2   tablespoons fish sauce (nam pla)
    1   8-ounce package square wonton skins
  1/2   cup water

    8   cups Chicken Stock (see Basics)
    1   cup sliced Red Roasted Pork (see chapter on Pork)
    3   tablespoons soy sauce
    2   cups sliced bok choy
  1/8   teaspoon pepper

In large bowl, combine ground pork or chicken, green onion, cilantro, and fish sauce. Mix well. Place 1 heaping teaspoon of the mixture into the center of a wonton skin. Dampen edges of skin with water and fold into triangle. Repeat with remaining wontons. Set aside.

In 5-quart Dutch oven, bring stock to boil, over high heat. Add Red Roasted Pork, wontons, and soy sauce. Allow to boil, until wonton are done, about 5 minutes, then add the rest of ingredients. Cook until bok choy softens, about 2 minutes more. Remove from heat and serve with Pickled Chili Sauce. Yields 6 servings.

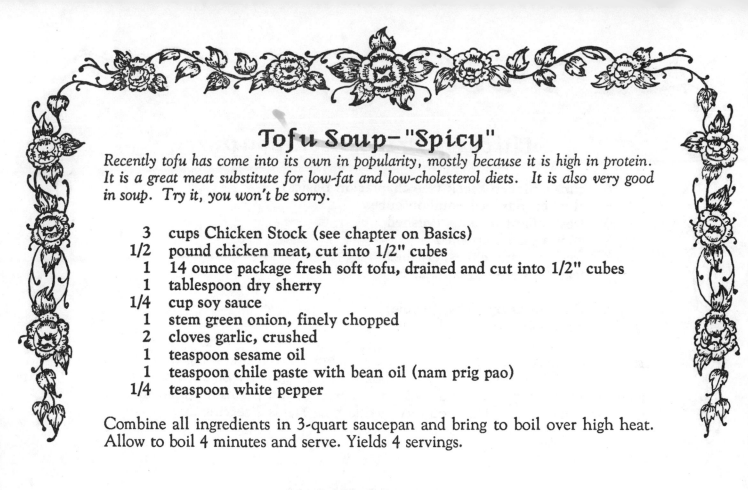

Tofu Soup–"Spicy"

Recently tofu has come into its own in popularity, mostly because it is high in protein. It is a great meat substitute for low-fat and low-cholesterol diets. It is also very good in soup. Try it, you won't be sorry.

3	cups Chicken Stock (see chapter on Basics)
1/2	pound chicken meat, cut into 1/2" cubes
1	14 ounce package fresh soft tofu, drained and cut into 1/2" cubes
1	tablespoon dry sherry
1/4	cup soy sauce
1	stem green onion, finely chopped
2	cloves garlic, crushed
1	teaspoon sesame oil
1	teaspoon chile paste with bean oil (nam prig pao)
1/4	teaspoon white pepper

Combine all ingredients in 3-quart saucepan and bring to boil over high heat. Allow to boil 4 minutes and serve. Yields 4 servings.

Hot & Sour Beef Soup
(Thom Yum Nuah)

8	medium, dried, black mushrooms (shi-i-take)
6	cups Chicken Stock (see chapter on Basics)
1	tomato, sliced thin
4	beef flavored bouillon cubes
3	shallots, smashed
3	tablespoons rice vinegar (seasoned gourmet)
1	tablespoon ground fresh chile paste
1 1/2	pounds sirloin steak, sliced bite-sized
2	cups fresh mushrooms

Soak black mushrooms in hot water for 20 minutes. Drain, remove bottom of stems and slice thin. Set aside. Combine the next 6 ingredients and black mushrooms in 5-quart Dutch oven, bring to boil, over high heat. Allow to boil for 1 minute. Add beef and fresh mushrooms, cook until beef is done, about 2 minutes. Remove from heat and serve while hot. Yields 4 servings.

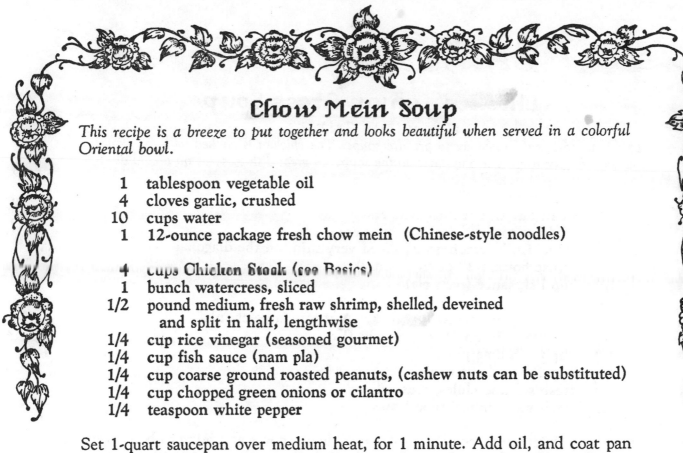

Chow Mein Soup

This recipe is a breeze to put together and looks beautiful when served in a colorful Oriental bowl.

1   tablespoon vegetable oil
4   cloves garlic, crushed
10 cups water
1   12-ounce package fresh chow mein (Chinese-style noodles)

4   cups Chicken Stock (see Basics)
1   bunch watercress, sliced
1/2 pound medium, fresh raw shrimp, shelled, deveined
      and split in half, lengthwise
1/4 cup rice vinegar (seasoned gourmet)
1/4 cup fish sauce (nam pla)
1/4 cup coarse ground roasted peanuts, (cashew nuts can be substituted)
1/4 cup chopped green onions or cilantro
1/4 teaspoon white pepper

Set 1-quart saucepan over medium heat, for 1 minute. Add oil, and coat pan evenly. Add garlic, and brown lightly. Set aside. Boil 10 cups water in 5-quart Dutch oven, over high heat. Add noodles, stir to separate and cook, until noodles are done, about 5 minutes. Drain, rinse with cold water and transfer to serving bowl. Mix with browned garlic and set aside.

Add chicken stock to Dutch oven, and bring to boil, over high heat. Add watercress and cook until limp. Remove watercress, lay on top of noodles. Add shrimp to stock and cook, until shrimp is done, about 1 minute. Remove shrimp, lay on top of watercress. Add vinegar and fish sauce to stock and stir to blend. Pour stock over noodles, top with ground peanuts, green onion, and pepper. Serve while hot, with Pickled Chiles as desired. Yields 4 servings.

Corn Beef & Zucchini Soup

1/4 pound corn beef, sliced very thin, bite size
4   cups Chicken Stock (see Basics)
4   beef flavored bouillon cubes
1   teaspoon coarse ground black pepper
2   cups sliced zucchini

Combine all ingredients in 5-quart Dutch oven, cover, and bring to boil over high heat. Cook until corn beef is done, about 3 minutes. Remove from heat and serve. Yields 2 servings.

Chicken Lemon Grass Soup

(Thom Yum Gai)

This is the original Thai way to prepare soup. The chicken is cooked with the bones and skin to give a good strong flavor to the soup. A great dish to serve on a cold day.

2	quarts water
1	small onion, cut into quarters
1	medium tomato, cut into quarters
3	stems fresh lemon grass, sliced very thin, on the diagonal (use bottom 2" of stems only)
1/4	cup fish sauce (nam pla)
1	3 to 3 1/2 pound whole chicken, cut into large chunks (leave skin and bones attached)
1/2	cup fresh lime juice
1/4	cup chopped cilantro
4	fresh serrano chiles, crushed
15	fresh mint or makrood leaves

In 5-quart Dutch oven, combine first 5 ingredients, cover and bring to boil, over high heat. Add chicken, cover and cook until chicken is done, about 40 minutes. Remove from heat and add the rest of ingredients. Stir to blend and serve. Yields 4 to 6 servings.

Chicken & Coconut Soup

(Thom Kah Gai)

Thom Kah Gai is a very traditional soup; a Thai favorite on family gatherings. The blend of Laos root and coconut gives the soup a wonderful aroma.

2	cups water
1/4	cup fish sauce (nam pla)
1	14-ounce can coconut milk
6	slices dried or fresh Laos roots
4	shallots, crushed
3	tablespoons Tamarind Sauce (see Basics)
1	pound chicken breast, cut into 1" x 2" chunks
2	tablespoons chopped cilantro
2	red serrano chiles, crushed
4	fresh makrood leaves (optional)

In 5-quart Dutch oven, combine first 6 ingredients. Bring to boil over high heat. Add chicken, cover and cook, until chicken is done, about 7 minutes. Remove from heat and add remaining ingredients. Stir to blend and serve with steamed rice. Yields 2 to 3 servings.

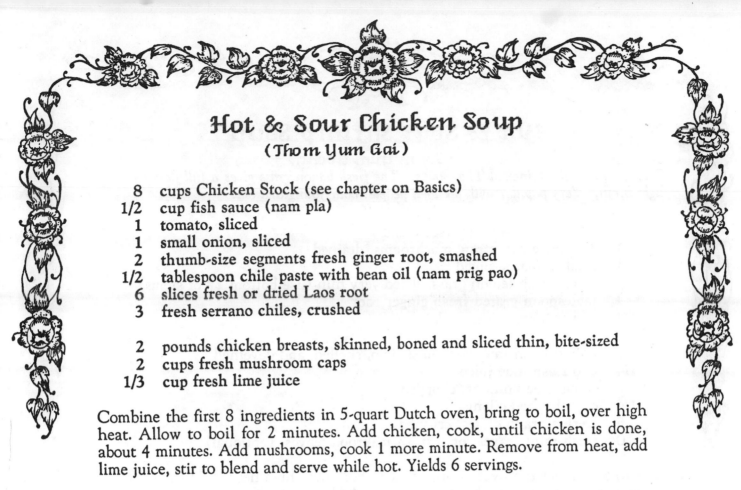

Hot & Sour Chicken Soup
(Thom Yum Gai)

   8   cups Chicken Stock (see chapter on Basics)
1/2   cup fish sauce (nam pla)
   1   tomato, sliced
   1   small onion, sliced
   2   thumb-size segments fresh ginger root, smashed
1/2   tablespoon chile paste with bean oil (nam prig pao)
   6   slices fresh or dried Laos root
   3   fresh serrano chiles, crushed

   2   pounds chicken breasts, skinned, boned and sliced thin, bite-sized
   2   cups fresh mushroom caps
1/3   cup fresh lime juice

Combine the first 8 ingredients in 5-quart Dutch oven, bring to boil, over high heat. Allow to boil for 2 minutes. Add chicken, cook, until chicken is done, about 4 minutes. Add mushrooms, cook 1 more minute. Remove from heat, add lime juice, stir to blend and serve while hot. Yields 6 servings.

Shrimp Wonton Soup
(Guiw Goong)

    4   medium, dried black mushrooms (shi-i-take)
    8   sheets square wonton skins
  1/4   pound fresh raw shrimp, cleaned, deveined and minced
         (or ground pork or chicken)
2 1/2 cups Chicken Stock (see Basics)

    1   teaspoon minced fresh ginger root
    1   cup bok choy or cabbage, shredded
    2   tablespoons fish sauce

  1/8   teaspoon white pepper
    1   green onion, sliced in 1/2" pieces

Soak mushrooms in hot water for 20 minutes, drain, remove bottom part of stems and cut mushrooms in quarters. Set aside. Place 1 heaping teaspoon of minced shrimp onto the center of a wonton skin. Dampen edges of wonton skin with hot water and fold into triangles, repeat with remaining wonton skins and shrimp. Set aside.

In 3-quart saucepan, bring chicken stock to boil over high heat. Add the next 3 ingredients, cover and cook, until wonton are soft, about 3 to 4 minutes. Add onion and pepper, stir to blend and serve. Yields 2 servings.

Hot & Sour Shrimp Soup
(Thom Yum Goong)

This is one of the principal Thai soups. The fresh lemon grass gives a full flavor to a light broth. Very popular with all Thai people, both young and old.

4 cups Chicken Stock (see Basics)
1 15-ounce can straw mushrooms, drained
1 small tomato, sliced
2 stems fresh lemon grass, sliced very thin (use bottom 2" of stems)
1 tablespoon grated fresh ginger root
1/4 cup fish sauce (nam pla)

1/2 pound fresh raw medium shrimp, shelled, and deveined
1/4 cup fresh lime juice
2 stems green onions, chopped
1/4 cup chopped cilantro
5 fresh serrano chiles, crushed
10 fresh mint leaves, or 4 fresh makrood leaves, (optional)

In 4 to 5-quart Dutch oven, bring stock to boil, over high heat. Add the next 5 ingredients and allow to boil 2 minutes. Add shrimp and cover, cook until shrimp turns pink, about 1 minute. Remove from heat, add the rest of ingredients, stir to blend and serve. Yields 2 servings.

Meatball Soup with Bean Sprouts

Thai meatballs are firm and full of flavors and blend well with the sprouts. They are quick to prepare.

6 cups Chicken Stock (see chapter on Basics)
4 whole cloves
2 8-ounce packages Thai meat balls (from Thai markets)
1/2 pound sirloin beef, sliced bite-sized

3 cups bean sprouts
4 stems green onions, chopped
1/2 cup chopped cilantro
1/4 cup Maggi Seasoning

In 4 to 5-quart Dutch oven, bring stock to boil, over high heat. Add meatballs, and cloves, cook until meatballs are thoroughly heated, about 2 minutes. Add beef and cook, until beef is done, about 1 minute. Add remaining ingredients. Serve with Pickled Chili. Yields 4 servings.

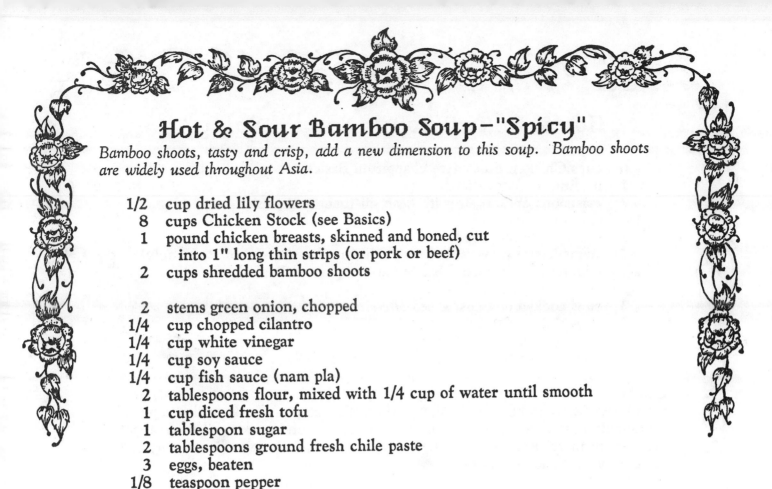

Hot & Sour Bamboo Soup–"Spicy"

Bamboo shoots, tasty and crisp, add a new dimension to this soup. Bamboo shoots are widely used throughout Asia.

- 1/2 cup dried lily flowers
- 8 cups Chicken Stock (see Basics)
- 1 pound chicken breasts, skinned and boned, cut into 1" long thin strips (or pork or beef)
- 2 cups shredded bamboo shoots

- 2 stems green onion, chopped
- 1/4 cup chopped cilantro
- 1/4 cup white vinegar
- 1/4 cup soy sauce
- 1/4 cup fish sauce (nam pla)
- 2 tablespoons flour, mixed with 1/4 cup of water until smooth
- 1 cup diced fresh tofu
- 1 tablespoon sugar
- 2 tablespoons ground fresh chile paste
- 3 eggs, beaten
- 1/8 teaspoon pepper

Soak lily flowers in hot water for 10 minutes. Drain, dice and set aside. In 4 to 5-quart Dutch oven, bring stock to boil, over high heat. Add chicken, bamboo shoots, and lily flowers. Cover and cook until chicken is done, about 4 minutes. Add remaining ingredients, stir and cook, until soup thickens lightly, about 2 minutes. Transfer to soup tureen and serve at once. Yields 6 to 8 servings.

Hot & Sour Fish Soup

(Thom Yum Pla)

Any fish can be used for the very rich and versatile soup.

- 6 cups Chicken Stock (see chapter on Basics)
- 1 small onion, chopped
- 1 medium tomato, sliced
- 1/4 cup fish sauce (nam pla)
- 2 stems lemon grass, sliced very thin (use bottom 2" of stems only)
- 1 16-ounce can golden mushrooms, drained
- 1/4 cup Tamarind Sauce (see chapter on Basics)
- 1 teaspoon ground fresh chile paste

- 1 1/2 pounds bass fillets, cut into 2" chunks

Combine the first 8 ingredients in 5-quart Dutch oven, bring to boil, over high heat. Add fish, cover and cook, until fish is done, about 3 minutes. Remove from heat and serve. Yields 4 servings.

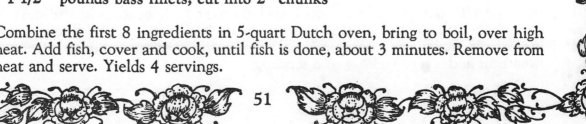

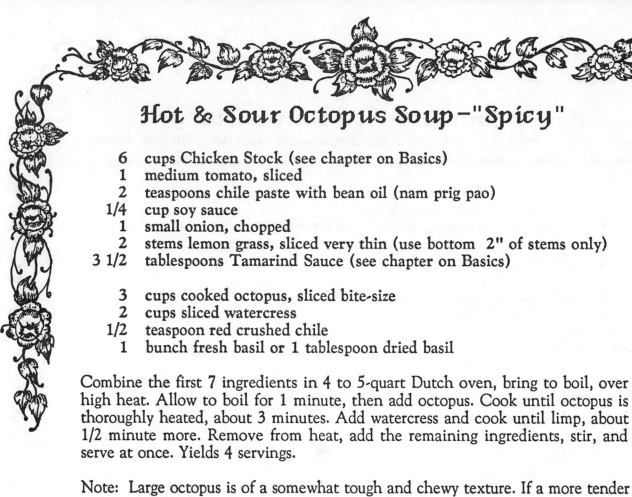

Hot & Sour Octopus Soup – "Spicy"

6 cups Chicken Stock (see chapter on Basics)
1 medium tomato, sliced
2 teaspoons chile paste with bean oil (nam prig pao)
1/4 cup soy sauce
1 small onion, chopped
2 stems lemon grass, sliced very thin (use bottom 2" of stems only)
3 1/2 tablespoons Tamarind Sauce (see chapter on Basics)

3 cups cooked octopus, sliced bite-size
2 cups sliced watercress
1/2 teaspoon red crushed chile
1 bunch fresh basil or 1 tablespoon dried basil

Combine the first 7 ingredients in 4 to 5-quart Dutch oven, bring to boil, over high heat. Allow to boil for 1 minute, then add octopus. Cook until octopus is thoroughly heated, about 3 minutes. Add watercress and cook until limp, about 1/2 minute more. Remove from heat, add the remaining ingredients, stir, and serve at once. Yields 4 servings.

Note: Large octopus is of a somewhat tough and chewy texture. If a more tender texture is desired, small octopus should be selected.

Flat Rice Noodle Soup

8 cups Chicken Stock (see chapter on Basics)
2 pounds fresh Chinese flat rice noodles (cut into 1"x 2" pieces)
1 8-ounce package shrimp balls
1 pound pork, beef, or chicken (sliced bite-sized)

3 cups sliced bok choy
1/2 cup fish sauce (nam pla)
1/4 cup catsup
1/2 cup chopped cilantro
1/4 cup white vinegar
1/4 cup sugar
1/4 teaspoon pepper
2 teaspoons ground fresh chile paste

In 5-quart Dutch oven, bring stock to boil, over high heat. Add the next 3 ingredients and cook until meat is done, about 4 minutes. Add the rest of the ingredients, cover and cook, until bok choy softens, about 1 minute. Remove from heat and serve. Yields 4 to 6 servings.

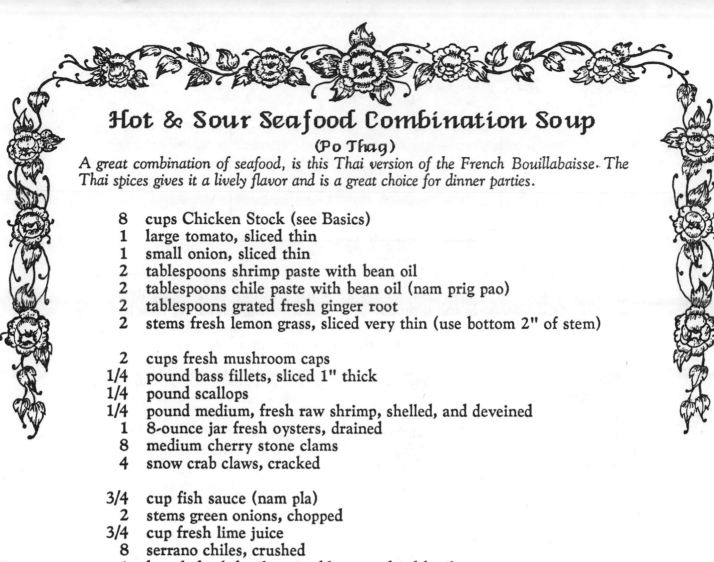

Hot & Sour Seafood Combination Soup

(Po Thag)

A great combination of seafood, is this Thai version of the French Bouillabaisse. The Thai spices gives it a lively flavor and is a great choice for dinner parties.

8	cups Chicken Stock (see Basics)
1	large tomato, sliced thin
1	small onion, sliced thin
2	tablespoons shrimp paste with bean oil
2	tablespoons chile paste with bean oil (nam prig pao)
2	tablespoons grated fresh ginger root
2	stems fresh lemon grass, sliced very thin (use bottom 2" of stem)
2	cups fresh mushroom caps
1/4	pound bass fillets, sliced 1" thick
1/4	pound scallops
1/4	pound medium, fresh raw shrimp, shelled, and deveined
1	8-ounce jar fresh oysters, drained
8	medium cherry stone clams
4	snow crab claws, cracked
3/4	cup fish sauce (nam pla)
2	stems green onions, chopped
3/4	cup fresh lime juice
8	serrano chiles, crushed
1	bunch fresh basil or 1 tablespoon dried basil

Combine the first 7 ingredients in 8 to 10-quart stock pot, bring to boil, over high heat. Allow to boil for 2 minutes. Then add the next 7 ingredients, cover and cook, until clam shells open and scallops are done. Remove from heat and add the rest of ingredients. Stir to blend and serve while hot. Yields 4 to 6 servings.

Thai Onion Soup

If you are looking for a quick soup dish, this is it. It goes well before any meal.

2	cups Chicken Stock (see Basics)
2	chicken-flavored bouillon cubes
2	stems green onions, finely chopped
1/2	cup thin sliced mushrooms
1/8	teaspoon pepper

In 2-quart saucepan, bring stock to boil, over high heat. Add remaining ingredients and bring to boil again. Stir to blend, remove from heat and serve while hot. Yields 2 servings.

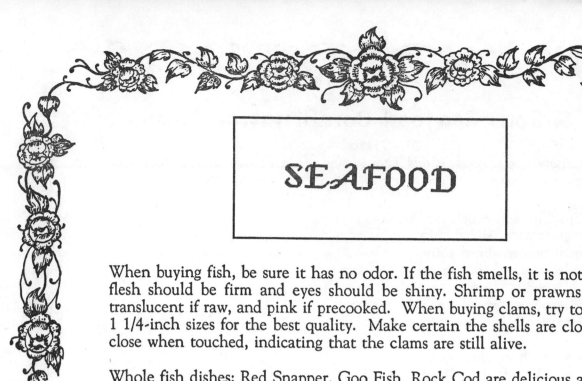

SEAFOOD

When buying fish, be sure it has no odor. If the fish smells, it is not fresh. The flesh should be firm and eyes should be shiny. Shrimp or prawns should be translucent if raw, and pink if precooked. When buying clams, try to select 1 to 1 1/4-inch sizes for the best quality. Make certain the shells are closed, or will close when touched, indicating that the clams are still alive.

Whole fish dishes: Red Snapper, Goo Fish, Rock Cod are delicious and just the right size for serving whole.

Stir fries: The Thais love catfish. They use it for stir frying along with snapper, bass, cod and orange roughy, which has an excellent texture. Shrimp, crab, and oysters are wonderful for stir frying. Do not overcook fish. It should be firm, not mushy. Shrimp should only be cooked for a few minutes or they will be tough.

Soups: Shrimp, bass, clams and any kind of fish or shell-fish of your choice is great to add to soups. Be sure to add the fish or shellfish at the very end or they will be overcooked.

Shrimp with Garlic & Pepper
(Goong Gratiam Prig Tai)

3	tablespoons vegetable oil
4	cloves garlic, crushed
1/2	pound medium raw fresh shrimp, shelled and deveined
1/2	teaspoon salt
1/2	teaspoon coarse ground black pepper

Set 10" frying pan over high heat for one minute. Add oil and coat bottom of pan evenly. Add garlic and cook until light brown. Add remaining ingredients, stir and cook, until shrimp are pink on both sides, about 2 minutes. Remove from heat and serve. Yields 2 servings.

Note: -You can use this recipe as an appetizer or as a main course.

Sweet & Sour Shrimp
(Paht Pril Wam Goong)

This is a Thai version of a very popular Chinese dish. Hope you like it.

3	tablespoons vegetable oil
3	cloves garlic, minced
1	small onion, sliced
1	pound medium, fresh raw shrimp, shelled and deveined
1	small tomato, sliced
1	small bell pepper, sliced
1	tablespoon catsup
2	tablespoons fish sauce (nam pla)
1/2	tablespoon sugar
1/2	tablespoon white vinegar
1/8	teaspoon pepper

Set wok over high heat for 1 minute. Add oil and coat sides of wok evenly. Add garlic and onion, stir and cook, until light brown. Add shrimp, stir and cook, until shrimp is pink, about 2 minutes. Add remaining ingredients, stir and cook, until bell pepper just begins to soften. Transfer to serving plate and serve with steamed rice. Yields 4 servings.

Shrimp Baked in Roasted Chili Paste
(Goong Ob Nam Prig Pao)

1/2	pound large fresh raw shrimp, shelled and deveined, leaving tails attached
2	10" x 10" pieces heavy-duty tinfoil
1/2	teaspoon salt
1/4	cup chile paste with bean oil (nam prig pao)
2	green onions, whole (white and green parts)

Preheat broiler. Arrange 1/4 pound of shrimp on each piece of tinfoil. Sprinkle with salt and spoon 2 tablespoons chile paste on each arrangement of shrimp. Place 1 whole green onion on top of each of the shrimp packages. Bring 4 corners of foil to center, twist to close securely.

Place packages in broiler and broil 10 to 12 minutes or until done. Remove from heat and cut open foil. Place shrimp on serving plate. Serve with steamed rice or bread. Yields 2 servings.

Shrimp in Orange Sauce

2   egg whites, beaten until foamy, reserve yolks
1   tablespoon corn starch
1/4 cup vegetable oil
1/2 pound medium, fresh raw shrimp, shelled, and deveined
12 dried red chile pods
1   tablespoon minced garlic
1   tablespoon minced fresh ginger root

1   small tomato, finely chopped
2   tablespoons soy sauce
1/2 cup fresh orange juice
1   tablespoon honey
2   tablespoons dry sherry
1/4 teaspoon white pepper
1   tablespoon cornstarch, mixed with 3 tablespoons of water

Make batter by combining egg whites with corn starch, mix until smooth. Set aside. Meanwhile heat oil in wok over high heat until sizzling hot, reduce to medium heat. Dip 4 shrimps in batter at a time and deep fry until golden brown on both sides, about 1 minute. Remove shrimp and drain on paper towel. Repeat remaining shrimp. Add chile pods to oil and quickly fry until pods darken, but do not burn, set aside.

Remove all but 2 tablespoons of oil from wok. Stir in garlic, and ginger, cook until fragrant. Add the rest of ingredients including egg yolks, stir and cook, until sauce thickens, about 1 minute. Return shrimp and chiles, gently stir to blend. Transfer to serving plate and serve at once. Yields 2 servings.

Shrimp with Snow Peas

2   tablespoons vegetable oil
3   cloves garlic, crushed
1/2 pound medium, fresh raw shrimp, shelled and deveined

1   cup snow peas
1   cup sliced mushrooms
3   tablespoons soy sauce
1/4 teaspoon pepper

Set wok over high heat for one minute. Add oil and coat sides of wok evenly. Add garlic and cook until light brown. Add shrimp, stir and cook, until shrimp is done, about 2 minutes. Add the rest of ingredients, stir and cook, until mushrooms just begin to soften, about 1 minute. Serve with steamed rice or fried rice. Yields 2 servings.

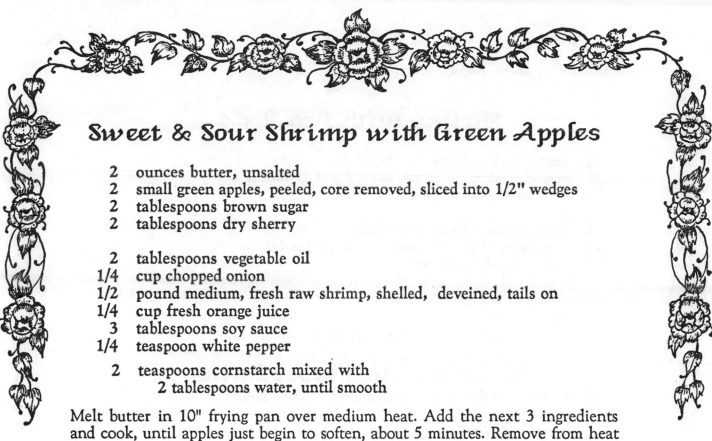

Sweet & Sour Shrimp with Green Apples

- 2   ounces butter, unsalted
- 2   small green apples, peeled, core removed, sliced into 1/2" wedges
- 2   tablespoons brown sugar
- 2   tablespoons dry sherry

- 2   tablespoons vegetable oil
- 1/4   cup chopped onion
- 1/2   pound medium, fresh raw shrimp, shelled, deveined, tails on
- 1/4   cup fresh orange juice
- 3   tablespoons soy sauce
- 1/4   teaspoon white pepper

- 2   teaspoons cornstarch mixed with
    2 tablespoons water, until smooth

Melt butter in 10" frying pan over medium heat. Add the next 3 ingredients and cook, until apples just begin to soften, about 5 minutes. Remove from heat and set aside.

Set wok over high heat for 1 minute. Add oil and coat sides of wok evenly. Add onion stir and cook, until fragrant. Add shrimp, stir and cook until shrimps turn pink, about 1/2 minute. Add cooked apples and rest of the ingredients, stir and cook, until sauce thickens, about 10 seconds. Transfer to serving dish and serve. Yields 2 servings.

Shrimp with Green Curry
(Goong Paht Prig Keiw)

Shrimp and green curry are a special flavor combination. Any firm textured fish can be substituted for the shrimp.

- 2   tablespoons vegetable oil
- 4   cloves garlic, crushed
- 2   tablespoons Green Curry Paste
- 1/2   pound medium fresh raw shrimp, shelled and deveined
- 1   cup shredded bamboo shoots
- 2   tablespoons fish sauce (nam pla)
- 2   stems green onions, cut into 1/2" pieces (white and green parts)

Set wok over high heat for 1 minute, add oil and coat sides of wok evenly. Add garlic and curry paste, stir and cook, until light brown. Add shrimp and bamboo, stir and cook, until shrimp is pink on both sides, about 2 minutes. Add fish sauce and green onion, stir to blend and remove from heat. Serve with steamed rice. Yields 2 servings.

Shrimp with Pea Pods

    2   cups Chicken Stock (see Basics)
    1/2 pound fresh raw shrimp, shelled and deveined,
    1   cup snow peas, cleaned
    1   cup sliced watercress
    2   chicken-flavored bouillon cubes
    1/4 cup chopped green onions (white part only)
    1/4 teaspoon white pepper

In 2-quart covered saucepan, bring chicken stock to boil, over high heat. Add the rest of ingredients, stir to blend and cook, until shrimp is done, about 1 minute. Remove from heat and serve. Yields 2 servings.

Shrimp with Herbal Butter

A fine combination of flavors, I suggest you serve this for lunch.

    1/2 cup Herbal Butter (see Basics)
    1/2 pound medium, fresh raw shrimp, shelled and deveined
           (leaving tails attached)
    1/4 cup white wine
    10   mushroom caps
    1   chicken-flavored bouillon cube, crushed

Melt Herbal Butter in 2-quart covered saucepan, over medium heat. Add remaining ingredients, stir, cover and cook, until shrimp is done, about 2 minutes. Remove from heat and serve with steamed rice or bread. Yields 2 servings.

Fried Prawns

(Goong Nang Dee)

Prawns are a little bigger variety of shrimp. Try this dish that is sometimes found as Heavenly Shrimp on a Japanese menu.

    1/4 pound medium, fresh raw shrimp, shelled, deveined and split
    2   egg yolks
    1/4 teaspoon salt
    2   tablespoons vegetable oil

Combine shrimp with egg yolk and salt, allow to marinate for 5 minutes. Set 10" frying pan over high heat for 1 minute. Add oil and coat bottom of pan evenly. Add marinated shrimp, stir to separate and cook, until shrimp is done, about 1/2 minute per side. Transfer to serving plate, and serve immediately. Yields 2 servings.

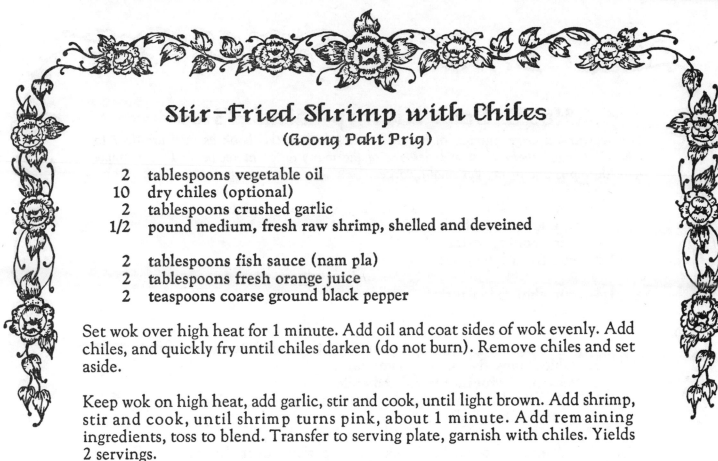

Stir-Fried Shrimp with Chiles
(Goong Paht Prig)

- 2 tablespoons vegetable oil
- 10 dry chiles (optional)
- 2 tablespoons crushed garlic
- 1/2 pound medium, fresh raw shrimp, shelled and deveined

- 2 tablespoons fish sauce (nam pla)
- 2 tablespoons fresh orange juice
- 2 teaspoons coarse ground black pepper

Set wok over high heat for 1 minute. Add oil and coat sides of wok evenly. Add chiles, and quickly fry until chiles darken (do not burn). Remove chiles and set aside.

Keep wok on high heat, add garlic, stir and cook, until light brown. Add shrimp, stir and cook, until shrimp turns pink, about 1 minute. Add remaining ingredients, toss to blend. Transfer to serving plate, garnish with chiles. Yields 2 servings.

Butterflied Garlic Shrimp

Oriental people often cook shrimp in their shell, to keep in the flavor and juices. It also can be fun to peel your own shrimp at the table. Some people eat them shell and all.

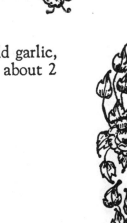

- 2 ounces butter or margarine, unsalted
- 1/2 pound fresh raw medium shrimp, in shell
- 6 cloves garlic, crushed
- 1/2 teaspoon, each, salt and pepper

Over medium heat, melt butter in 10" frying pan. Add shrimp, toss. Add garlic, pepper, and salt. Increase heat, stir and cook until shrimp turns pink, about 2 minutes. Remove from heat and serve. Yields 2 Servings.

Grilled Lobster

- 1 pound fresh raw slipper lobster tails or
- 2 whole Pacific lobsters (about 1 pound, each)
- 2 metal skewers
  juice from 1 whole lemon

Preheat broiler. Insert a skewer lengthwise through half of the lobster tails, or a whole lobster, to prevent curling. Repeat with second skewer. Place in broiler and broil, about 5 minutes, turn and brush with lemon juice. Broil until done, about 5 more minutes. Serve with Ginger Sauce and sliced cucumbers. Yields 2 servings.

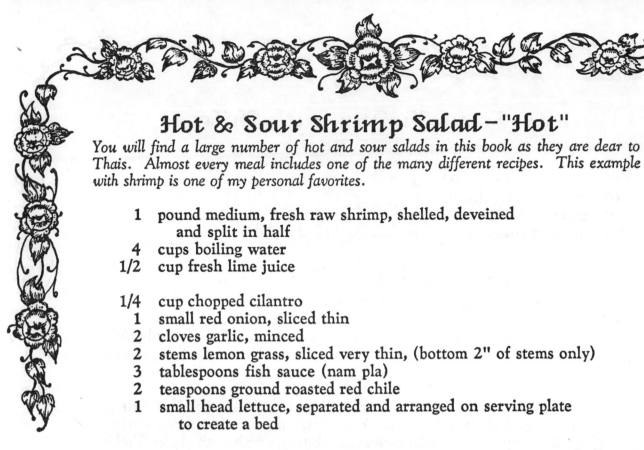

Hot & Sour Shrimp Salad – "Hot"

You will find a large number of hot and sour salads in this book as they are dear to Thais. Almost every meal includes one of the many different recipes. This example with shrimp is one of my personal favorites.

- 1 pound medium, fresh raw shrimp, shelled, deveined and split in half
- 4 cups boiling water
- 1/2 cup fresh lime juice

- 1/4 cup chopped cilantro
- 1 small red onion, sliced thin
- 2 cloves garlic, minced
- 2 stems lemon grass, sliced very thin, (bottom 2" of stems only)
- 3 tablespoons fish sauce (nam pla)
- 2 teaspoons ground roasted red chile
- 1 small head lettuce, separated and arranged on serving plate to create a bed

Place shrimp into medium bowl, pour boiling water over shrimp and allow to stand for 1 minute, drain. Add lime juice, mix well. Add next 6 ingredients, toss to blend. Serve on bed of lettuce, with steamed rice and your choice of fresh raw vegetables. Yields 2 to 3 servings.

Sweet & Sour Fish
(Paht Pril Wam Pla)

- 3 tablespoons vegetable oil
- 3 cloves garlic, crushed
- 1 small onion, sliced thin
- 2 pounds fish fillets, sliced bite size (any firm-fleshed fish like bass, catfish, red snapper or shark)

- 2 carrots, peeled, sliced very thin
- 2 tablespoons catsup or Sweet and Sour Chile Sauce
- 1/4 cup soy sauce
- 3 teaspoons sugar
- 2 tablespoons rice vinegar (seasoned gourmet)
- 1/4 teaspoon pepper

Set wok over high heat for 1 minute. Add oil and coat sides of wok evenly. Add garlic and onion, stir and cook, until light brown. Add fish, cook and gently stir, until fish is done, about 3 minutes. Add remaining ingredients, cook until carrots just begin to soften, about 1 minute. Transfer to serving dish and serve with steamed rice. Yields 4 servings.

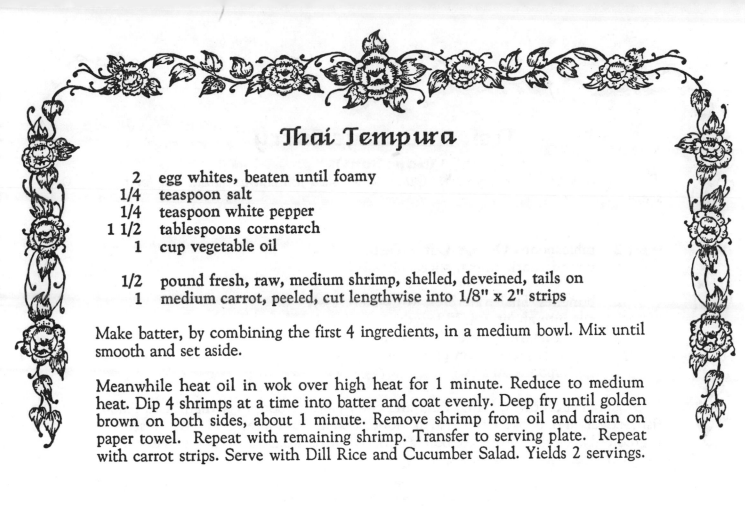

Thai Tempura

2 egg whites, beaten until foamy
1/4 teaspoon salt
1/4 teaspoon white pepper
1 1/2 tablespoons cornstarch
1 cup vegetable oil

1/2 pound fresh, raw, medium shrimp, shelled, deveined, tails on
1 medium carrot, peeled, cut lengthwise into 1/8" x 2" strips

Make batter, by combining the first 4 ingredients, in a medium bowl. Mix until smooth and set aside.

Meanwhile heat oil in wok over high heat for 1 minute. Reduce to medium heat. Dip 4 shrimps at a time into batter and coat evenly. Deep fry until golden brown on both sides, about 1 minute. Remove shrimp from oil and drain on paper towel. Repeat with remaining shrimp. Transfer to serving plate. Repeat with carrot strips. Serve with Dill Rice and Cucumber Salad. Yields 2 servings.

Spicy Shrimp in Shells

Serve this as part of a cold buffet or picnic lunch. It is great with fresh, hot garlic bread.

2 ounces butter or margarine
1/2 pound medium, fresh raw shrimp, in shell
1/2 teaspoon ginger powder
1/2 teaspoon garlic powder
1 teaspoon coarse ground black pepper
1 teaspoon mustard powder
1/2 teaspoon salt

2 tablespoons Tamarind Sauce (see Basics)
2 tablespoons dry sherry
1 tablespoon dried parsley flakes

Melt butter in 10" frying pan over high heat. Add shrimp, toss gently a few times. Add the next 5 ingredients, stir and cook, until shrimps turn pink, about 2 minutes. Add the rest of ingredients, stir and cook for 1/2 minute. Remove from heat and serve. Yields 2 servings.

Fish in Orange Curry
(Gang Som)

This is a very popular curry dish. Other firm-fleshed fish can be substituted for the shark.

3 cups water
2 tablespoons Orange Curry Paste
1 pound shark fillets, sliced bite-size

2 bunches Thai watercress (or watercress),
   cut into about 1 1/2" length
1/4 cup Tamarind Sauce (see Basics)
1/4 cup fish sauce (nam pla)
2 tablespoons sugar

In 5-quart Dutch oven, bring water and curry paste to boil, over high heat. Add fish, cover and cook, until fish is done, about 2 minutes. Add the rest of ingredients, cover, bring to boil again. Remove from heat and serve with steamed rice. Yields 2 servings.

Steamed Rock Cod
(Pla Nueng)

4 dried black mushrooms (shi-i-take)
1 2 to 2 1/2 pound whole fish (snapper or cod)
3 tablespoons light soy sauce
1 tablespoon yellow bean sauce
1 small onion, sliced thin
1 thumb-size segment fresh ginger, slivered
1 cup water

2 stems green onions, sliced (white and green parts)
3 stalks cilantro

Soak mushrooms in hot water for 30 minutes. Drain, cut off bottom parts, and set aside. Preheat oven to 500 degrees. Clean fish and make deep diagonal slashes on each side of fish, about 4 to each side. Rub soy sauce and bean condiment all over fish, inside and out. Place some of the onion and ginger inside stomach cavity. Arrange the mushrooms and the remaining onion and ginger over the top of the fish. Pour water in bottom of fish steamer and place the fish on the rack. Put steamer in oven and cook for 35 minutes or until fish is done. (Fish becomes opaque.)

Remove from oven and place on serving platter. Garnish with shredded green onion and cilantro. Pour juice from steamer over fish and serve with steamed rice. Yields 2 to 3 servings.

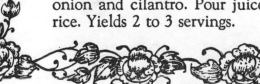

Barbecued Whole Fish-"Hot"
(Pla Yang)

1   2 1/2 to 3 pound whole fish (trout or bass)
2   tablespoons fish sauce (nam pla)
1/2 teaspoon salt
1   18" x 18" piece tin foil (heavy duty)

1   thumb size segment fresh ginger root, grated
1   small onion, sliced thin
3   jalapeno chiles, sliced thin
1/4 cup chopped cilantro

Cut 3 to 4 deep diagonal slashes on each side of fish. Sprinkle fish sauce and salt all over fish, inside and out. Place fish on tin foil, arrange remaining ingredients on top of fish. Bring 4 corners of tin foil to center, twist to close securely, allowing room for expansion. Grill fish over medium hot coals about 30 to 40 minutes or until done. Serve with Garlic Noodles or steamed rice. Yields 4 servings.

Catfish in Curry Sauce
(Gang Pla Dook)

1   14-ounce can coconut milk
2   tablespoons Masman Curry Paste
3   small potatoes, peeled and quartered
1   tablespoon curry powder

1/4 cup water
1   pound catfish, cut into 3/4" thick slices
2   tablespoons fish sauce (nam pla)
1   tablespoon Tamarind Sauce (see Basics)
1   red serrano chile, quartered
1   green serrano chile, quartered

In 5-quart Dutch oven, cook 1/2 cup of the coconut milk, over high heat, until the milk separates. Add masman curry paste, stir to blend, then reduce heat. Add potatoes, curry powder and remaining coconut milk. Stir, cover and cook for approximately 10 minutes. Add water, stir, and increase heat. Bring to a boil, then add fish and fish sauce. Gently stir, cover and cook, until fish is done, about 4 minutes. Add quartered chiles and remove from heat. Serve with Cucumber Salad, choice of bread or steamed rice. Yields 2 servings.

Note: - If sauce becomes to thick while cooking, add a little water. Do not overcook the fish. Fish should be firm, not mushy. The sauce should be of a light consistency with some coconut oil floating on top.

Stuffed Squid
(Pla Muik Yad Sai)

This may be just the dish for your next party. Unusual, but it has good texture and good taste.

1/2	pound ground pork
1/4	cup finely chopped onion
1	tablespoon fish sauce (nam pla)
1/2	teaspoon pepper
4	whole, raw squid (about 5" long), cleaned, skinned and tentacles removed
1	cup vegetable oil
1/2	small cucumber, sliced
1	carrot, sliced

In small bowl, combine first 4 ingredients, mix well. Stuff about 4 tablespoons of meat mixture into each squid. Heat oil in wok, over medium, until sizzling hot. Add the stuffed squid and fry until golden brown, turning often, about 15 minutes. Remove squid from oil and drain on paper towel. Place on serving plate and garnish with sliced cucumbers and carrots. Yields 2 servings.

Stir-Fried Squid-"Hot"
(Paht Pla Muik)

3	tablespoons vegetable oil
4	cloves garlic, crushed
1	small onion, sliced thin
6	jalapeno chiles, sliced thin
2	pounds fresh squid, cleaned and cut into 2" strips
2	tablespoons fish sauce (nam pla)
1/2	cup chopped parsley
	juice from 1/2 lemon

Set 10" frying pan over high heat for 1 minute. Add oil and coat bottom of pan evenly. Add garlic, onion, and chiles, stir and cook, until light brown. Add squid, stir and cook, until squid is done, about 2 minutes. Add remaining ingredients, stir to blend. Remove from heat and serve. Yields 4 servings.

Steamed Fish with
Red Curry & Coconut Milk – "Spicy"

1	14-ounce can coconut milk
2	stems green onions, cut in 1/2" pieces (white and green parts)
3	tablespoons fish sauce (nam pla)
2 1/2	tablespoons Red Curry Paste
1	thumb-size segment fresh ginger root, grated
1	bunch fresh basil
4	jalapeno chiles, sliced thin
2	eggs, beaten
1/8	teaspoon pepper
2	pounds catfish fillets, cut into 2" square chunks

Combine first 9 ingredients in medium bowl, mix well. Add fish, gently stir to blend. Pour the mixture into a 2-quart heat-proof container and place in steamer. Add 5 cups water to steamer pan, steam over high heat, until fish is done, about 35 minutes. Serve with steamed rice. Yields 4 servings.

Thai Braised Shrimp

2	tablespoons vegetable oil
1/2	pound medium, fresh raw shrimp, shelled, deveined, leaving tail attached
2	tablespoons chopped onion
1	teaspoon minced garlic
1	teaspoon minced fresh ginger root
1/8	teaspoon white pepper

Sauce:

3	tablespoons catsup
2 1/2	tablespoons soy sauce
2	tablespoons dry sherry
2	teaspoons brown sugar
2	teaspoons cornstarch, mixed with 2 tablespoons of water
2	teaspoons light sesame oil
2	green onions, finely chopped (white part only)

Set wok over high heat, for 1 minute. Add oil, and coat sides of wok evenly. Add shrimp and cook until pink, about 1 minute. Remove shrimp and set aside.

Add next 4 ingredients to wok stir and cook until fragrant, about 20 seconds. Add sauce ingredients, stir and cook, until sauce thickens, about 1 minute. Return shrimp, stir to blend. Remove from heat, and serve with steamed rice. Yields 2 servings.

Note: -This exotic dish is quick, easy and always a big hit at parties.

Steamed Crab Claws
(Galm Pu Nueng)

Old-style clay pots are available at most Oriental markets. They are used to steam and serve seafood. If you enjoy steamed mussels and clams, you may like to purchase one. For this recipe and many others, these clay pots add a special Oriental feel.

- 6 slices bacon, diced
- 3 cloves garlic, minced
- 1 small onion, sliced
- 1 pound cooked crab claws, cracked
- 3 tablespoons oyster sauce
- 1/4 cup water
- 1/2 cup chopped cilantro
- 1 teaspoon coarse ground black pepper

Set 2-quart covered saucepan over high heat for one minute. Add bacon and fry until brown. Add garlic, and onion, stir and cook, until light brown. Add remaining ingredients, cover and cook, until crab claws are thoroughly heated, about 10 minutes. Remove from heat and serve with steamed rice. Yields 2 servings.

Stir-Fried King Crab Legs

- 1/4 cup chopped bacon
- 1 small onion, sliced
- 2 pounds king crab legs, cut into 2" sections, cracked
- 1 cup thin sliced celery
- 2 tablespoons soy bean condiment

Set wok over high heat for 1 minute. Add bacon and fry, until brown. Add onion and cook, until light brown. Add crab legs, stir and cook, until crab is thoroughly heated, about 3 minutes. Add remaining ingredients, stir and cook, until celery just begins to soften. Remove from heat and serve with steamed rice. Yields 2 to 3 servings.

Crab Meat or Shrimp with Curry

- 2 tablespoons vegetable oil
- 1/2 pound crab meat or fresh raw shrimp, shelled and deveined
- 1/2 tablespoon fish sauce (nam pla)
- 1/2 tablespoon curry powder
- 2 stems green onions, cut into 1/2" pieces (white and green parts)

Set 10" frying pan over high heat for 1 minute. Add oil and coat bottom of pan evenly. Add the rest of ingredients, stir and cook, until shrimp is pink or crab meat is thoroughly heated, about 2 minutes. Transfer to serving dish and serve with Garlic Noodles or steamed rice. Yields 2 servings.

Grilled Squid
(Pla Muik Yiang)

1   pound squid, cleaned
    roasted Serrano Chile Sauce (see Index)
1   cucumber, sliced

Place squid on hot grill and cook until done, about 5 minutes, or broil squid in oven for 5 minutes. Slice into bite-size pieces and set aside. Place chile sauce in small bowl, in center of serving plate. Arrange squid and cucumber slices around bowl, alternating sections of squid and cucumber slices. Serve as side dish or appetizer. Yields 2 servings.

Stir-Fried Oysters with Ginger

2   tablespoons vegetable oil
3   tablespoons minced fresh ginger root
1   8-ounce jar fresh oysters, drained
3   tablespoons oyster sauce
2   stems green onions, cut in 1/2" pieces (white and green parts)

Set 10" frying pan over high heat for 1 minute. Add oil and coat bottom of pan evenly. Add ginger, stir and cook, until fragrant. Add oysters, gently stir and cook, until oysters are done, about 2 minutes. Add remaining ingredients, stir and remove from heat. Serve with steamed rice. Yields 2 servings.

Abalone with Vegetables

1   cup dried black mushrooms (shi-i-take)
2   tablespoons vegetable oil
3   cloves garlic, minced
1   16-ounce can abalone, drained (reserving juice), sliced bite-size

4   cups sliced napa cabbage
1   cup sliced bell pepper
1/4   cup soy sauce
1/4   teaspoon pepper
2   tablespoons all-purpose flour, mixed with reserved abalone juice

Soak mushrooms in hot water for 20 minutes. Drain, remove bottom of stems and slice thin. Set aside. Set wok over high heat for 1 minute. Add oil and coat sides of wok evenly. Add garlic, abalone and mushrooms, stir and cook, until abalone is thoroughly heated, about 2 minutes. Add remaining ingredients, stir and cook, until sauce thickens, about 2 minutes. Remove from heat and serve with steamed rice. Yields 4 servings.

Scallops with Vegetables

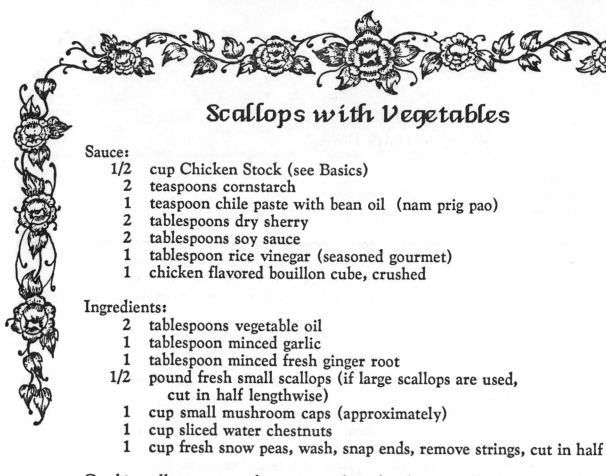

Sauce:
- 1/2   cup Chicken Stock (see Basics)
- 2   teaspoons cornstarch
- 1   teaspoon chile paste with bean oil (nam prig pao)
- 2   tablespoons dry sherry
- 2   tablespoons soy sauce
- 1   tablespoon rice vinegar (seasoned gourmet)
- 1   chicken flavored bouillon cube, crushed

Ingredients:
- 2   tablespoons vegetable oil
- 1   tablespoon minced garlic
- 1   tablespoon minced fresh ginger root
- 1/2   pound fresh small scallops (if large scallops are used, cut in half lengthwise)
- 1   cup small mushroom caps (approximately)
- 1   cup sliced water chestnuts
- 1   cup fresh snow peas, wash, snap ends, remove strings, cut in half

Combine all sauce ingredients in medium bowl, mix well. Set aside. Set wok over high heat for 1 minute. Add oil, coat sides of wok evenly. Stir in garlic, and ginger, cook until fragrant. Add scallops, stir and cook, until scallops are done, about 1 minute. Add the next 3 ingredients and cook, until mushroom just begin to soften, about 1 minute. Add sauce mixture, stir and cook, until sauce thickens. Remove to serving dish and serve at once. Yields 4 servings.

Stir-Fried Octopus

This is an original and established Thai dish. It is an old and trusted recipe. You may substitute your favorite fish for the octopus.

- 3   tablespoons vegetable oil
- 4   cloves garlic, crushed
- 1   small onion, sliced thin
- 2   pounds cooked octopus, cut into 1" chunks

- 2   tablespoons chile paste with bean oil (nam prig pao)
- 2   tablespoons fish sauce (nam pla)
- 2   tablespoons oyster sauce
- 1   tablespoon dried basil

Set 10" frying pan over high heat for 1 minute. Add oil and coat bottom of pan evenly. Add garlic and onion, cook until light brown. Add octopus, stir and cook, until octopus is thoroughly heated, about 2 minutes. Add remaining ingredients, stir to blend. Remove from heat and serve with steamed rice. Yields 4 servings.

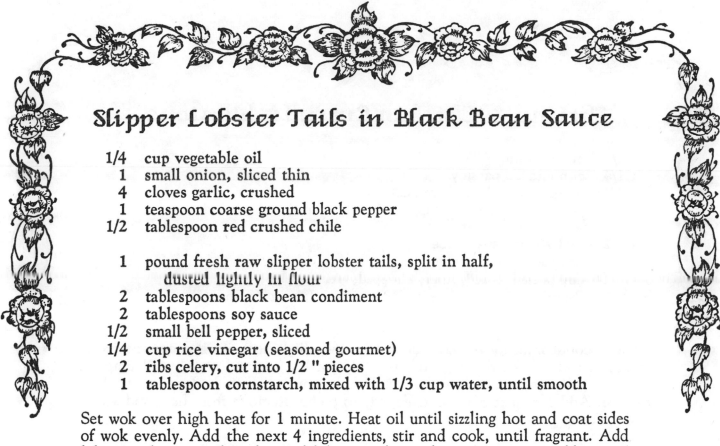

Slipper Lobster Tails in Black Bean Sauce

1/4 cup vegetable oil
1 small onion, sliced thin
4 cloves garlic, crushed
1 teaspoon coarse ground black pepper
1/2 tablespoon red crushed chile

1 pound fresh raw slipper lobster tails, split in half,
dusted lightly in flour
2 tablespoons black bean condiment
2 tablespoons soy sauce
1/2 small bell pepper, sliced
1/4 cup rice vinegar (seasoned gourmet)
2 ribs celery, cut into 1/2 " pieces
1 tablespoon cornstarch, mixed with 1/3 cup water, until smooth

Set wok over high heat for 1 minute. Heat oil until sizzling hot and coat sides of wok evenly. Add the next 4 ingredients, stir and cook, until fragrant. Add lobster tails, stir and cook, until lobster is done, about 5 minutes. Add next 5 ingredients, stir and cook, until vegetables just begin to soften, about 1 minute. Stir in cornstarch and cook until sauce thickens. Remove from heat and serve with Garlic Noodles. Yields 2 servings.

Spicy Slipper Lobster Tails

1/4 cup cooking oil
4 cloves of garlic, crushed
1 pound fresh raw slipper lobster tails, split in half,
coated lightly with flour

1 tablespoon chile paste with bean oil (nam prig pao)
2 tablespoons hot chile oil
1/2 tablespoon dried, ground orange peel
1 cup fresh orange juice
3 tablespoons fish sauce (nam pla)

Set wok over high heat for 1 minute. Heat oil until sizzling hot and coat sides of wok evenly. Add garlic, stir and cook, until fragrant. Add lobster tails, stir and cook, until lobster is done, about 5 minutes. Add remaining ingredients, stir to blend. Reduce heat, cover and simmer for 2 to 3 minutes. Serve over Garlic Noodles. Yields 2 servings.

Shrimp & Chicken Curry in Wontons

1/2 cup coconut milk
1/4 cup minced parsley
1/4 pound minced chicken meat
1/4 pound fresh raw shrimp, shelled, deveined and minced

1 1/2 tablespoons soy sauce
1 teaspoon curry powder
1 cup peeled, cored, finely chopped, green apples
1 8-ounce package square wonton skins (about 25 sheets)
1 cup vegetable oil

Cook coconut milk in 5-quart Dutch oven over high heat, until coconut milk separates (oil will be floating on top). Add parsley, stir and cook, until limp. Add the chicken, and shrimp, stir and cook, until chicken is done, about 1 minute. Add the next 3 ingredients, stir to blend. Remove from heat and set aside to cool.

To prepare wontons, scoop 1 tablespoon of mixture into center of a wonton skin. Dampen edges with hot water and fold into a triangle. Fill remaining skins.

Add oil to wok and place over medium heat for 2 minutes. Drop a small piece of wonton skin into hot oil. The piece will rise to the top right away if the oil is ready. Add a few wontons at a time and fry until crisp and golden brown on both sides, about 2 minutes. Remove wontons from oil and drain on paper towel. Repeat with remaining wontons and serve. Yields about 25 pieces.

Dill Fish Fillets

1 cup fresh orange juice
3 tablespoons soy sauce
2 tablespoons dry sherry
1/4 teaspoon paprika
1 tablespoon dried dill

1 pound shark fillets, cut into 2" x 2" chunks
2 teaspoons cornstarch, mixed with 2 tablespoons of water

Combine the first 5 ingredients in 3 quart saucepan. Bring to boil over high heat. Add fish, cover and cook, until fish is done, about 5 minutes. Add cornstarch mixture, stir and cook, until sauce thickens. Remove from heat and serve with noodles or rice. Yields 2 servings.

Steamed Catfish or Mahi Mahi

Catfish is very popular with Thais. This recipe can be cooked with any type of firm-fleshed fish. But since the popularity of Southern cooking has brought catfish into many American kitchens, it is readily available now.

1/4	pound bacon, chopped
1	pound catfish or mahi mahi fillets, cut into 4 pieces
1	tablespoon thin soy sauce
1/2	tablespoon yellow soy bean condiment
1	tablespoon oyster sauce
1	tablespoon dry sherry
1/4	teaspoon coarse ground black pepper
1/4	teaspoon ground coriander
4	stems green onion, cut in half (white and green parts)
4	ribs celery, cut in half
1	bunch fresh dill or 1/2 tablespoon dried dill
1/4	cup water

Line bottom of 5-quart Dutch oven with bacon. Spread the rest of ingredients over the bacon, cover and cook, over medium heat, until fish is done, about 15 minutes. Transfer to serving dish and serve. Yields 2 servings.

Abalone in Garlic Sauce

3	tablespoons vegetable oil
4	cloves of garlic, crushed
2	thumb-size segments of fresh ginger root, slivered
1/4	cup finely chopped green onion
1	15-ounce can abalone, drained, reserve juice, slice thin, bite-size
1	15-ounce can oyster mushrooms, drained and quartered
3	chicken flavored bouillon cubes, crushed
	juice from 1 lemon
1/2	teaspoon white pepper
2	teaspoons cornstarch, mixed with reserved abalone juice
2	egg whites

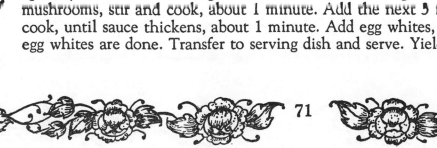

Set wok over high heat for about 1 minute. Add oil and coat sides of wok evenly. Quickly add the next 3 ingredients and cook until fragrant. Add abalone, and mushrooms, stir and cook, about 1 minute. Add the next 5 ingredients, stir and cook, until sauce thickens, about 1 minute. Add egg whites, stir and cook, until egg whites are done. Transfer to serving dish and serve. Yields 4 servings.

Steamed Eastern Mussels with Lemon Grass

2 pounds large fresh raw Eastern mussels
1/2 teaspoon sesame oil
1 cup water

3 stems fresh lemon grass, sliced very thin (use bottom 2" of stems)
4 makrood leaves
2 tablespoons fish sauce (nam pla)
2 large shallots, sliced
1 stalk cilantro
2 fresh serrano chiles, crushed
1 tablespoon fresh lime juice

Soak mussels in cold water, mixed with 1/2 teaspoon of sesame oil, for 2 hours, scrub and debeard. Wash and set aside.

In 5-quart Dutch oven, bring 1 cup of water to boil, add mussels, and the next 6 ingredients. Cover and steam over high heat until mussels open, about 8 minutes (do not overcook). Remove from heat, add lime juice, stir to blend and serve. Yields 2 servings.

Steamed Sea Bass

Sit back and enjoy your company while your dinner cooks in the oven. This recipe is not only easy, but also, very, very good.

2 pounds sea bass fillets
1/4 cup soy sauce
1/4 cup water

4 stems green onions, cut in half (white and green parts)
2 thumb-size segments of fresh ginger root, mashed
1 10-ounce can golden mushroom, drained
1 bunch fresh basil leaves (optional)
  parsley for garnish

Preheat oven to 500 degrees. Rub soy sauce over fish and lay the fish on the steamer rack. Pour water, and remaining soy sauce in bottom of fish steamer. Arrange the remaining ingredients over the top of the fish and cover. Place steamer in oven, cook about 20 minutes or until fish is done. Remove from oven, place fish, and vegetable on serving plate, pour sauce from steamer over fish. Garnish with parsley and serve with fried rice. Yields 4 servings.

Shrimp with Lobster Sauce

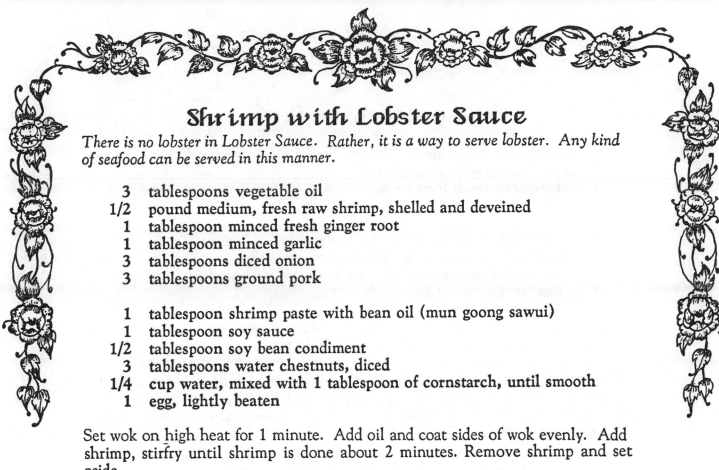

There is no lobster in Lobster Sauce. Rather, it is a way to serve lobster. Any kind of seafood can be served in this manner.

- 3   tablespoons vegetable oil
- 1/2 pound medium, fresh raw shrimp, shelled and deveined
- 1   tablespoon minced fresh ginger root
- 1   tablespoon minced garlic
- 3   tablespoons diced onion
- 3   tablespoons ground pork

- 1   tablespoon shrimp paste with bean oil (mun goong sawui)
- 1   tablespoon soy sauce
- 1/2 tablespoon soy bean condiment
- 3   tablespoons water chestnuts, diced
- 1/4 cup water, mixed with 1 tablespoon of cornstarch, until smooth
- 1   egg, lightly beaten

Set wok on high heat for 1 minute. Add oil and coat sides of wok evenly. Add shrimp, stirfry until shrimp is done about 2 minutes. Remove shrimp and set aside.

Keep wok on high heat, add ginger, garlic, and onion, stir and cook until fragrant. Add ground pork, stir to separate. Add the next 5 ingredients, bring to boil, and cook until sauce thickens, about 1 minute. Return shrimp, then gently stir egg into sauce and cook until egg is done. Remove at once and serve. Yields 4 servings.

Basil Shrimp

This is a simple dish that is very appealing. Easy to make, it has a unique flavor and will be a treat for the hard-to-please.

- 2   tablespoons vegetable oil
- 4   cloves garlic, crushed
- 1   thumb size segment of fresh ginger root, slivered
- 1/2 teaspoon coarse ground pepper
- 1/2 pound fresh raw shrimp, shelled, deveined, leaving tails attached

- 1   tablespoon fish sauce (nam pla)
- 1   teaspoon hot chile oil
- 1   bunch fresh basil leaves
      juice of a half lemon

Set wok over high heat for 1 minute. Add oil and coat sides of wok evenly. Add garlic, ginger and pepper, stir and cook, until light brown. Add shrimp, stir and cook, until shrimp turns pink, about 1 minute. Add remaining ingredients, stir and cook, until basil leaves are limp. Remove from heat and serve. Yields 2 servings.

Steamed Blue Crab

2   tablespoons fish sauce
1   tablespoon soy bean condiment
3   tablespoons fresh lemon juice
1   tablespoon grated fresh ginger root

6   large, fresh raw blue crabs (approximately 2 1/2 pounds)
1   thumb-size segment fresh ginger root, mashed
1   stem fresh lemon grass, cut into 4 sections and mashed
3   slices fresh or dried Laos root

In small bowl combine first 4 ingredients, mix well and set aside to use as dipping sauce. Rinse crabs with cold water and drain.

Add 5 cups of water to vegetable steamer and set over high heat. Place crabs on steamer rack and arrange ginger, lemon grass and Laos root on top of crabs. Steam until crabs are done, about 20 minutes. Remove crabs to serving plate. Serve with sauce. Yields 2 to 3 servings.

Clams with Black Beans

2   pounds fresh raw clams*
1   teaspoon sesame oil
3   tablespoons vegetable oil
1   thumb-size segment of fresh ginger root, slivered
4   cloves garlic, crushed

2   tablespoons fermented black beans, smashed
2   tablespoons oyster sauce
1   tablespoon dry sherry
1   teaspoon chile paste with bean oil (nam prig pao)
1/4 teaspoon pepper
2   stems green onions, cut into 1/2" piece (white and green parts)
1/2 cup Chicken Stock (see Basics) mixed with 1 teaspoon corn starch
2   egg whites, lightly beaten

Soak clams in cold water, mixed with 1 teaspoon sesame oil, for 2 hours. Rinse thoroughly. Set aside. Set wok over high heat for 1 minute. Add oil and coat sides of wok evenly. Add ginger and garlic, stir and cook, until light brown. Add clams stir and cook, until shells are open, about 5 minutes. Add the next 7 ingredients, stir and cook, until sauce thickens, about 1/2 minute. Stir in egg whites and cook until egg whites are done. Transfer to serving dish and serve over Garlic Noodles. Yields 4 servings.

Note: -*For best results, use Eastern steamers.

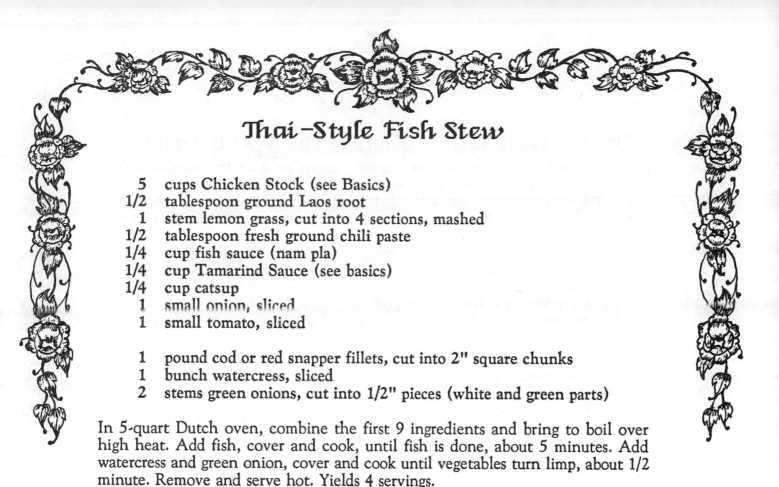

Thai-Style Fish Stew

5 cups Chicken Stock (see Basics)
1/2 tablespoon ground Laos root
1 stem lemon grass, cut into 4 sections, mashed
1/2 tablespoon fresh ground chili paste
1/4 cup fish sauce (nam pla)
1/4 cup Tamarind Sauce (see basics)
1/4 cup catsup
1 small onion, sliced
1 small tomato, sliced

1 pound cod or red snapper fillets, cut into 2" square chunks
1 bunch watercress, sliced
2 stems green onions, cut into 1/2" pieces (white and green parts)

In 5-quart Dutch oven, combine the first 9 ingredients and bring to boil over high heat. Add fish, cover and cook, until fish is done, about 5 minutes. Add watercress and green onion, cover and cook until vegetables turn limp, about 1/2 minute. Remove and serve hot. Yields 4 servings.

Abalone with Black Mushrooms

8 medium, dried black mushrooms (shi-i-take)
3/4 cup Chicken Stock (see Basics)
1 tablespoon corn starch
1 1/2 tablespoons oyster sauce

3 tablespoons vegetable oil
1 thumb-size segment fresh ginger root, minced
4 cloves garlic, minced
1 15-ounce can abalone, drained, sliced thin

Soak mushrooms in hot water for 20 minutes. Drain, remove bottom part of stems and slice thin. Set aside. Mix chicken stock, corn starch and oyster sauce until smooth and set aside.

Set 10" frying pan over high heat. Add oil and coat bottom of pan evenly. Add ginger and garlic, stir and cook, until fragrant. Add mushrooms and abalone stir and cook, until abalone is thoroughly heated, about 3 minutes. Add reserved sauce mixture, stir and cook, until sauce thickens. Remove from heat and serve with fried rice. Yields 4 servings.

Deep Fried Whole Fish with Spicy Sauce

This wonderful recipe is tasty and has a great presence on a dinner or buffet table. When teaching this recipe to my students, I found some had reservations about cooking the whole fish with the head. If this troubles you, feel free to remove the head. It will not change the flavor of the recipe. Don't miss out on this truly stunning dish.

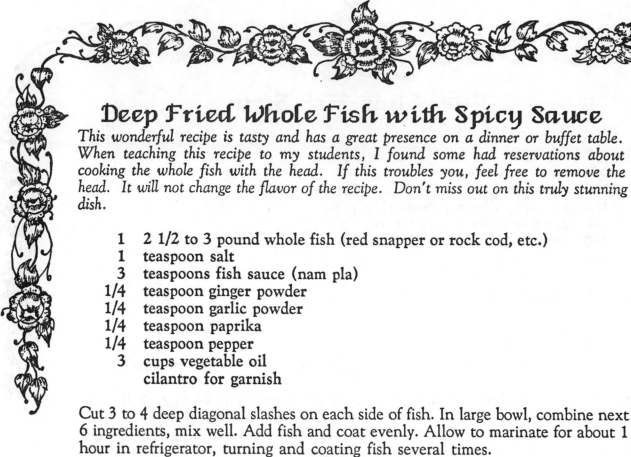

1	2 1/2 to 3 pound whole fish (red snapper or rock cod, etc.)
1	teaspoon salt
3	teaspoons fish sauce (nam pla)
1/4	teaspoon ginger powder
1/4	teaspoon garlic powder
1/4	teaspoon paprika
1/4	teaspoon pepper
3	cups vegetable oil
	cilantro for garnish

Cut 3 to 4 deep diagonal slashes on each side of fish. In large bowl, combine next 6 ingredients, mix well. Add fish and coat evenly. Allow to marinate for about 1 hour in refrigerator, turning and coating fish several times.

Heat oil in 12" frying pan, over medium heat, until oil is sizzling hot. Deep fry fish, until golden brown on both sides and cooked through, about 20 minutes on each side. Place fish on serving plate and pour spicy sauce over top. Garnish with cilantro. Yields 4 servings.

Spicy Sauce:

3	tablespoons vegetable oil
1	tablespoon grated fresh ginger root
1	small onion, chopped
4	serrano chile, chopped
3	cloves garlic, minced
4	tablespoons soy sauce
1	tablespoon brown sugar
2	tablespoons white vinegar
2	tablespoons chopped cilantro
2	stems green onion, chopped (white and green parts)
1	small tomato, finely chopped
1/4	cup all purpose flour mixed with 1 1/2 cups water until smooth

Set 2-quart saucepan over high heat for 1 minute. Add oil and coat bottom of pan evenly. Add the next 4 ingredients, stir and cook, until light brown. Add the remaining ingredients, Stir and cook, until sauce thickens. Remove from heat and set aside.

Grilled Clams & Mussels

This is a terrific way to start a meal. This will put everyone in the best frame of mind and set a positive mood for the whole evening.

    2   pounds fresh raw cherry stone clams
    2   pounds fresh raw mussels
    1   teaspoon vegetable oil
    1   medium cucumber, sliced
    1/2 cup pickled ginger (optional)

Soak clams and mussels in cold water, mixed with oil, for 2 hours. Scrub mussels and debeard, rinse clams and mussels thoroughly.

To cook: Grill clams and mussels over hot coals, until shells open, about 5 minutes. Then serve with sliced cucumber, pickled ginger, and Chile Sauce. Yields 4 to 6 servings.

Steamed Mussels with Lemon Grass

    2   pounds fresh raw mussels
    1   teaspoon vegetable oil

    3   stems fresh lemon grass, cut into 4 sections each, then mashed
    1   tablespoon paprika
    1   small cucumber, sliced

Soak mussels with cold water, mixed with vegetable oil, for 2 hours. Scrub and debeard mussels, wash with cold water. Place mussels in steamer, arrange lemon grass on top and sprinkle with paprika. Add 5 cups of water to steamer, cover and steam over high heat about 10 minutes, or until mussel shells are open (do not over cook). Transfer to serving plate, serve with sliced cucumber and Chile Sauce. Yields 2 to 4 servings.

Quick Sautéed Shrimp

    2   ounces butter or margarine, unsalted
    4   cloves garlic, crushed
    1/2 teaspoon coarse ground black pepper
    1/2 pound medium, fresh raw shrimp, in shell
    1/4 teaspoon salt
    2   tablespoons dry sherry
    1/4 cup fresh orange juice

In 10" frying pan, melt butter or margarine, over high heat. Quickly toss in garlic, and pepper, cook until fragrant. Add shrimp, and salt, stir and cook, until shrimp turns pink, about 1 minute. Add sherry, and orange juice, stir to blend and serve over Garlic or Soy Noodles. Yields 2 to 3 servings.

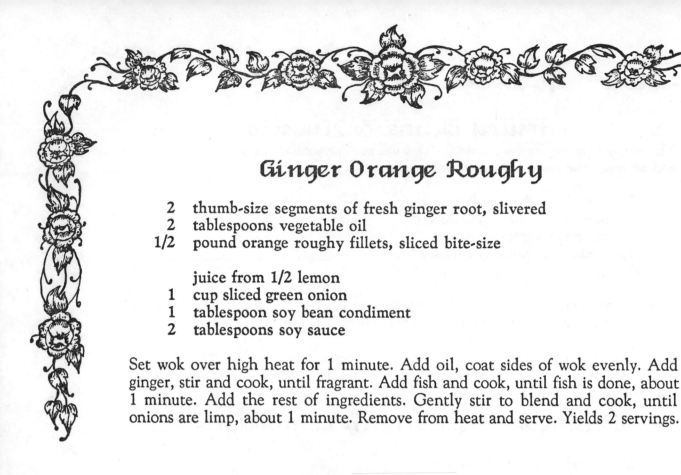

Ginger Orange Roughy

2   thumb-size segments of fresh ginger root, slivered
2   tablespoons vegetable oil
1/2   pound orange roughy fillets, sliced bite-size

     juice from 1/2 lemon
1   cup sliced green onion
1   tablespoon soy bean condiment
2   tablespoons soy sauce

Set wok over high heat for 1 minute. Add oil, coat sides of wok evenly. Add ginger, stir and cook, until fragrant. Add fish and cook, until fish is done, about 1 minute. Add the rest of ingredients. Gently stir to blend and cook, until onions are limp, about 1 minute. Remove from heat and serve. Yields 2 servings.

Scallops in Herbal Butter Sauce

1/4   cup Herbal Butter (see Basics)
1/2   pound small, fresh raw scallops, or large scallops cut in half
2   cups thin sliced carrots

1   tablespoon fresh lemon juice
1/2   teaspoon salt
1   cup milk
1   tablespoon of cornstarch, mixed with 3 tablespoons of water
1/4   teaspoon fresh ground chile paste

In 10" frying pan, melt Herbal Butter, over high heat. Add scallops and carrots, stir and cook, until scallops turn white, about 2 minutes. Add the rest of ingredients, stir, cover and continue cooking, until sauce thickens, about 1/2 minute. Remove from heat and serve with fried rice. Yields 2 servings.

FOWL

When buying chicken, select a good 3-pound or larger chicken, with not much fat. You can buy the chicken cut up, but it is just as easy and more economical to buy the whole chicken and cut it up yourself. All parts can be used. White or dark meat can be used for stir fries and the bones and skin should be saved to make stock.

Chopping the chicken parts with the bones and skin left in place, is the more authentic way of Thai cooking. The Thais feel, there is more flavor to the dish, if this method is followed. When making stewed chicken you can use the skin and bones that you saved and put them in with the whole chicken for a double rich flavor.

Thai Kung Pao Chicken

3	tablespoons vegetable oil
15	dried red chile pods
4	cloves garlic, crushed
1	pound chicken breasts, boned, skinned, and sliced thin, bite-size
2	tablespoons chile paste with bean oil (nam prig pao)
1/2	cup diced water chestnuts
1/4	cup very thin sliced carrots
1/4	cup diced bamboo shoots
1/2	cup very thin sliced celery
1	tablespoon fish sauce (nam pla)
2	tablespoons soy sauce
1 1/2	tablespoons dry sherry
1	tablespoon corn starch, mixed with 3 tablespoons of water

Set wok over high heat for 1 minute. Add oil, and coat sides of wok evenly. Add chiles, and cook until chiles darken (do not burn). Remove chiles right away and set aside

Keep wok on heat, add garlic and cook until fragrant. Add chicken, stir and cook, until chicken is done, about 2 minutes. Add chile paste, stir to blend. Add next 4 ingredients, stir and cook for 1 minute. Add remaining ingredients, stir and cook, until sauce thickens, about 1 more minute. Arrange on serving plate and garnish with chiles. Yields 3 servings.

Thai Roasted Chicken
(Gai Ob)

1	3 1/2 to 4 pound whole chicken
1/2	tablespoon salt
1/2	tablespoon ground ginger
1/2	tablespoon paprika

Stuffing:
1	tablespoon minced fresh ginger root
1/4	teaspoon salt
1	small onion, chopped
1	16-ounce can straw mushrooms, drained

Baste:
2	ounces butter or margarine, unsalted
1	tablespoon dry sherry
2	tablespoons honey
2	tablespoons dark soy sauce

Preheat oven to 350 degrees. Wash chicken with cold water, pad with paper towel to dry, trim off fat. Rub salt, ground ginger, and paprika over chicken inside and out. In medium bowl combine all stuffing ingredients, mix well. Spoon stuffing into chicken. Lay chicken on a rack in a baking pan. Bake for about 1 to 1 1/2 hours (allowing 18 minutes per pound).

While chicken is roasting, melt butter or margarine, in 1-quart saucepan, over low heat. Add dry sherry, honey, and soy sauce, stir to blend. Remove from heat and set aside. Just 5 minutes before chicken is done, brush chicken evenly with butter mixture, increase oven temperature to 400 degrees to brown. When done, remove chicken from oven, place on cutting board. Scoop out stuffing, place on center of serving platter. Cut chicken into serving pieces and arrange around stuffing. Yields 4 to 6 servings.

Steamed Garlic Chicken

1	whole chicken (3 pounds or more)
1	whole garlic, crushed
1	tablespoon salt
2	tablespoons sesame oil
1/4	cup water

Preheat oven to 450 degrees. Rub garlic and salt over chicken inside and out. Lay chicken on rack of steamer. Sprinkle sesame oil on top of chicken. Add water to steamer, cover and place steamer in oven and bake about 60 minutes or until chicken is done. Remove from oven. Yields 4 to 6 servings.

Broiled Cornish Hens in Herbal Butter

1   cup Herbal Butter (see Basics)
1/2   cup finely chopped onions
1   tablespoon paprika
1   tablespoon celery seed
1   teaspoon salt
4   1 to 1 1/2 pound Cornish game hens

Garnish:
1   lime, cut into 8 wedges
8   sprigs of parsley

In 1-quart saucepan, melt Herbal Butter over low heat. Add next 4 ingredients and mix well (do not cook). Remove from heat. Place hens in large bowl. Pour butter mixture over and into hens. Allow to stand for 1/2 hour at room temperature, turning occasionally to coat hens evenly.

Preheat oven to 350 degrees. Place hens breast down, on a rack in a baking pan. Reserve butter mixture. Bake until hens are golden brown and done, about 40 minutes, brushing occasionally with reserved butter mixture. Garnish with lime wedges and parsley. Yields 4 to 6 servings.

Chicken Tamarind

3   tablespoons vegetable oil
4   cloves garlic, crushed
1   thumb-size segment of fresh ginger root, slivered
1   pound chicken thighs, cut into 3 pieces each,
      (leave skin and bones attached)

1   bunch fresh basil or 2 tablespoons of dried basil
2   tablespoons Tamarind Sauce (see Basics) or fresh lemon juice
1   tablespoon oyster sauce
1   tablespoon fish sauce (nam pla)

Set wok over high heat, for 1 minute. Add oil, coat sides of wok evenly. Add ginger and garlic, stir and cook until light brown. Add chicken pieces, stir and cook, until chicken is done, about 10 minutes. Add the rest of ingredients, stir to blend. Transfer to serving plate. Yields 4 servings.

Thai Barbecued Chicken—"Spicy"
(Gai Yang)

This is my own special barbecue favorite. I always like barbecued food, so I have worked especially hard to create this special Thai barbecue chicken recipe. You can roast the chicken in the oven, if the weather is not good for an outdoor barbecue.

    1   cup coconut milk
    3   tablespoons red curry paste
    3   tablespoons fish sauce
    1   tablespoon curry powder
    1/2 teaspoon garlic powder
    1/2 teaspoon ginger powder
    1/2 teaspoon pepper
    1   3 to 3 1/2 pound whole chicken, split in half

In large bowl, combine first 7 ingredients. Add chicken and coat with marinade. Cover and refrigerate for several hours. Place chicken halves, bone side down, over medium hot coals, reserving marinade. Grill chicken about 15-20 minutes on each side, or until done, turning often. Brush frequently with reserved marinade. Serve with Sweet and Sour Chili Sauce. Yields 4 servings.

Barbecued Chicken with Lemon & Butter

    8   ounces butter or margarine, unsalted

    2   tablespoons salt
    1/2 teaspoon onion powder
    1/2 teaspoon ground ginger
    1/2 teaspoon pepper
    2   cups fresh lemon juice
    12   cloves garlic, crushed

    2   3 to 3 1/2 pound whole chickens, split in half

Melt butter, in 2-quart saucepan, over low heat (do not cook). Add the next 6 ingredients and stir until smooth. Place chicken in large bowl. Pour butter mixture over chicken and coat chicken evenly. Cover and marinate at room temperature for 2 to 3 hours or more.

Drain chicken, reserving marinade. Place chicken halves, bone side down, over medium hot coals. Grill chicken about 15 to 20 minutes on each side or until done, turning often. Brush frequently with reserved marinade. Serve with Sweet and Sour Chili Sauce. Yields 6 to 8 servings.

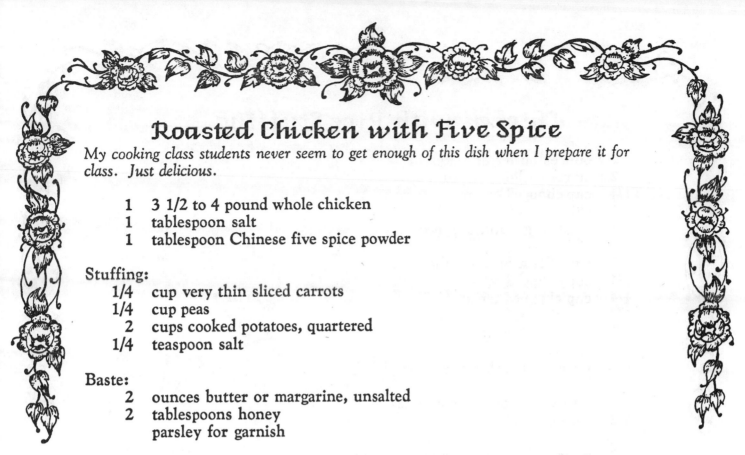

Roasted Chicken with Five Spice

My cooking class students never seem to get enough of this dish when I prepare it for class. Just delicious.

1	3 1/2 to 4 pound whole chicken
1	tablespoon salt
1	tablespoon Chinese five spice powder

Stuffing:

1/4	cup very thin sliced carrots
1/4	cup peas
2	cups cooked potatoes, quartered
1/4	teaspoon salt

Baste:

2	ounces butter or margarine, unsalted
2	tablespoons honey
	parsley for garnish

Preheat oven to 450 degrees. Wash chicken with cold water, pat dry with paper towel and trim off fat. Mix salt and five spice together then rub over chicken inside and out.

In medium bowl, combine all stuffing ingredients, mix well. Spoon stuffing into chicken. Lay chicken on a rack, in a baking pan. Reduce heat to 350 degrees. Bake about 1 hour and 20 minutes (allowing 20 minutes per pound).

About 5 minutes before chicken is done, combine butter and honey in 1 quart saucepan. Set over low heat to melt. Brush evenly over chicken. Increase temperature to 400 degrees to brown. Brush chicken again just before removing from oven. When done, remove chicken from oven and place on cutting board. Scoop out stuffing and place in center of large serving platter. Carve chicken into serving pieces and arrange around stuffing, on platter. Garnish with parsley and serve. Yields 4 servings.

Note: -In Thailand to roast is "Ob," chicken is "Gai". This dish should be called "Gai Ob". I would love for you to learn the Thai names for the dishes you will be serving.

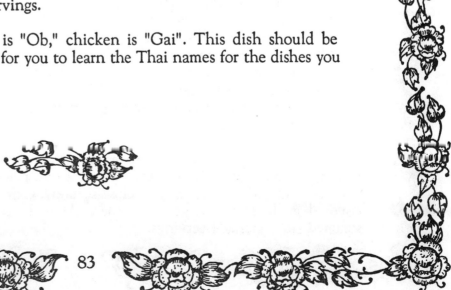

Chicken with Rice Stuffing

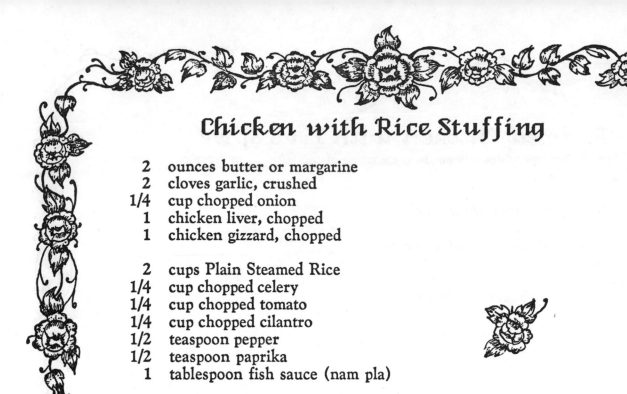

    2   ounces butter or margarine
    2   cloves garlic, crushed
  1/4   cup chopped onion
    1   chicken liver, chopped
    1   chicken gizzard, chopped

    2   cups Plain Steamed Rice
  1/4   cup chopped celery
  1/4   cup chopped tomato
  1/4   cup chopped cilantro
  1/2   teaspoon pepper
  1/2   teaspoon paprika
    1   tablespoon fish sauce (nam pla)

    1   3 to 3 1/2 pound whole chicken
  1/2   teaspoon salt

    2   ounces butter or margarine, melted

Melt butter in 2-quart saucepan over medium heat. Add garlic and onion, stir and cook, until light brown. Add liver and gizzard, cook until done. Add next 7 ingredients, stir to blend. Stuff rice mixture into chicken, tie and sprinkle salt over chicken. Set aside.

Preheat oven to 350 degrees. Place chicken, breast side up, on a rack in a baking pan. Bake about 1 1/2 hours or until done, brushing often with melted butter or margarine. Yields 4 servings.

Grilled Chicken with Oyster Sauce

    4   chicken breast halves, skinned and boned
    3   cloves garlic, crushed
    1   small onion, chopped
  1/4   cup chopped cilantro
  1/4   teaspoon pepper
    1   teaspoon brown sugar
    2   tablespoons sesame seed
    1   tablespoon grated fresh ginger root
    4   tablespoons oyster sauce

In medium bowl, combine all ingredients, mix well. Tear off four 18x18-inch pieces of heavy-duty foil. On each piece of foil, place 1 chicken breast. Bring 4 corners of foil to center, twist to close securely. Grill chicken over slow coals in covered grill, until chicken is tender, about 20 to 25 minutes. Serve with steamed rice. Yields 4 servings.

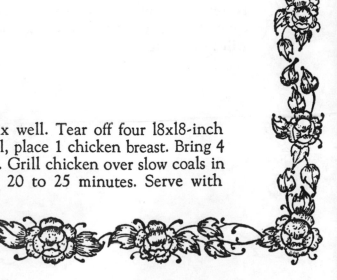

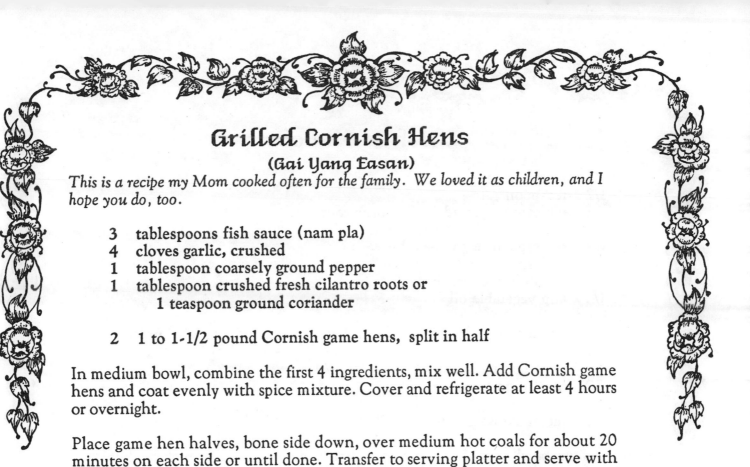

Grilled Cornish Hens
(Gai Yang Easan)

This is a recipe my Mom cooked often for the family. We loved it as children, and I hope you do, too.

3	tablespoons fish sauce (nam pla)
4	cloves garlic, crushed
1	tablespoon coarsely ground pepper
1	tablespoon crushed fresh cilantro roots or
	1 teaspoon ground coriander
2	1 to 1-1/2 pound Cornish game hens, split in half

In medium bowl, combine the first 4 ingredients, mix well. Add Cornish game hens and coat evenly with spice mixture. Cover and refrigerate at least 4 hours or overnight.

Place game hen halves, bone side down, over medium hot coals for about 20 minutes on each side or until done. Transfer to serving platter and serve with Roasted Serrano Chile Sauce and Steamed Sweet Rice. Yields 2 to 3 servings.

Spicy Lemonade Barbecued Chicken

3	cloves garlic, crushed
6	chicken flavored bouillon cubes, dissolved in 1/4 cup of hot water
1/2	cup chopped onions
1/2	cup catsup
1	6-ounce can frozen lemonade concentrate, thawed
1	tablespoon grated fresh ginger root
1	tablespoon ground coriander
1	tablespoon brown sugar
1/2	tablespoon dry mustard
2	tablespoons ground fresh chili paste
1	tablespoon ground orange peel
1/2	teaspoon pepper
2	3 to 3 1/2 pound whole chickens, split in half

In medium bowl, combine all the ingredients, stir to blend together well. Coat chicken halves evenly, cover and refrigerate for several hours. Drain chicken, reserving marinade. Place chicken halves, bone side down, over medium hot coals. Grill for 15 to 20 minutes on each side or until done, turning and brushing with reserved marinade. Transfer to serving platter and serve with Steamed Sweet Rice and raw vegetables of your choice. Yields 4 servings.

Chicken Kabobs

1	teaspoon pepper
1/2	teaspoon salt
1	tablespoon grated fresh ginger root
3	tablespoons fresh lemon juice
1/2	tablespoon dry mustard
3	tablespoons soy sauce
3	cloves garlic, crushed
1/2	cup vegetable oil
2	pounds chicken breasts, skinned and boned, cut into 2" chunks
6	cups boiling water
30	mushroom caps
6	metal skewers

In medium bowl, combine first 8 ingredients, mix well. Add chicken chunks, stir, to coat chicken evenly. Cover and refrigerate several hours or overnight. Pour boiling water over mushrooms caps, let stand for a few minutes, drain. Thread mushrooms on skewers alternately with chicken. Grill over medium hot coals about 15-20 minutes, or until done, turning often. Yields 6 servings.

Chicken or Shrimp with Broccoli
(Kang Gai Liew Goong)

This can also be made with Chinese broccoli, which is available at Oriental markets.

3	tablespoons vegetable oil
3	cloves garlic, crushed
1	pound chicken breasts, skinned and boned, sliced thin, bite-size or medium, fresh raw shrimp, shelled and deveined
6	cups sliced Chinese broccoli, or broccoli
3 1/2	tablespoons soy sauce

Set wok over high heat for 1 minute. Add oil and coat sides of wok evenly. Add garlic, stir and cook, until light brown. Add chicken or shrimp, stir and cook, until done. Add broccoli, stir, then add soy sauce. Stir and cook, until broccoli just begins to soften, about 2 minutes. Serve with steamed rice. Yields 4 servings.

Note: - Chicken cooks in about 3 minutes, shrimp cooks quickly in about 1 minute. Do not overcook.

Stir-Fried Chicken, Beef, Pork, Shrimp or Fish with Chiles & Mint-"Hot"

Most of my friends ask for the recipe of this hot and spicy dish. Remember, you can adjust the chile to your taste.

1	tablespoon vegetable oil
4	cloves garlic, crushed
6	jalapeno chiles, quartered lengthwise
2	pounds chicken breasts, skinned and boned, or beef, pork, fresh raw shrimp, or fish fillets, sliced thin, bite-size
2	tablespoons fish sauce (nam pla)
20	fresh Thai mint or basil leaves
2	stems green onions, cut in 1/2" pieces (white and green parts)

Set wok over high heat for 1 minute. Add oil and coat sides of wok evenly. Add garlic and chiles, stir and cook, until garlic is light brown. Add meat, stir and cook, until meat is done. Add remaining ingredients, stir to blend and serve with Steamed Rice. Yields 4 servings.

Note: -Cooking time will vary depending on the type of meat used. Chicken and pork will take about 3 minutes, while beef, shrimp or fish will be done in about 1 minute. Do not overcook.

Chicken, Beef or Pork with Cabbage

When I was still very "new" to this country, I had a party for my American friends. One of them told me that she hated cabbage. Both of us were very surprised when this dish turned out to be one of her favorites. Even now, after many years, she still asks me to prepare it for her.

3	tablespoons vegetable oil
3	cloves garlic, crushed
1	pound chicken breasts, skinned and boned, or beef, or pork, sliced thin, bite-size
6	cups thinly sliced cabbage
3	tablespoons fish sauce (nam pla)

Set wok over high heat for 1 minute. Add oil and coat sides of wok evenly. Add garlic and fry until light brown. Add meat, stir and cook, until meat is done. Add cabbage and fish sauce, stir and cook, until cabbage just begins to soften. Remove from heat and serve with Steamed Rice. Yields 4 servings.

Note: -Chicken and pork cook in about 3 minutes, beef cooks in only 1 minute.

Stir-Fried Chicken or Shrimp with Roasted Chile Paste

Roasted chile paste is a spicy addition to many different Thai dishes. In this recipe, it is used to add spice, flavor and color to the food. Some Thai people like the taste of the chile paste so much, that they even use it as a spread on toast.

1	tablespoon vegetable oil
3	cloves garlic, crushed
2	tablespoons chile paste with bean oil (nam prig pao)
1	pound chicken breasts, skinned and boned, sliced, bite-size or fresh raw shrimp, shelled and deveined
2	tablespoons fish sauce (nam pla)
2	stems green onions, cut into 1/2" pieces (white and green parts)

Set wok over high heat for 1 minute. Add oil and coat sides of wok evenly. Add garlic and cook until light brown. Add chile paste and meat, stir and cook, until meat is done. Add fish sauce and green onions. Stir to blend and serve with Steamed Rice. Yields 4 servings.

Note: -Chicken cooks in about 3 minutes, shrimp cooks in only 1 minute,

Chicken, Beef or Pork with Ginger
(Gai Paht Keing)

Oyster sauce is made from oyster extract. It adds a rich flavor to this recipe. As it is salty, do not add salt.

8	medium, dried black fungus (wood ear) mushrooms
2	tablespoons vegetable oil
3	cloves garlic, crushed
2	thumb-size segments fresh ginger root, slivered
2	pounds chicken breasts, skinned and boned, or beef, or pork, sliced thin, bite size
1/4	cup very thin sliced carrots
3	stems green onions, cut into 1/2" pieces
3	tablespoons soy sauce

Soak mushrooms in hot water for 30 minutes, drain and slice very thin. Set aside. Set wok over high heat for 1 minute. Add oil and coat sides of wok evenly. Add garlic and ginger, stir and cook, until light brown. Add mcat, stir and cook, until meat is done. Add remaining ingredients, stir to blend and serve with Steamed Rice. Yields 4 servings.

Note: -Chicken and pork cook in about 3 minutes, beef cooks in only 1 minute.

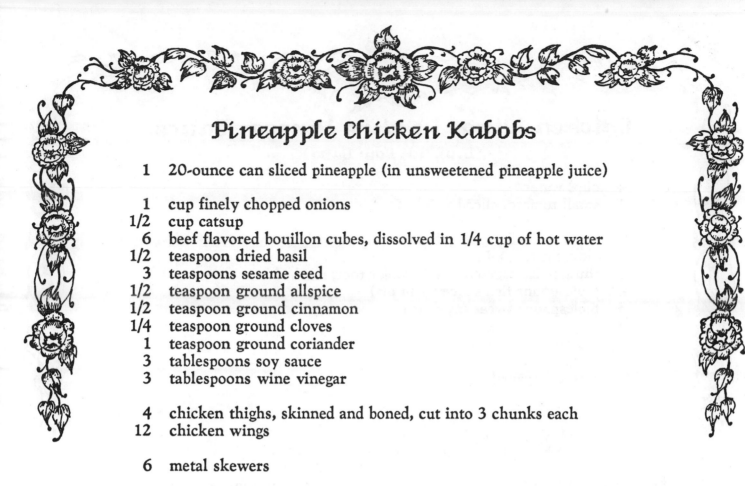

Pineapple Chicken Kabobs

1   20-ounce can sliced pineapple (in unsweetened pineapple juice)

1   cup finely chopped onions
1/2   cup catsup
6   beef flavored bouillon cubes, dissolved in 1/4 cup of hot water
1/2   teaspoon dried basil
3   teaspoons sesame seed
1/2   teaspoon ground allspice
1/2   teaspoon ground cinnamon
1/4   teaspoon ground cloves
1   teaspoon ground coriander
3   tablespoons soy sauce
3   tablespoons wine vinegar

4   chicken thighs, skinned and boned, cut into 3 chunks each
12   chicken wings

6   metal skewers

Drain pineapple, reserving juice, cover and refrigerate pineapple. In medium bowl, combine pineapple juice and the next 11 ingredients, stir to blend. Add chicken thighs and wings, coat pieces evenly with marinade. Cover and refrigerate for several hours.

Drain chicken, reserve marinade. Quarter each pineapple slice, place two pieces together. Thread pineapple on skewers alternating with chicken. Grill over hot coals, until done, about 20 minutes, turning and brushing occasionally with reserved marinade. Yields 6 servings.

Stir-Fried Chicken with Oyster Sauce
(Gai Paht Nam Mun Hoi)

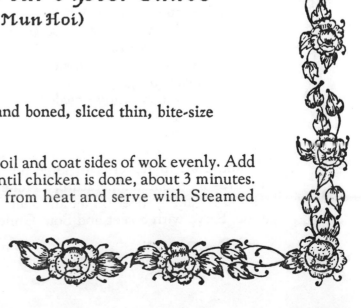

3   tablespoons vegetable oil
1   small onion, sliced thin
3   cloves garlic, crushed
1   pound chicken breasts, skinned and boned, sliced thin, bite-size
2   tablespoons oyster sauce

Set wok over high heat for 1 minute. Add oil and coat sides of wok evenly. Add onion, garlic and chicken, stir and cook, until chicken is done, about 3 minutes. Add oyster sauce, stir to blend. Remove from heat and serve with Steamed Rice. Yields 4 servings.

Chicken Wings in Wine Vinegar Sauce
(Beak Gai Low Dang)

4 cups water
1 small tomato, sliced
1 small onion, sliced
1 small red bell pepper, sliced
4 cloves garlic, minced
1 thumb-size segment fresh ginger root, mashed
4 tablespoons fish sauce (nam pla)
3 tablespoons sweet soy sauce
1/4 cup red wine vinegar
2 tablespoons catsup
1/2 teaspoon pepper
1/2 teaspoon paprika

3 pounds chicken wings
3 tablespoons all-purpose flour,
   mixed with 1/2 cup of water until smooth

Bring water to boil in 5-quart Dutch oven, over high heat. Add next 11 ingredients, stir and bring to boil again. Add chicken, cover and cook until chicken wings are tender, about 20 minutes. Add flour mixture, stir and cook, until sauce thickens, about 2 minutes. Remove from heat and serve with Plain Steamed Rice. Yields 4 servings.

Crispy Chicken Wings
(Beak Gai Grob)

Chicken wings are expensive in Thailand. When I first arrived in the United States, I was pleasantly surprised to see how inexpensive they were here. These crispy chicken wings will also make a tasty appetizer or a nice addition to a buffet table.

4 pounds chicken wings
3 tablespoons fish sauce (nam pla)
1 teaspoon salt
1 teaspoon garlic powder
1 teaspoon ginger powder
1 teaspoon onion powder
1 teaspoon paprika
1 teaspoon pepper

Combine all ingredients in large bowl. Mix well, cover and marinate for 15 minutes at room temperature. Preheat oven to 400 degrees. Place chicken wings on baking sheet on middle shelf of oven. Bake about 35 minutes or until done. Serve with Sweet and Sour Chile Sauce. Yields 4 servings.

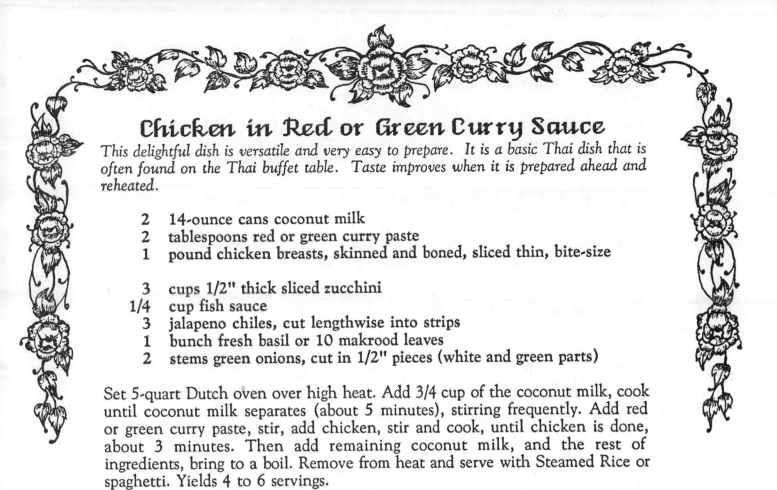

Chicken in Red or Green Curry Sauce

This delightful dish is versatile and very easy to prepare. It is a basic Thai dish that is often found on the Thai buffet table. Taste improves when it is prepared ahead and reheated.

2   14-ounce cans coconut milk
2   tablespoons red or green curry paste
1   pound chicken breasts, skinned and boned, sliced thin, bite-size

3   cups 1/2" thick sliced zucchini
1/4   cup fish sauce
3   jalapeno chiles, cut lengthwise into strips
1   bunch fresh basil or 10 makrood leaves
2   stems green onions, cut in 1/2" pieces (white and green parts)

Set 5-quart Dutch oven over high heat. Add 3/4 cup of the coconut milk, cook until coconut milk separates (about 5 minutes), stirring frequently. Add red or green curry paste, stir, add chicken, stir and cook, until chicken is done, about 3 minutes. Then add remaining coconut milk, and the rest of ingredients, bring to a boil. Remove from heat and serve with Steamed Rice or spaghetti. Yields 4 to 6 servings.

Pa Lo Chicken Wings

(Beak Gai Pa Lo)

Pa lo powder, used to give this dish its distinctive flavor, is a brown, mild sort of curry. It is commonly used in the Thai kitchen.

3   tablespoons vegetable oil
1   small onion, chopped
3   cloves garlic, crushed
1   tablespoon grated fresh ginger root
2   pounds chicken wings

6   hard boiled eggs, peeled
4   cups chicken stock (see Basics)
3   tablespoons pa lo powder (available at Thai markets)
2   tablespoons brown sugar
1/3   cup soy sauce
3   tablespoons chopped cilantro
1   tablespoon coarse ground black pepper

Set 5-quart Dutch oven over high heat. Add oil and coat bottom of pot evenly. Add onion, garlic, and ginger, stir and cook, until light brown. Add chicken wings, stir and cook, until wings are light brown. Add remaining ingredients, stir to blend, cover and cook, until chicken wings are done, about 20 minutes. Remove from heat and serve with steamed rice. Yields 4 servings.

Stir-Fried Chicken & Pork with Baby Corn & Mushrooms

    3   tablespoons vegetable oil
    3   cloves garlic, crushed
    1/2 pound chicken breasts, skinned and boned, sliced thin, bite-size
    1/2 pound pork, sliced thin, bite-size
    1   12-ounce can straw mushrooms, drained
    1   15-ounce can baby corn, drained

    2   tablespoons soy sauce
    2   tablespoons fish sauce (nam pla)
    2   stems green onions, cut in 1/2" pieces (white and green parts)
    1/4 teaspoon pepper
    1   tablespoon flour, mixed with 3 tablespoons water until smooth

Set wok over high heat for 1 minute. Add oil and coat sides of wok evenly. Add garlic and cook until light brown. Add pork, stir fry until lightly browned, about 2 minutes. Add chicken, stir and cook, until chicken and pork is done, about 3 minutes. Add mushrooms and baby corn, stir and cook, until baby corn is thoroughly heated, about 2 minutes. Add remaining ingredients, stir and cook, until sauce thickens, about 1 minute. Remove from heat and serve with Steamed Rice. Yields 4 servings.

Chicken with Cashew Nuts – "Spicy"

(Gai Na Mooang Himapan)

This is a well-known Thai dish and all of my American friends are very fond of this recipe. If you like it less hot, cut the amount of red curry paste and chile paste in half.

    3   tablespoons vegetable oil
    3   cloves garlic, crushed
    1   tablespoon red curry paste
    1   tablespoon chile paste with bean oil (nam prig pao)
    1   pound chicken breast, skinned and boned, sliced thin, bite-size
    2   tablespoons fish sauce (nam pla)
    2   stems green onions, cut in 1/2" pieces (white and green parts)
    1/2 cup roasted cashew nuts

Set wok over medium heat for 1 minute. Add oil and coat sides of wok evenly. Add garlic, red curry paste, and chile paste, stir and cook until garlic is light brown. Increase heat, add chicken, stir and cook, until chicken is done, about 3 minutes. Add fish sauce and onion, stir to blend. Transfer to serving plate and garnish with cashew nuts. Serve with steamed rice. Yields 4 servings.

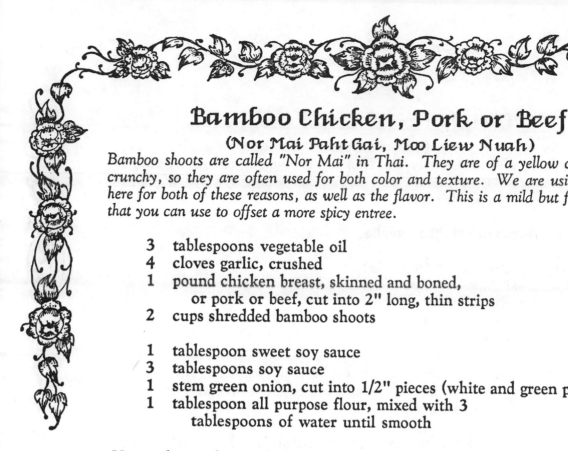

Bamboo Chicken, Pork or Beef
(Nor Mai Paht Gai, Moo Liew Nuah)

Bamboo shoots are called "Nor Mai" in Thai. They are of a yellow color and are crunchy, so they are often used for both color and texture. We are using the shoots here for both of these reasons, as well as the flavor. This is a mild but flavorful dish, that you can use to offset a more spicy entree.

3   tablespoons vegetable oil
4   cloves garlic, crushed
1   pound chicken breast, skinned and boned,
        or pork or beef, cut into 2" long, thin strips
2   cups shredded bamboo shoots

1   tablespoon sweet soy sauce
3   tablespoons soy sauce
1   stem green onion, cut into 1/2" pieces (white and green parts)
1   tablespoon all purpose flour, mixed with 3
        tablespoons of water until smooth

Heat oil in wok over high heat for 1 minute. Add garlic and cook until light brown. Add meat and bamboo shoots, stir and cook, until meat is done, about 5 minutes. Add remaining ingredients, stir and cook, until sauce thickens, about 1 minute. Remove from heat and serve with steamed rice. Yields 4 servings.

Note: -Cooking time for beef, is about 2 minutes.

Ground Turkey Breast with Green Beans

2   tablespoons vegetable oil
1/2   tablespoon minced fresh ginger root
1/2   tablespoon minced garlic
1   pound ground turkey breast or ground pork
1/2   cup very thin sliced Chinese long green beans or green beans
1 1/2   tablespoons fish sauce (nam pla)

Set wok over high heat for 1 minute. Add oil and coat sides of wok evenly. Add ginger and garlic, stir and cook until fragrant. Add meat, stir and cook, until meat is done, about 2 minutes. Add beans and fish sauce, stir and cook for 1 minute. Remove from heat. Yields 2 servings.

Note: -This recipe is good, served with rice, or use as a filling for pita, or any other kind of pocket bread.

Quick Fried Chicken
(Taud Gai)

"Taud" means fried in Thai. Usually, the Thai way of frying is without breading or batter, so that the meat does not retain too much oil and become greasy. We like to serve this over a bed of Garlic Noodles.

4	chicken legs with thighs attached

1 1/2	tablespoons fish sauce (nam pla)
1/2	teaspoon salt
1/2	teaspoon garlic powder
1/2	teaspoon Laos root powder
1	cup vegetable oil

With a sharp knife make 3 diagonal slashes on both sides of each chicken leg. Place legs in medium bowl and add the next 4 ingredients. Mix well and allow to marinate for 30 minutes or more.

In wok, heat oil over high heat for 1 minute, or until sizzling hot. Add chicken and fry, until chicken is golden brown and done, about 7 minutes. Turn frequently to keep from burning. Remove legs from oil and drain on paper towel. Transfer to serving platter and serve with Garlic Noodles, or steamed rice and your choice of vegetables. Yields 2 servings.

Peanut Chicken

1 1/2	cups water
1 1/2	tablespoons Maggi Seasoning
1/4	teaspoon ground cloves
1/4	teaspoon ground ginger
1/4	teaspoon ground Laos root
1/4	teaspoon ground coriander
2	teaspoons brown sugar
1	teaspoon lemon juice
3	star aniseed
1/2	cup roasted peanuts, unsalted
1	pound chicken breasts, boned and sliced bite-size

In 3-quart covered saucepan, combine first 10 ingredients and bring to boil, over high heat. Reduce heat, cover and simmer, until peanuts soften, about 20 minutes. Add chicken, increase heat, cover and cook, until chicken is done, about 5 minutes. Remove from heat and serve with Garlic Noodles. Yields 2 servings.

Orange Chicken

      2   egg whites, beaten until soft peaks form
  2 1/2   tablespoons corn starch
    1/2   cup vegetable oil
      1   pound chicken breasts, skinned, boned, cut into 1" x 1/4" pieces

Sauce:
      3   cloves of garlic, crushed
      1   thumb-size segment of fresh ginger root, slivered
    1/4   cup roasted, slivered almonds
      1   tablespoon dried ground orange peel

    1/4   cup honey
    1/4   cup Tamarind Sauce (see Basics)
      2   tablespoons soy sauce

Make batter by combining egg whites with corn starch and mix until smooth. Meanwhile heat oil in wok, over medium high heat until sizzling hot. Dip a few chicken pieces at a time, into the batter. Fry until golden brown on both sides, approximately 1 minute. Remove and drain on paper towel, set aside. Repeat with remaining chicken.

Remove all but 2 tablespoons of oil from wok. Return wok to medium high heat. Stir in the first 4 sauce ingredients, cook until light brown. Add the rest of sauce ingredients, stir and cook about 1/2 minute, or until sauce thickens. Add chicken, toss to blend, then serve. Yields 4 servings.

Stir-Fried Chicken with Five Spice

      2   tablespoons vegetable oil
      1   pound chicken breasts, skinned, boned and sliced thin, bite-size

      1   teaspoon Chinese five spice seasoning
      2   tablespoons soy sauce
    1/4   cup chicken stock mixed with
               1 teaspoon of cornstarch until smooth

Set wok over high heat for 1 minute. Add oil, coat sides of wok evenly. Add chicken, stir and cook until chicken is done, about 2 minutes. Add remaining ingredients, stir and cook, until sauce thickens, about 1 minute. Yields 2 servings.

Chicken & Bean Thread Noodles in Red Curry Sauce

This dish is from my home region and I have been eating this since I was a little girl. My mother always cooked a big pot of these noodles, because everyone in the family liked it so much.

2	2-ounce packages mung bean thread noodles
1	14-ounce can coconut milk
2	tablespoons red curry paste
1	pound deboned chicken meat, sliced thin, bite-size
1/2	cup shredded bamboo shoots
1	cup water
1/4	cup fish sauce (nam pla)
3	stems green onions, cut into 1/2" pieces (white and green parts)
1/2	bunch fresh basil, or 1 teaspoon dried basil

Soak noodles in hot water for 10 minutes. Drain, cut into 2" pieces. Set aside. In 5-quart Dutch oven, bring a 1/4 cup of the coconut milk to boil, over high heat, until coconut milk separates, stirring frequently, about 1 minute. Add red curry paste, stir and cook to blend, about 1/2 minute. Add chicken, stir and cook, until chicken is done, about 2 minutes. Add the remaining coconut milk, noodles, and the rest of ingredients. Bring to boil and allow to boil, until mixture is thoroughly heated, about 1 minute. Remove from heat and serve. Yields 4 servings.

Easy Chicken

1	3 1/2 to 4 pound whole chicken
1	tablespoon salt
1/2	tablespoon garlic powder
1/2	tablespoon ground ginger
1/2	tablespoon pepper
1/2	tablespoon paprika

Preheat oven to 450-degrees. Split chicken in half and trim off fat. Wash chicken with cold water, pat with paper towel to dry. Sprinkle all ingredients evenly over both sides of chicken halves. Place chicken on a rack, in a baking pan. Bake for 1 hour, or until chicken is done. Remove from oven, cut into serving portions and arrange on platter. Serve with Garlic Noodles or Soy Sauce Noodles. Yields 4 to 6 servings.

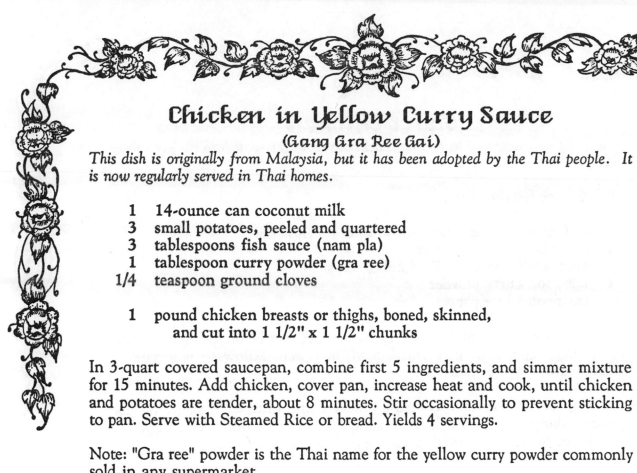

Chicken in Yellow Curry Sauce
(Gang Gra Ree Gai)

This dish is originally from Malaysia, but it has been adopted by the Thai people. It is now regularly served in Thai homes.

- 1   14-ounce can coconut milk
- 3   small potatoes, peeled and quartered
- 3   tablespoons fish sauce (nam pla)
- 1   tablespoon curry powder (gra ree)
- 1/4   teaspoon ground cloves

- 1   pound chicken breasts or thighs, boned, skinned, and cut into 1 1/2" x 1 1/2" chunks

In 3-quart covered saucepan, combine first 5 ingredients, and simmer mixture for 15 minutes. Add chicken, cover pan, increase heat and cook, until chicken and potatoes are tender, about 8 minutes. Stir occasionally to prevent sticking to pan. Serve with Steamed Rice or bread. Yields 4 servings.

Note: "Gra ree" powder is the Thai name for the yellow curry powder commonly sold in any supermarket.

Almond Chicken

Chicken and almonds seem to be a natural together. We like this recipe over a bed of noodles.

- 2   tablespoons vegetable oil
- 4   cloves garlic, crushed
- 1/4   cup slivered almonds
- 1/2   pound chicken breast, skinned, boned, and sliced thin, bite-size

- 1   slice canned pineapple, drained, cut into small pieces
- 1   tablespoon soy sauce
- 1   tablespoon dry sherry
- 1   stem green onion, cut into 1/2 " pieces (white and green parts)
- 1/4   cup pineapple juice mixed with
    - 1 teaspoon of cornstarch until smooth

Set wok over high heat for 1 minute. Add oil and coat sides of wok evenly. Quickly toss in garlic, and almonds, cook until light brown. Add chicken, stir and cook, until chicken is done, about 2 minutes. Add the rest of ingredients, stir and cook, until sauce thickens, about 1/2 minute and serve. Yields 2 servings.

Yogurt Chicken

This is a dish that I urge you to try. It is delicious and light enough to eat even when on a diet.

8   6" wooden skewers
1   pound chicken breasts, boned and skinned.
      Cut each breast lengthwise into 4 strips.
1   cup plain low fat yogurt
2   chicken-flavored bouillon cubes, crushed
1   teaspoon curry powder
1/4 teaspoon white pepper

Soak skewers in water for at least 1/2 hour. Remove just before using. Combine the remaining ingredients in a small bowl, mix well. Allow to marinate at room temperature for 15 minutes.

Preheat oven to 500 degrees. Thread a chicken strip onto each skewer. Place skewers on baking sheet and bake on middle shelf of oven, until done, about 15 minutes. Remove from oven and serve. Yields 8 skewers.

Ginger Chicken Livers

4   large, dried fungus (wood ear) mushrooms

3   tablespoons vegetable oil
15 dried red chile pods
1   thumb-size segment of fresh ginger root, slivered
4   cloves garlic, crushed
1/2 pound chicken livers, sliced very thin
1/2 pound chicken gizzards, sliced very thin

1   tablespoon fish sauce (nam pla)
1/2 tablespoon soy bean condiment
2   ribs celery, sliced thin, on the diagonal

Soak mushrooms in hot water for 30 minutes. Drain, remove stems. Then slice very thin. Set aside. Set wok over high heat for 1 minute. Add oil, coat sides of wok evenly. Add chiles, ginger, and garlic, stir and cook, until lightly brown. Add livers, and gizzards, stir fry until gizzards are done, about 3 minutes. Add remaining ingredients, stir and cook, until celery just begins to soften, about 1 minute. Remove from heat and serve. Yields 2 servings.

Steamed Chicken with Bamboo Shoots

4 small, dried black mushrooms (shi-i-take)
4 cups Chicken Stock (see Basics)
4 chicken drumsticks
1 thumb-size segment of fresh ginger root, mashed
2 cloves garlic, crushed
1 tablespoon oyster sauce
3 tablespoons soy sauce
1 cup diced bamboo shoots

Soak mushrooms in hot water for 20 minutes. Drain, remove bottom part of stems. Set aside. Bring chicken stock to boil, in 5-quart Dutch oven, over high heat. Add mushrooms and the rest of ingredients, cover and cook, until chicken is done, about 20 minutes. Stir occasionally to avoid sticking to pot. Serve hot, with plain cooked noodles, or steamed rice. Yields 2 servings.

Chicken with Cauliflower & Chiles
(Gang Kare)

1/2 small red onion, chopped
2 red fresh jalapeno chiles, chopped
1 tablespoon chopped fresh Laos roots
3 cloves garlic, chopped
3 cups water

3 tablespoons fish sauce (nam pla)
1 tablespoon anchovy paste

1 pound chicken breasts, boned, skinned and sliced bite-size
1 cup drained canned baby corn
1 cup shredded bamboo shoots
1 cup sliced cauliflower

2 cups sliced watercress

In blender, combine first 5 ingredients, blend on medium speed, until coarse ground. Pour the mixture into 1 quart Dutch oven. Add fish sauce, and anchovy, cover, bring to boil over high heat. Add the next 4 ingredients, cover and cook, until chicken is done, about 3 minutes. Add watercress and cook until watercress is limp. Remove to serving dish and serve at once. Yields 4 servings.

Golden Chicken Nuggets

This is a nice appetizer for a party. It is also a delicious snack. Served over Garlic Noodles, it is a fine main course.

1	cup all-purpose flour
2/3	cup water
1	teaspoon sugar
2	teaspoons baking powder
2	teaspoons salt
2	tablespoons roasted sesame seeds, crushed

1	cup vegetable oil
1	pound chicken breasts, boned, skinned, and cut into 2" squares
1	cucumber, sliced about 1/4" thick
12	cherry tomatoes, halved

In medium bowl combine first 6 ingredients and mix until smooth. Set aside. Heat oil in wok, over medium heat, until sizzling hot. Dip 4 to 5 chicken pieces at a time into batter, and coat evenly. Deep fry until chicken is golden brown on both sides, about 6 minutes. Remove chicken pieces from oil and drain on paper towel. Repeat with remaining chicken. Place chicken nuggets on platter, garnish with cucumber and tomatoes. Yields about 14 nuggets.

Sweet Crispy Drumsticks

1	cup all-purpose flour
1/2	teaspoon white pepper
1/2	teaspoon ground ginger
1	teaspoon sugar
1	teaspoon baking powder
1/2	tablespoon salt
1/8	teaspoon ground allspice

8	chicken drumsticks
4	sprigs cilantro or parsley (for garnish)

Sauce:
1/4	cup honey mixed with
	1/2 teaspoon ground fresh chile paste

Preheat oven to 450 degrees. In medium bowl, combine first 7 ingredients. Transfer to 1-quart plastic bag. Add drumsticks and shake to coat drumsticks evenly. Place drumsticks on a rack in a baking pan. Bake for about 45 minutes or until done. Remove to serving plate and garnish with cilantro or parsley and serve with sauce. Yields 4 servings.

Stewed Duck or Chicken
(Phed Liew Gai Thoon)

    4   cups water
   10   thin slices of fresh ginger root
    5   star aniseed
    1   small onion, quartered
    4   cloves garlic, crushed
  1/2   cup Maggi Seasoning
  1/4   cup sweet soy sauce
    1   tablespoon ground coriander
    1   tablespoon coarse ground pepper

    1   4 1/2 to 5 pound fresh duck or chicken

In 8 to 10-quart stew pot, combine the first 9 ingredients, bring to boil over high heat. Add duck or chicken, fold legs under belly and press belly down to bottom of pot. Cook covered for about 20 minutes. Move duck or chicken occasionally while cooking to keep from sticking to pot, turn duck or chicken over, reduce heat and cook until done, about 35 minutes. Remove from heat and carve duck or chicken into serving pieces. Transfer to serving plate and pour sauce from pot over it. Garnish with shredded carrot or cilantro. Serve with Garlic Noodles or steamed rice. Yields 4 servings.

Note: Duck or chicken should not be overcooked. Allow meat to be firm, not soft, for better flavor. Chicken will take slightly less cooking time.

Grilled Chicken & Vegetables

    6   chicken drumsticks
    6   chicken thighs
    1   cup green beans, cut in half (approximately)
    1   cup sliced carrots
    1   cup sliced bell pepper
  1/2   cup soy sauce
    2   ounces margarine, melted
    1   small red onion, sliced and separated into rings
    2   tablespoons sesame seed
    2   tablespoons grated fresh ginger root
  1/8   teaspoon pepper

Combine all ingredients in large bowl, mix well. Tear off six 18x18 inch pieces of heavy-duty foil. Place 1 chicken drumstick, 1 chicken thigh and an equal amount of vegetables into each piece of foil. Bring 4 corners of foil to center, twist to close securely. Repeat with remaining packages. Grill over slow coals, on covered grill, for about 45 minutes or until done. Yields 6 servings.

Hot & Sour Chicken or Duck Salad – "Hot"
(Larb Gai Lieu Phed)

"Larb" is the Thai name for ground meat mixed with hot spices and lime juice. The hot and sour flavor make this a wonderful beginning to a meal. It is also a great main course. It is always present, in one form or another, at a Thai party. It is well-liked and is usually served with Steamed Sweet Rice and plenty of fresh, raw vegetables.

1	pound ground chicken or duck breast
10	cups boiling water
1/4	cup fresh lime juice
1/4	pound chicken or duck skin, boiled, sliced into 2" strips (optional)
1/4	pound chicken or duck giblets, boiled, sliced thin, (optional)
1/4	cup fish sauce (nam pla)
1/4	cup chopped cilantro
1/4	cup ground, roasted sweet rice
1	tablespoon ground, roasted red chili
2	stems fresh lemon grass, sliced very thin (use bottom 2" of stems)
4	fresh makrood leaves, sliced very thin
20	fresh mint leaves (sa ra nea)
1	small red onion, sliced very thin
1/4	teaspoon ground Laos root
	cilantro for garnish

Place ground chicken or duck meat into medium bowl. Pour boiling water over meat and mix well. Let stand for 2 minutes, drain. Add lime juice, mix well. Add the rest of ingredients, toss, and serve with your choice of fresh raw vegetables. Garnish with cilantro. Yields 4 servings.

Chicken Teriyaki

4	chicken breasts, skinned and boned
3	tablespoons teriyaki sauce
1/8	teaspoon ground ginger
1/8	teaspoon garlic powder
1/8	teaspoon onion powder
1/8	teaspoon pepper
2	tablespoons vegetable oil

In medium bowl, combine first 6 ingredients, mix well. Cover and marinate 10 minutes at room temperature. Set 10" covered frying pan over medium heat for 1 minute. Add oil and coat bottom of pan evenly. Add chicken, cover and cook until light brown. Turn chicken over and cook until done, about 4 minutes on each side. Serve with steamed rice and your choice of vegetables. Yields 4 servings.

Roasted Duck

A wonderful dinner entree, juicy and full of flavor. Leftovers can be used in many Thai dishes.

1   4 1/2 to 5 pound fresh whole duck

1/2 tablespoon salt
3   tablespoons dry sherry
2   tablespoons soy sauce
1   tablespoon sweet soy sauce
1   teaspoon ginger powder
2   teaspoons coarse ground black pepper
1   teaspoon flour
1/2 teaspoon ground laos root

12   star aniseeds
    parsley for garnish

Preheat oven to 450 degrees. Wash duck with cold water and pat with paper towel to dry. Trim off fat and pierce duck with meat fork to allow grease to drain. Combine the next 8 ingredients, mix well. Rub duck inside and out with this marinade, reserving left over marinade. Stuff aniseeds inside stomach cavity.

Place duck, breast side down, on a rack, in a baking pan. Reduce heat to 350 degrees and roast duck for 1 hour or until done, allowing 15 minutes per pound. After 45 minutes, turn duck over. During the last 5 minutes of cooking time, increase temperature to 400 degrees to brown and brush duck evenly with reserved marinade. Remove duck from oven, place on cutting board, and cut into serving pieces. Arrange on serving plate and garnish with parsley. Yields 4 to 6 servings.

Steamed Chicken Breast in Red Sauce

1/2 cup water
1   pound chicken breasts, boned, skinned, cut into about 1" x 1" chunks
1   tablespoon chile paste with bean oil (nam prig pao)
1/2 teaspoon paprika
2   chicken-flavored bouillon cubes

Combine all ingredients, in 2-quart covered saucepan. Cover and cook, over medium heat, until chicken is done, about 30 minutes (water should have evaporated). Remove from heat and serve. Yields 2 Servings.

Orange Duck

Great for your next dinner party. It will make for a delicious meal. A must for anyone who loves duck.

- 1 5-pound fresh whole duck
- 1 tablespoon salt

Glaze:
- 1/2 cup fresh orange juice
- 1/2 teaspoon salt
- 2 tablespoons dry sherry
- 2 tablespoons orange liqueur
  parsley for garnish

Preheat the oven to 450 degrees. Wash duck with cold water, pat dry with paper towel and trim off fat. Pierce duck with fork, to allow grease to drain. Rub salt over duck inside and out.

Place duck, breast side down, on a rack, in a baking pan. Reduce heat to 350 degrees. Bake about 1 hour and 15 minutes (allowing 15 minutes per pound).

While duck is roasting, combine glaze ingredients in 1-quart saucepan, cook over medium heat for 10 minutes, stirring occasionally (glaze will thicken and reduce to about 1/4 cup). Set aside.

Baste duck with glaze after about 45 minutes. Turn duck over and continue baking. Baste duck again during the last 5 minutes of cooking time and increase heat to 400 degrees to brown. When done, remove duck from oven, place on cutting board and carve into serving pieces. Arrange on serving platter and garnish with parsley. Serve at once. Yields 6 to 8 servings.

Roasted Duck with Cauliflower

- 2 tablespoons vegetable oil
- 3 cloves garlic, crushed
- 1 pound Roasted Duck*, cut into serving pieces
- 6 cups sliced cauliflower
- 3 tablespoons soy sauce

Set wok over high heat for 1 minute or until sizzling hot. Add oil and coat sides of wok evenly. Add garlic and cook until fragrant. Add duck, stir and cook, until duck is thoroughly heated. Add cauliflower and soy sauce, stir and cook, until cauliflower just begins to soften. Remove from heat and serve with steamed rice. Yields 4 servings.

Note: *-Roasted Duck can be purchased in Oriental markets.

Thai Roasted Turkey

1   whole fresh turkey, about 10 to 12 pounds

1   tablespoon salt
1   tablespoon brown sugar
1/2   tablespoon ground ginger
1/2   tablespoon ground laos root
1   teaspoon white pepper

Stuffing:
4   stems lemon grass, cut into 4 sections and crushed
12   slices dried laos root
2   thumb-size segments fresh ginger root, sliced
1   large onion, chopped
8   cloves garlic, crushed
1   tablespoon coarse ground black pepper
1   6" wooden skewer

Glaze:
4   ounces butter or margarine, unsalted, melted
1   cup honey
1   cup Tamarind Sauce (see Basics)
4   tablespoons dry sherry
2   teaspoons salt

Remove innards and any excess fat from turkey. Wash turkey with cold water and pad dry with paper towel. Combine the next 5 ingredients and rub over turkey inside and out. Allow to marinate at room temperature for 15 minutes.

Preheat oven to 350 degrees. Combine all stuffing ingredients and stuff into stomach cavity of turkey. Close with wooden skewer. Place turkey breast side down (to keep breast nice and juicy) on a rack, in a baking pan. Cover turkey with tin foil and bake for about 3 to 3 1/2 hours or until done, allowing 18 minutes per pound.

Heat together glaze ingredients until blended. Set aside. About 30 minutes before turkey is done, remove tin foil and turn turkey breast side up. Frequently brush with glaze during the last 30 minutes of cooking time. When done, remove turkey from oven. Remove and discard stuffing, carve and pour remaining glaze over meat. Serve with Ginger Dipping Sauce and Plain Steamed Rice. Yields 10 to 12 servings.

BEEF

Beef cuts should have a nice deep, rich red color if fresh. If the meat has a purplish cast, it is old. Trim as much fat as possible but meat should have a little marble of fat running through it for juiciness.

I prefer top sirloin for my stir fries and beef salad. I even use it for the curries, but you can use less expensive cuts like chuck steak or flank steak which have a good flavor but tend to be tough. I would recommend these cuts for braising.

Barbecued Short Ribs

3	pounds beef plate short ribs, cut into serving size pieces
3	cloves garlic, minced
1	small onion, finely chopped
1/2	cup catsup
1/2	cup soy sauce
2	tablespoons fish sauce (nam pla)
1/2	tablespoon dry mustard
1/2	tablespoon lemon pepper
1/2	tablespoon all spice
1/2	tablespoon paprika

Combine all ingredients in large bowl, mix well. Cover and refrigerate for several hours or overnight. Drain, reserving marinade. Place ribs over slow coals. Grill 15 to 20 minutes or until done. Turn ribs often, basting occasionally with reserved marinade. Serve with Garlic Noodles or steamed rice. Yields 4 servings.

Stir-Fried Beef or Pork with Broccoli
(Paht Nuah Liew Moo Kana)

3	tablespoons vegetable oil
3	cloves garlic, crushed
1	pound beef or pork, sliced thin, bite-size
6	cups sliced broccoli (or Chinese broccoli)
3 1/2	tablespoons oyster sauce

Heat oil in wok over high heat until sizzling hot. Add garlic and cook, until light brown. Add beef or pork, stir and cook, until meat is done, about 1 minute for beef and 3 minutes for pork. Add broccoli, stir, then add oyster sauce. Stir and cook, until broccoli just begins to soften, about 2 minutes. Transfer to serving dish and serve with steamed rice. Yields 3 servings.

Thai Hamburger

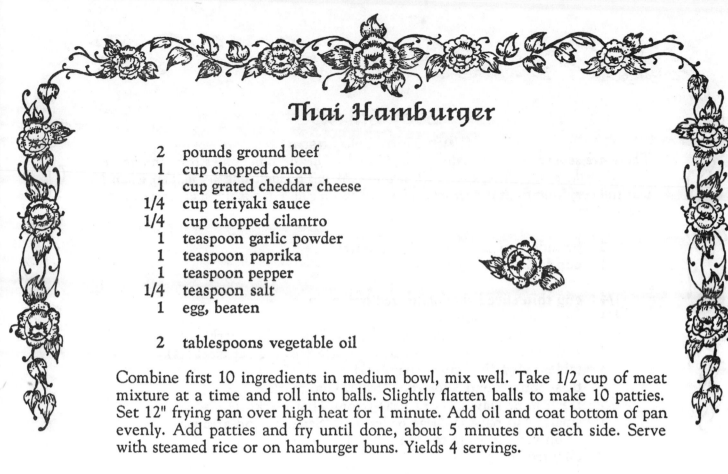

2 pounds ground beef
1 cup chopped onion
1 cup grated cheddar cheese
1/4 cup teriyaki sauce
1/4 cup chopped cilantro
1 teaspoon garlic powder
1 teaspoon paprika
1 teaspoon pepper
1/4 teaspoon salt
1 egg, beaten

2 tablespoons vegetable oil

Combine first 10 ingredients in medium bowl, mix well. Take 1/2 cup of meat mixture at a time and roll into balls. Slightly flatten balls to make 10 patties. Set 12" frying pan over high heat for 1 minute. Add oil and coat bottom of pan evenly. Add patties and fry until done, about 5 minutes on each side. Serve with steamed rice or on hamburger buns. Yields 4 servings.

Beef Kabobs

2 pounds beef top sirloin, cut into 2" square chunks
1/2 cup soy sauce
1 tablespoon brown sugar
1 teaspoon dry mustard
1/2 teaspoon chile powder
1 teaspoon onion powder
1/4 teaspoon pepper
1 teaspoon salt
1 teaspoon ground coriander
3 cloves garlic, minced

16 mushroom caps
2 onions, cut into wedges
16 cherry tomatoes
3 green sweet peppers, cut into 1" squares
8 12" wooden skewers, soaked in water for 1/2 hour,
    remove just before using

Combine first 10 ingredients in medium bowl, mix well. Cover and refrigerate several hours, turning meat occasionally. Drain meat, reserving marinade. Alternate meat, mushrooms, onion, tomato, and sweet pepper on skewers, 2 sets per skewer. Grill over medium hot coals until done, about 8 minutes for rare, turning and brushing often with reserved marinade. Serve with fried rice. Yields 6 servings.

Beef Salad
(Yum Nam Tok Easan)

There are several different types of beef salad. This version comes from my home region, to the east of Bangkok. I learned to cook this by watching my mother when I was still very young. It is a strong, spicy and exciting dish and is normally served with steamed rice.

2	pounds beef steak (sirloin or skirt)
1/4	cup fresh lime juice
1/4	cup thin sliced shallots or red onion
1/4	cup coarsely chopped cilantro
1	tablespoon ground roasted red chile (from Thai markets)
3	tablespoons ground roasted sweet rice (from Thai markets)
3	tablespoons fish sauce (nam pla)
1	teaspoon ground Laos root (from Thai markets)
25	fresh mint leaves (sa ra nea) (from Thai markets)
1	small head napa cabbage or lettuce. Separate and arrange on serving plate to create a bed.
	cilantro for garnish

Broil steak in oven, until medium rare. Remove and slice thin, bite-size. In medium bowl, combine sliced steak and lime juice, mix well. Add the next 7 ingredients and toss to blend. Serve on bed of napa cabbage, or lettuce, garnish with cilantro. Yields 4 to 6 servings.

Hot & Sour Beef with Cucumber
(Yum Yai)

Another in a series of hot and sour salads. This is a milder variety that can be served as a light lunch.

1	pound beef top sirloin steak
1/4	cup fresh lime juice
1	cucumber, split in half, then sliced very thin
1	small red onion, sliced very thin
2	tablespoons fish sauce (nam pla)
1/2	teaspoon ground roasted chile or red crushed chile
1	tablespoon ground roasted peanuts
1	teaspoon sugar
5	large lettuce leaves
	cilantro for garnish

Broil steak in oven, until medium rare, slice thin, bite-size. In medium bowl, combine sliced steak and lime juice, mix well. Add the next 6 ingredients and toss to blend. Serve on bed of lettuce leaves, garnish with cilantro. Yields 3 servings.

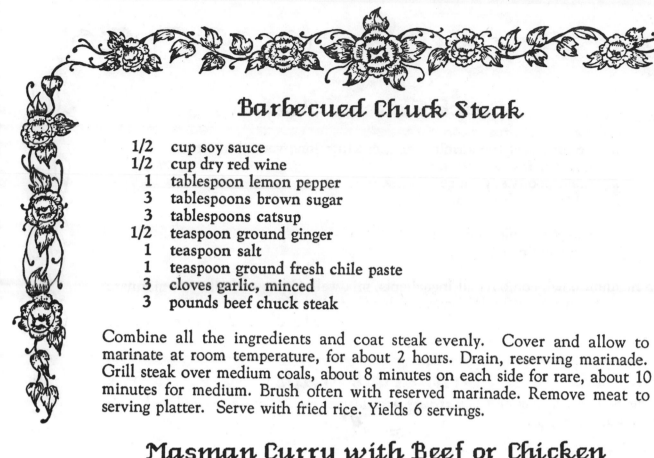

Barbecued Chuck Steak

1/2   cup soy sauce
1/2   cup dry red wine
1   tablespoon lemon pepper
3   tablespoons brown sugar
3   tablespoons catsup
1/2   teaspoon ground ginger
1   teaspoon salt
1   teaspoon ground fresh chile paste
3   cloves garlic, minced
3   pounds beef chuck steak

Combine all the ingredients and coat steak evenly. Cover and allow to marinate at room temperature, for about 2 hours. Drain, reserving marinade. Grill steak over medium coals, about 8 minutes on each side for rare, about 10 minutes for medium. Brush often with reserved marinade. Remove meat to serving platter. Serve with fried rice. Yields 6 servings.

Masman Curry with Beef or Chicken
(Gang Masman)

Like so many native Thai dishes, this is an exotic blend of curry and coconut milk. Unlike other Thai curry dishes, this dish uses potatoes and is very much like a stew. My family likes it served only with bread.

2   tablespoons vegetable oil
1/4   cup Masman Curry Paste
2   14-ounce cans coconut milk

1   pound boneless stew beef, or chicken breasts, cut into 2" squares
1/3   cup roasted peanuts
3   small potatoes, peeled, cut into quarters
1   small onion, cut into quarters
2   tablespoons fish sauce (nam pla)
2   tablespoons sugar
2   tablespoons Tamarind Sauce (see Basics)

Heat oil in 1-quart saucepan, until sizzling hot, and coat bottom of pan evenly. Add masman curry, stir and cook, until brown. Set aside.

Set 5-quart Dutch oven over high heat. Add 3/4 cup of the coconut milk and cook, until coconut milk separates, about 5 minutes, stirring frequently. Add the browned masman curry paste and stir to blend. Add meat, stir and cook, until meat is lightly browned, about 3 minutes. Add the rest of coconut milk and remaining ingredients, cover and cook, until meat and potatoes are tender, about 20 minutes. Serve with steamed rice or bread. Yields 4 servings.

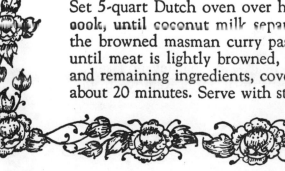

Quick Roasted Beef

2	pounds beef top sirloin steak, cut into long very thin strips
2	tablespoons sesame seed
2	tablespoons soy sauce
1/2	tablespoon brown sugar
1/2	teaspoon garlic powder
1/2	teaspoon onion powder
1/4	teaspoon pepper

In medium bowl, combine all ingredients, mix well. Cover and allow to marinate at room temperature for 1/2 hour. Preheat oven to 450 degrees. Place beef on a rack, in a baking pan, in middle shelf of oven. Bake about 12 to 15 minutes or until done and serve. Yields 4 servings.

Pan-Fried Steak

This is a rich tasting dish that is very easy to prepare. It can be served with plain steamed rice or fried rice.

2	pounds beef top sirloin steak
2	tablespoons teriyaki sauce
2	tablespoons oyster sauce
1/8	teaspoon pepper
1/8	teaspoon garlic powder
1/8	teaspoon onion powder
3	tablespoons vegetable oil
1	small onion, sliced thin

Combine first 6 ingredients in medium bowl, mix well. Cover and allow to marinate at room temperature for 15 minutes. Drain, reserving marinade. Set 10" covered frying pan over high heat for 1 minute. Add oil and coat bottom of pan evenly. Add onion and cook, until light brown. Remove onion from oil and set aside. Add steak to pan, cover and cook, until steak is done, about 4 minutes on each side. Place onion on top of steak and pour reserved marinade over it. Cover and simmer 1 minute. Remove from heat and serve. Yields 4 servings.

Stir-Fried Beef in Herbal Butter

1/2	cup Herbal Butter (see Basics)
1/4	cup chopped parsley
1/4	teaspoon salt
1	pound beef sirloin steak, sliced thin, bite-size

Melt Herbal Butter in 10" frying pan over high heat. Add parsley and salt, cook, until limp. Add beef, stir fry about 1 minute or until done. Remove from heat and serve. Yields 2 servings.

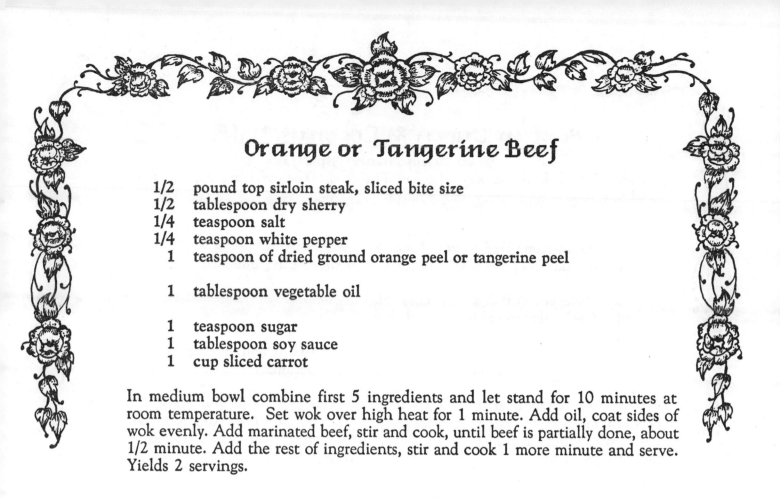

Orange or Tangerine Beef

1/2	pound top sirloin steak, sliced bite size
1/2	tablespoon dry sherry
1/4	teaspoon salt
1/4	teaspoon white pepper
1	teaspoon of dried ground orange peel or tangerine peel
1	tablespoon vegetable oil
1	teaspoon sugar
1	tablespoon soy sauce
1	cup sliced carrot

In medium bowl combine first 5 ingredients and let stand for 10 minutes at room temperature. Set wok over high heat for 1 minute. Add oil, coat sides of wok evenly. Add marinated beef, stir and cook, until beef is partially done, about 1/2 minute. Add the rest of ingredients, stir and cook 1 more minute and serve. Yields 2 servings.

Green Curry with Beef or Chicken
(Gang, Kiew Warn)

This dish is always served at Thai gatherings. Thai people never seem to get tired of it. I hope you will try it soon.

2	14-ounce cans coconut milk
3	tablespoons Green Curry Paste
1	pound beef sirloin steak or chicken breasts, sliced bite-size
1 1/2	cups frozen sweet green peas, thawed
3	tablespoons fish sauce (nam pla)
1	tablespoon sugar
2	jalapeno chiles, cut lengthwise
2	stems green onions, cut into 1/2" pieces (white and green parts)
20	fresh mint leaves (sa ra nea) or basil leaves

Set 5-quart Dutch over high heat. Add 3/4 cup of the coconut milk, cook until coconut milk separates, about 5 minutes, stirring occasionally. Add green curry paste and stir to blend. Add beef, stir and cook, until meat is done, about 1 minute for beef and about 3 minutes for chicken. Add the rest of the coconut milk, peas, and fish sauce. Cover and bring to boil. Add the remaining ingredients, stir and remove from heat. Serve with steamed rice or spaghetti. Yields 4 servings.

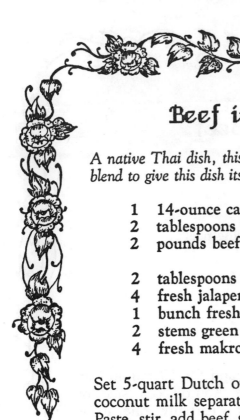

Beef in Curry & Coconut Milk
(Pha Nang Nuah– "Spicy")

A native Thai dish, this is very typical of Thai food. The curry and coconut flavors blend to give this dish its truly unique flavor.

1   14-ounce can coconut milk
2   tablespoons Red Curry Paste
2   pounds beef steak (sirloin or skirt), sliced thin, bite-size

2   tablespoons fish sauce (nam pla)
4   fresh jalapeno chiles, sliced thin
1   bunch fresh basil
2   stems green onions, cut into 1/2" pieces (white and green parts)
4   fresh makrood leaves, sliced very thin (optional)

Set 5-quart Dutch oven over high heat. Add coconut milk and cook, until coconut milk separates, stirring frequently, about 5 minutes. Add Red Curry Paste, stir, add beef, stir and cook, until beef is done, about 1 minute. Add the rest of ingredients, stir to blend and serve. Yields 4 servings.

Thai Mongolian Beef

1/2   pound flank steak, trimmed, sliced thin, bite-size, across the grain
3   beef-flavored bouillon cubes, dissolved in 2 tablespoons hot water
1   tablespoon light sesame oil
1   teaspoon coarse ground black pepper
1/8   teaspoon red crushed chile
1   tablespoon corn starch
    juice from 1/2 lemon

2   tablespoons vegetable oil
1   tablespoon slivered fresh ginger root
1   tablespoon crushed garlic
4   stems green onions, cut into 1/2" pieces (white and green parts)

In medium bowl, combine first 7 ingredients, mix well. Allow to marinate at room temperature for 10 minutes. Set wok over high heat for 1 minute. Add oil and coat sides of wok evenly. Add ginger, and garlic, cook until fragrant. Add marinated beef, stir and cook, until beef is done, about 1 minute. Add onion, stir and cook, until onions are limp, about 1/2 minute. Remove from heat and serve. Yields 2 servings.

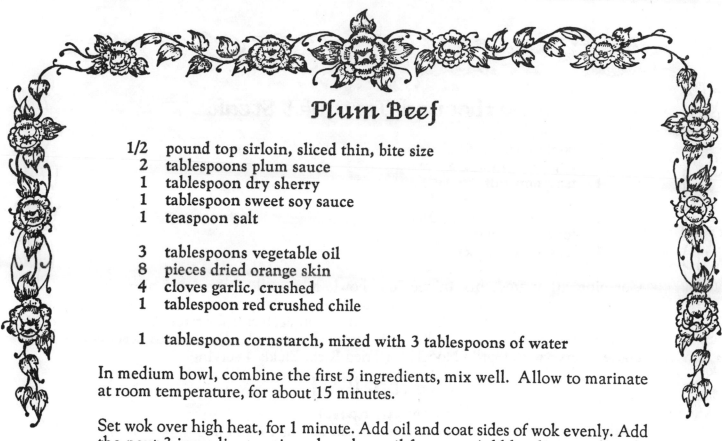

Plum Beef

1/2	pound top sirloin, sliced thin, bite size
2	tablespoons plum sauce
1	tablespoon dry sherry
1	tablespoon sweet soy sauce
1	teaspoon salt
3	tablespoons vegetable oil
8	pieces dried orange skin
4	cloves garlic, crushed
1	tablespoon red crushed chile
1	tablespoon cornstarch, mixed with 3 tablespoons of water

In medium bowl, combine the first 5 ingredients, mix well. Allow to marinate at room temperature, for about 15 minutes.

Set wok over high heat, for 1 minute. Add oil and coat sides of wok evenly. Add the next 3 ingredients, stir and cook, until fragrant. Add beef, stir and cook, until beef is done, about 1/2 minute. Add cornstarch mixture and cook until sauce thickens. Remove from heat and serve. Yields 2 servings.

Meat Balls with Vegetables

2	tablespoons vegetable oil
1	small onion, cut lengthwise
3	cloves garlic, minced
1	pound ground beef, rolled into 1" diameter balls
2	bell peppers, sliced into strips
1	carrot, peeled and sliced thin
1	small tomato, quartered
2	stems green onions, cut into 1/2" pieces (white and green parts)
2	ribs celery, cut into 1/2" pieces
2	tablespoons oyster sauce
1	tablespoon catsup

Set 2 to 3 quart covered saucepan over high heat for one minute. Add oil and coat bottom of pan evenly. Add onion and garlic, cook until light brown. Add meat balls, gently stir and cook, until meat is lightly browned. Add remaining ingredients, reduce heat, cover and cook, until meat is done, about 3 minutes. Transfer to serving dish and serve with steamed rice. Yields 4 servings.

Barbecued Teriyaki Steak

- 2 pounds beef sirloin steak
- 1/2 cup teriyaki sauce
- 1 teaspoon salt
- 1 teaspoon garlic powder
- 1 teaspoon onion powder
- 1 teaspoon pepper
- 1 teaspoon paprika

Combine all ingredients in medium bowl, mix well. Cover and allow to marinate at room temperature for about 2 hours. Drain, reserving marinade. Grill steak over medium coals about 8 minutes on each side for rare, 10 minutes for medium. Brush occasionally with reserved marinade. Remove to serving platter. Serve with Garlic Noodles or Fried Rice. Yields 4 servings.

Dried Beef
(Nuah Hang)

Try this Thai beef jerky sometime soon. It can be eaten warm and fresh from the oven. It can be stored in the refrigerator and eaten cold.

- 2 pounds lean beef, cut into very thin, long strips
- 4 tablespoons soy sauce
- 1/2 tablespoon brown sugar
- 1 teaspoon garlic powder
- 1 teaspoon onion powder
- 1 teaspoon pepper
- 1 teaspoon ground coriander
- 2 teaspoons paprika

In medium bowl, combine all ingredients. Cover and allow to marinate at room temperature for 2 hours, or refrigerate overnight. Preheat oven to 250 degrees. Place beef on a rack, in a baking pan, in middle shelf of oven. Bake about 2 hours or until crisp. Yields 4 servings.

Beef Liver with Onion

- 3 tablespoons vegetable oil
- 1 small red onion, sliced
- 1 pound beef liver, sliced thin, bite-size
- 1 tablespoon fish sauce (nam pla)
- 1/2 tablespoon oyster sauce
- 1/2 teaspoon red crushed chile

Set wok over high heat for 1 minute. Add oil, coat sides of wok evenly. Stir in onion, cook until fragrant. Add liver, stir and cook, until liver is done, about 2 minutes. Add remaining ingredients, stir to blend and serve. Yields 3 to 4 servings.

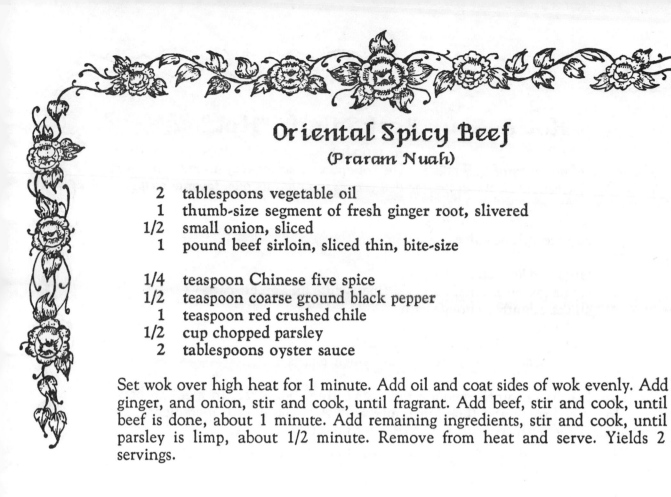

Oriental Spicy Beef
(Praram Nuah)

2 tablespoons vegetable oil
1 thumb-size segment of fresh ginger root, slivered
1/2 small onion, sliced
1 pound beef sirloin, sliced thin, bite-size

1/4 teaspoon Chinese five spice
1/2 teaspoon coarse ground black pepper
1 teaspoon red crushed chile
1/2 cup chopped parsley
2 tablespoons oyster sauce

Set wok over high heat for 1 minute. Add oil and coat sides of wok evenly. Add ginger, and onion, stir and cook, until fragrant. Add beef, stir and cook, until beef is done, about 1 minute. Add remaining ingredients, stir and cook, until parsley is limp, about 1/2 minute. Remove from heat and serve. Yields 2 servings.

Pepper Steak

1/2 pound beef flank or sirloin steak, trimmed, sliced thin, bite-size
1 tablespoon dry sherry
2 tablespoons oyster sauce
1 beef-flavored bouillon cube, dissolved in 1 tablespoon hot water
1 teaspoon coarse ground black pepper

2 tablespoons vegetable oil
1 small onion, sliced thin
1 medium bell pepper, sliced thin

In medium bowl, combine first 5 ingredients and marinate at room temperature for 15 minutes. Set wok over high heat for 1 minute. Add oil and coat sides of wok evenly. Add onion, stir and cook, until fragrant. Add beef, and bell pepper, cook until beef is done, about 1 1/2 minutes. Transfer to serving plate and serve. Yields 2 to 3 servings.

Hot & Sour Beef Salad—"Hot"
(Yum Nuah)

This is one of a variety of beef salads. The hot and sour salads play an important part in the Thai kitchen. It is not surprising that every region has its own favorite recipe.

2	pounds beef top sirloin steak
1/4	cup fresh lime juice
1	large tomato, sliced thin
2	stems green onions, chopped fine (white and green parts)
4	stalks cilantro, chopped fine
1	tablespoon red chrushed chile
3	tablespoons fish sauce (nam pla)
1	small head lettuce, broken into small pieces

Broil steak in oven, until medium rare. Slice thin, bite-size. In medium bowl, combine sliced steak and lime juice, mix well. Add the next 6 ingredients, toss to blend. Serve with steamed rice. Yields 4 to 6 servings.

Beef with Green Onion

2	tablespoons vegetable oil
3	cloves garlic, crushed
1/2	pound beef sirloin steak, sliced thin, bite-size
1	tablespoon fish sauce (nam pla)
5	stems green onion, cut into 1/2" pieces (white and green parts)

Heat wok over high heat for 1 minute. Add oil and coat sides of wok evenly. Quickly stir in garlic and cook until light brown. Add beef, stir and cook, until beef is done, about 1/2 minute. Add fish sauce and green onion, stir and cook, about 1/2 minute and serve with Garlic Noodles. Yields 2 servings.

Beef with Straw Mushrooms

Straw mushrooms are very common in Thailand and used in a wide variety of dishes. This is an especially nice dish to serve.

3	tablespoons vegetable oil
3	cloves garlic, minced
2	pounds beef top sirloin steak, sliced thin, bite-size
1	15-ounce can straw mushrooms, drained
2	stems green onions, cut into 1/2" pieces (white and green parts)
3	tablespoons oyster sauce

Set wok over high heat for 1 minute. Add oil and coat sides of wok evenly. Add garlic and cook until light brown. Add beef, stir and cook, until beef is done, about 1 minute. Add remaining ingredients, stir and cook, until mushrooms are thoroughly heated, about 1 minute. Remove to serving plate and serve with steamed rice. Yields 4 to 6 servings.

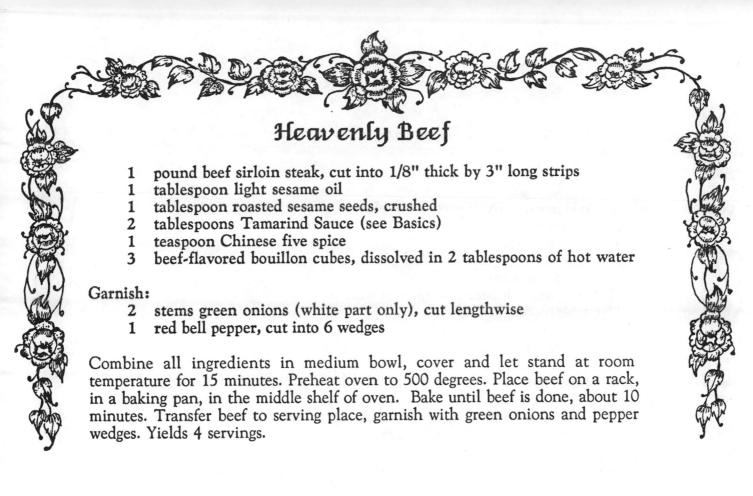

Heavenly Beef

1   pound beef sirloin steak, cut into 1/8" thick by 3" long strips
1   tablespoon light sesame oil
1   tablespoon roasted sesame seeds, crushed
2   tablespoons Tamarind Sauce (see Basics)
1   teaspoon Chinese five spice
3   beef-flavored bouillon cubes, dissolved in 2 tablespoons of hot water

Garnish:
2   stems green onions (white part only), cut lengthwise
1   red bell pepper, cut into 6 wedges

Combine all ingredients in medium bowl, cover and let stand at room temperature for 15 minutes. Preheat oven to 500 degrees. Place beef on a rack, in a baking pan, in the middle shelf of oven. Bake until beef is done, about 10 minutes. Transfer beef to serving place, garnish with green onions and pepper wedges. Yields 4 servings.

Lamb Curry

My neighbors always know when I cook a curry dish. It has a wonderful appetite-generating aroma. The lamb with potatoes is a nice dish for cooler days.

3   tablespoons vegetable oil
1/4 cup chopped parsley
4   cloves garlic, crushed
1   tablespoon Red Curry Paste
1   pound lean lamb, sliced thin, bite-size

1   teaspoon curry powder
2   tablespoons fish sauce (nam pla)
2   small cooked potatoes, diced into 1/2" cubes

Heat oil in wok, until sizzling hot, and coat sides of wok evenly. Add parsley, garlic, and curry paste, stir and cook, until fragrant. Add lamb, stir and cook, until lamb is done, about 2 minutes. Add remaining ingredients, stir and cook, until potatoes are thoroughly heated, about 1 more minute. Transfer to serving dish and serve. Yields 4 servings.

Tongue Stew

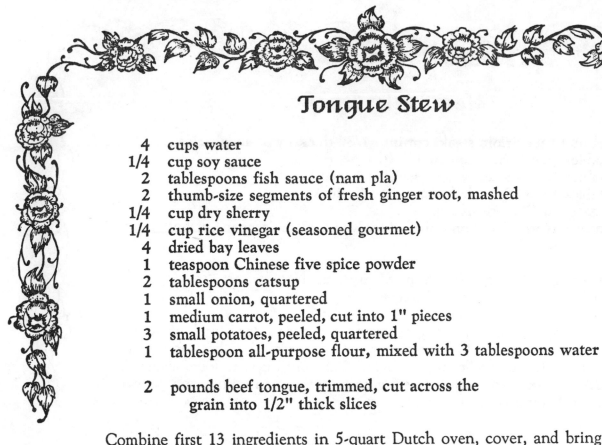

4	cups water
1/4	cup soy sauce
2	tablespoons fish sauce (nam pla)
2	thumb-size segments of fresh ginger root, mashed
1/4	cup dry sherry
1/4	cup rice vinegar (seasoned gourmet)
4	dried bay leaves
1	teaspoon Chinese five spice powder
2	tablespoons catsup
1	small onion, quartered
1	medium carrot, peeled, cut into 1" pieces
3	small potatoes, peeled, quartered
1	tablespoon all-purpose flour, mixed with 3 tablespoons water
2	pounds beef tongue, trimmed, cut across the grain into 1/2" thick slices

Combine first 13 ingredients in 5-quart Dutch oven, cover, and bring to boil over high heat. Add tongue, cover, bring to boil again. Reduce heat and simmer, until tongue is tender, about 1 hour. Stir occasionally while cooking to prevent sticking to pot. Sauce will have thickened to a stew like consistency. Transfer to soup tureen and serve while hot. Yields 4 to 6 servings.

Thai Sticks

25	6" wooden skewers
1	pound London broil steak, cut into 1/8" thick by 3" long strips
2 1/2	tablespoons soy sauce
2	tablespoons catsup
2	tablespoons dry sherry
1/4	teaspoon ground ginger
1/4	teaspoon ground Laos root
1/4	teaspoon garlic powder
1	teaspoon coarse ground black pepper
1	teaspoon brown sugar

Soak wooden skewers in water at least 1/2 hour. Remove just before using. Set aside. In medium bowl combine all ingredients. Let stand at room temperature for 15 minutes. Thread 1 piece of meat on top half of each skewer. Grill over hot coals about 1 minute on each side and serve. Can be served as an appetizer. Yields about 25 sticks.

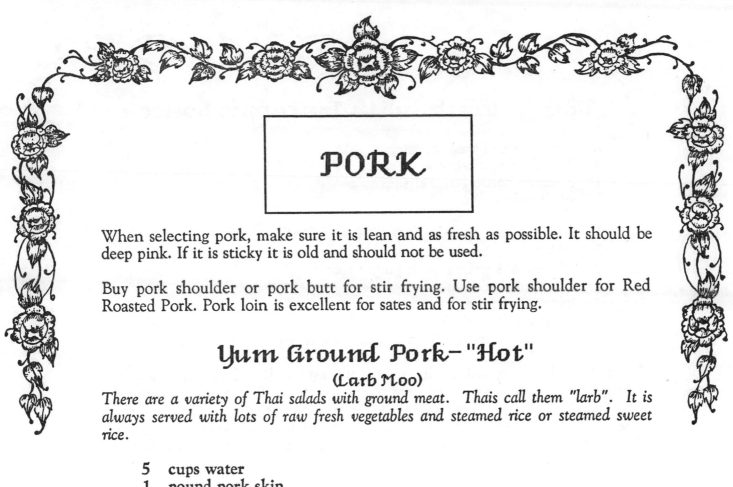

PORK

When selecting pork, make sure it is lean and as fresh as possible. It should be deep pink. If it is sticky it is old and should not be used.

Buy pork shoulder or pork butt for stir frying. Use pork shoulder for Red Roasted Pork. Pork loin is excellent for sates and for stir frying.

Yum Ground Pork–"Hot"
(Larb Moo)

There are a variety of Thai salads with ground meat. Thais call them "larb". It is always served with lots of raw fresh vegetables and steamed rice or steamed sweet rice.

5	cups water
1	pound pork skin
1/4	pound pork liver
2	pounds very lean, ground pork
10	cups boiling water
3/4	cup fresh lime juice
1	small red onion, sliced thin
1	thumb-size segment fresh ginger root, slivered
1/4	cup chopped cilantro
1/2	cup ground roasted sweet rice (from Thai markets)
1/2	cup fish sauce (nam pla)
2	tablespoons ground roasted red chile
2	stems fresh lemon grass, sliced very thin, use bottom 2" of stems
4	fresh makrood leaves, sliced very thin
20	fresh mint leaves (sa ra nea)

Bring 5-cups of water to boil, in 3-quart saucepan, over high heat. Add pork skin and boil until tender, about 20 minutes. Remove skin from water. Add liver and boil until liver is done, about 3 to 4 minutes, drain. Slice skin into about 2" long thin strips. Slice liver into 1" long thin strips.

Place ground pork into medium bowl. Pour 10 cups boiling water over pork, stir, and let stand for 2 minutes, then drain. Combine pork, pork skin, liver, and lime juice, mix well. Add the rest of ingredients and mix well. Serve with your choice of fresh raw vegetables and steamed rice. Yields 6 servings.

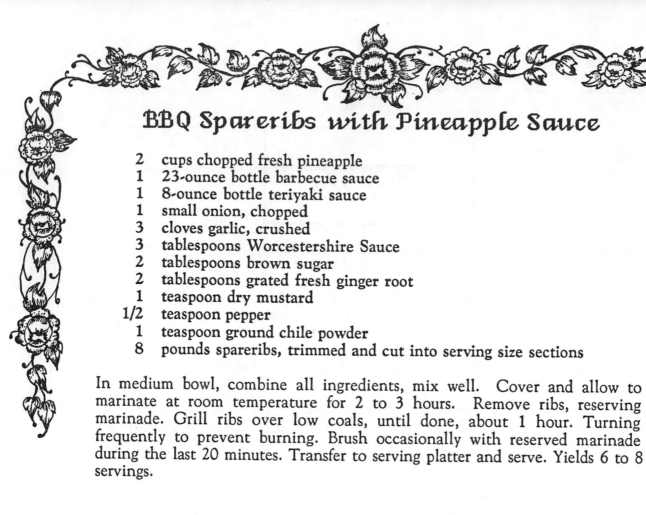

BBQ Spareribs with Pineapple Sauce

2   cups chopped fresh pineapple
1   23-ounce bottle barbecue sauce
1   8-ounce bottle teriyaki sauce
1   small onion, chopped
3   cloves garlic, crushed
3   tablespoons Worcestershire Sauce
2   tablespoons brown sugar
2   tablespoons grated fresh ginger root
1   teaspoon dry mustard
1/2   teaspoon pepper
1   teaspoon ground chile powder
8   pounds spareribs, trimmed and cut into serving size sections

In medium bowl, combine all ingredients, mix well. Cover and allow to marinate at room temperature for 2 to 3 hours. Remove ribs, reserving marinade. Grill ribs over low coals, until done, about 1 hour. Turning frequently to prevent burning. Brush occasionally with reserved marinade during the last 20 minutes. Transfer to serving platter and serve. Yields 6 to 8 servings.

Stir-Fried Ground Pork with Bean Threads
(Moo Paht Wun Sen)

8   medium, dried black fungus (wood ear) mushrooms or
     1 cup sliced mushrooms
2   2-ounce packages mung bean thread noodles

3   tablespoons vegetable oil
1   thumb-size section fresh ginger root, slivered
1   small onion, sliced thin
1   pound ground pork

2   cups shredded bamboo shoots
1/4   cup fish sauce (nam pla)

Soak black fungus mushrooms in hot water for 30 minutes. Drain and slice very thin. Set aside. Soak bean thread noodles in hot water for 10 minutes. Drain and cut into 2" lengths. Set aside.

Heat oil in wok until sizzling hot and coat sides of wok evenly. Add ginger, and onion, stir and cook, until light brown. Add pork, stir and cook, until pork is done, about 2 minutes. Add bean threads, mushrooms, and remaining ingredients, stir and cook, until mixture is thoroughly heated, about 2 minutes. Remove from heat and serve. Yields 4 servings.

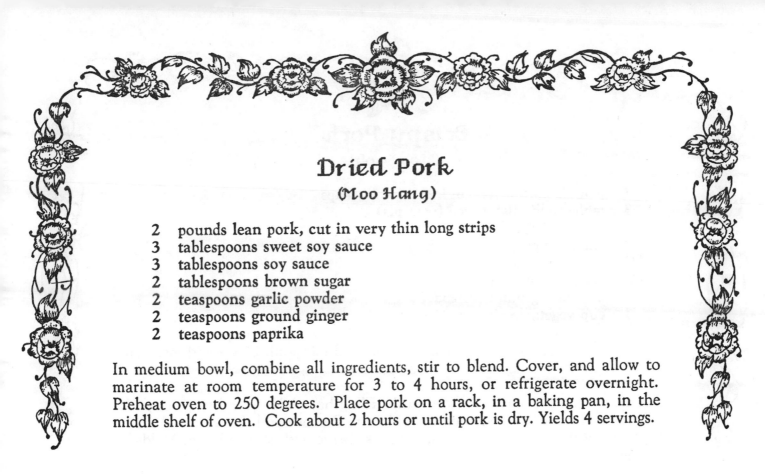

Dried Pork
(Moo Hang)

2 pounds lean pork, cut in very thin long strips
3 tablespoons sweet soy sauce
3 tablespoons soy sauce
2 tablespoons brown sugar
2 teaspoons garlic powder
2 teaspoons ground ginger
2 teaspoons paprika

In medium bowl, combine all ingredients, stir to blend. Cover, and allow to marinate at room temperature for 3 to 4 hours, or refrigerate overnight. Preheat oven to 250 degrees. Place pork on a rack, in a baking pan, in the middle shelf of oven. Cook about 2 hours or until pork is dry. Yields 4 servings.

Barbecued Spareribs
(Seek Klong Moo Yang)

1 23-ounce bottle barbecue sauce
1 8-ounce bottle teriyaki sauce
1/4 cup grated fresh ginger root
1 small onion, chopped
6 cloves garlic, crushed
1 teaspoon pepper
1 teaspoon paprika
1 teaspoon salt
8 pounds spareribs

Combine first 8 ingredients in blender. Blend on medium speed until smooth. Set aside. Cut spareribs into sections, trim and remove excess fat. Place in large bowl and pour sauce over spareribs, coat ribs evenly with sauce. Cover and allow to marinate at room temperature, or refrigerate overnight.

To cook: Remove spareribs, reserving marinade. Grill ribs over low coals until done, about 1 hour. Brush frequently with reserved marinade during the last 20 minutes. Yields 6 to 8 servings.

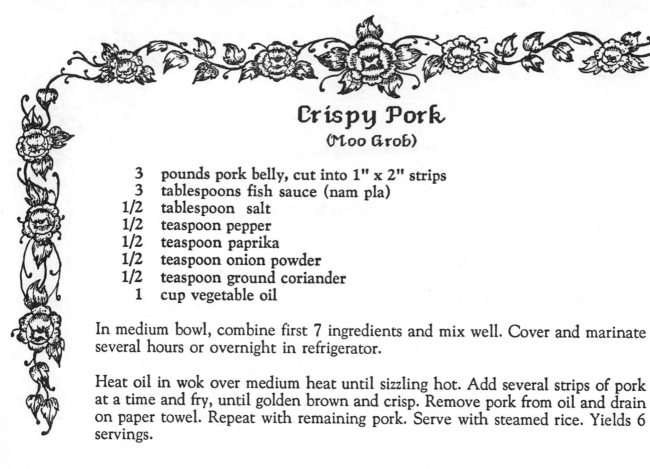

Crispy Pork
(Moo Grob)

3 pounds pork belly, cut into 1" x 2" strips
3 tablespoons fish sauce (nam pla)
1/2 tablespoon salt
1/2 teaspoon pepper
1/2 teaspoon paprika
1/2 teaspoon onion powder
1/2 teaspoon ground coriander
1 cup vegetable oil

In medium bowl, combine first 7 ingredients and mix well. Cover and marinate several hours or overnight in refrigerator.

Heat oil in wok over medium heat until sizzling hot. Add several strips of pork at a time and fry, until golden brown and crisp. Remove pork from oil and drain on paper towel. Repeat with remaining pork. Serve with steamed rice. Yields 6 servings.

Sweet & Sour Pork with Pineapple
(Paht Pril Warn Moo)

3 tablespoons vegetable oil
1 small onion, sliced thin
3 cloves garlic, crushed
2 pounds pork, sliced thin, bite-size

2 cups fresh pineapple, sliced bite-size
1/3 cup fish sauce (nam pla)
1/4 cup white vinegar
3 ribs celery, cut into 1/2" pieces
3 tablespoons catsup
1 tablespoon brown sugar
1 red bell pepper, cut into strips
1 green bell pepper, cut into strips
1/8 teaspoon pepper

2 tablespoons all-purpose flour mixed with 1/4 cup of water

Set 10" frying pan over high heat for 1 minute. Add oil and coat bottom of pan evenly. Add onion, and garlic, stir and cook, until light brown. Add pork, stir and cook, until pork is done, about 4 minutes. Add the next 9 ingredients, stir and cook, until celery just begins to soften. Add flour mixture, stir and cook, until sauce thickens. Transfer to serving plate and serve with steamed rice. Yields 4 servings.

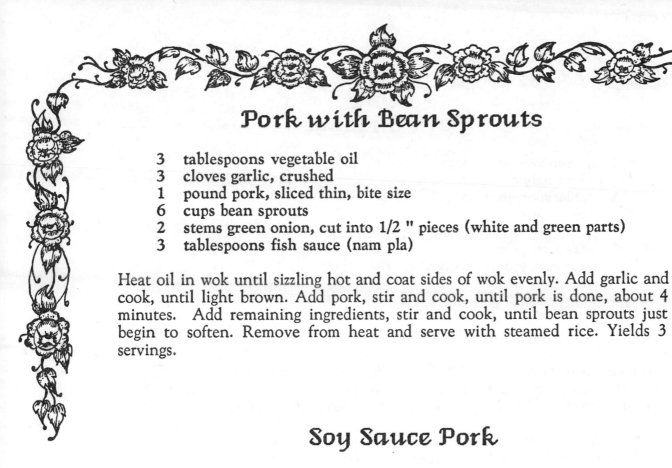

Pork with Bean Sprouts

3   tablespoons vegetable oil
3   cloves garlic, crushed
1   pound pork, sliced thin, bite size
6   cups bean sprouts
2   stems green onion, cut into 1/2 " pieces (white and green parts)
3   tablespoons fish sauce (nam pla)

Heat oil in wok until sizzling hot and coat sides of wok evenly. Add garlic and cook, until light brown. Add pork, stir and cook, until pork is done, about 4 minutes. Add remaining ingredients, stir and cook, until bean sprouts just begin to soften. Remove from heat and serve with steamed rice. Yields 3 servings.

Soy Sauce Pork

2   pounds pork belly, cut into 1 1/2 x 1" pieces
3   tablespoons soy sauce
1/4   cup vegetable oil

In medium bowl combine pork and soy sauce, cover and let stand at room temperature for about half hour. Heat oil in wok until sizzling hot. Add marinated pork and fry until golden brown on both sides, turn pork occasionally, to brown evenly. Remove pork and drain on paper towel. Transfer to serving plate and serve with Sweet and Sour Sauce or any other hot sauce of your choice. Yields 3 to 4 servings.

Crispy Pork

2   pounds pork belly, cut into 1 1/2"x 1" chunks
1/2   tablespoon salt
1   tablespoon pepper
1   tablespoon garlic powder
1/4   cup vegetable oil

In small bowl combine pork, salt, pepper, and garlic powder, cover and let stand at room temperature for half hour. Heat oil in wok over medium heat until sizzling hot. Add marinated pork and fry, turning occasionally, until crispy and golden brown, on all sides, about 30 minutes. Remove pork and drain on paper towel. Transfer to serving plate and serve while hot, with Sweet & Sour Sauce for dipping. Yields 3 to 4 servings.

Pork Sausage

1	pound ground pork or ground turkey
1/4	cup finely chopped onion
1	tablespoon paprika
1	teaspoon ground ginger
1	teaspoon onion powder
1/2	teaspoon pepper
1/2	teaspoon ground coriander
1/2	teaspoon salt
1/4	cup crushed, peeled pine nuts
2	tablespoons vegetable oil

In medium bowl combine first 9 ingredients, knead until well mixed. Place in covered container and refrigerate over night. Before cooking, separate into 8 equal portions, roll each into a ball, then flatten to make patties.

Set 10-12-inch frying pan over high heat, add oil and coat pan evenly. Add pork patties, reduce heat and fry patties until crisp and light brown on both sides, and meat is well-done, about 3 minutes on each side. Remove patties from pan and drain on paper towel. Transfer to serving plate and serve. Yields 4 servings.

Pan-Fried Pork Chops

2	pounds thick cut pork chops
2	tablespoons teriyaki sauce
1	tablespoon oyster sauce
1/4	teaspoon pepper
1/4	teaspoon ground sage
1	small onion, sliced thin
1	thumb-size segment fresh ginger root, slivered
3	tablespoons vegetable oil

Combine first 5 ingredients in medium bowl, mix well. Allow to marinate for 15 minutes at room temperature. Remove pork chops, reserving marinade.

Set 10 to 12-inch covered frying pan over high heat for 1 minute. Add oil and coat bottom of pan evenly. Add onion, and ginger, cook until light brown. Remove onion, and ginger from oil and reserve. Add pork chops to frying pan, reduce heat and cover. Cook until pork chops are done, about 8 minutes on each side. Place onion, and ginger on top of chops and pour reserved marinade over chops. Cover and simmer for 1-2 minutes. Remove from heat and serve with steamed rice. Yields 4 servings.

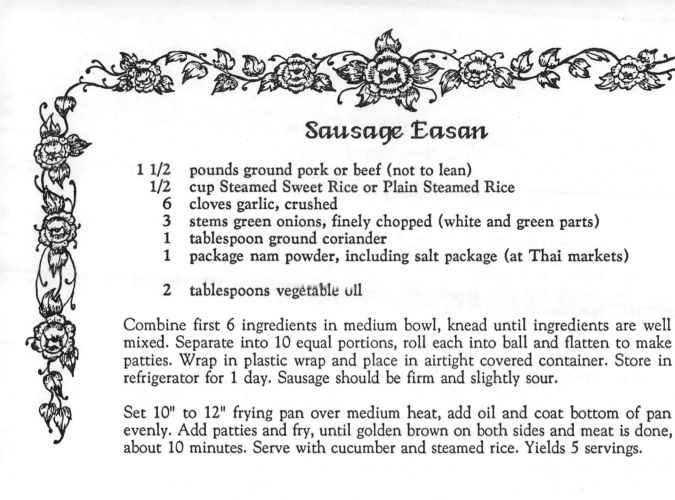

Sausage Easan

1 1/2   pounds ground pork or beef (not to lean)
1/2   cup Steamed Sweet Rice or Plain Steamed Rice
6   cloves garlic, crushed
3   stems green onions, finely chopped (white and green parts)
1   tablespoon ground coriander
1   package nam powder, including salt package (at Thai markets)

2   tablespoons vegetable oil

Combine first 6 ingredients in medium bowl, knead until ingredients are well mixed. Separate into 10 equal portions, roll each into ball and flatten to make patties. Wrap in plastic wrap and place in airtight covered container. Store in refrigerator for 1 day. Sausage should be firm and slightly sour.

Set 10" to 12" frying pan over medium heat, add oil and coat bottom of pan evenly. Add patties and fry, until golden brown on both sides and meat is done, about 10 minutes. Serve with cucumber and steamed rice. Yields 5 servings.

Steamed Country-Style Spareribs

4   small black mushrooms (shi-i-take)
1/4   cup vegetable oil
2   pounds country style spareribs

1   thumb-size segment of fresh ginger root, slivered
1   small red onion, sliced
4   cloves garlic, minced
1   tablespoon coarse ground black pepper

1   8-ounce can sweet corn, whole kernel, drained
1/4   cup chopped red bell pepper
2   cups chicken stock (see Basics)
1/4   cup soy sauce

Soak mushrooms in hot water for 20 minutes, drain, remove bottom part of stems and set aside. Set wok over high heat about 1 minute. Add oil and coat sides of wok evenly. Add spareribs and fry until golden brown, about 5 minutes. Remove ribs and drain on paper towel.

Remove all but 2 tablespoons of oil from wok. Reduce heat and add next 4 ingredients, stir and cook, until lightly brown. Return spareribs to wok, toss, and add the rest of ingredients. Cover and cook, until ribs are tender, about 45 minutes. Yields 4 servings.

Red Roasted Pork
(Moo Dang)

This is a great entree on its own. It is also a main ingredient in many different Thai and Chinese recipes.

3	pounds pork shoulder, cut in 6" long strips
1/2	cup brown sugar
1/4	cup soy sauce
1/4	cup sweet soy sauce
1/2	teaspoon ground ginger
1/2	teaspoon garlic powder
1/2	teaspoon onion powder
1	teaspoon red food coloring
1/4	teaspoon pepper
1	tablespoon all-purpose flour mixed with 3 tablespoons of water

Preheat oven to 400-degrees. In medium bowl, combine all ingredients and mix well. Cover and refrigerate several hours or overnight.   Drain pork, reserving marinade. Place pork on a rack, in a baking pan, in the middle shelf of oven. Brush several times with reserved marinade while roasting, for about 45 minutes or until done. Remove pork, slice thin and arrange on serving plate. Garnish with parsley. Serve with steamed rice. Yields 6 servings.

Country-Style Ribs with BBQ Sauce

This recipe is almost Malaysian in nature. It will be a brand new flavor on the backyard grill.

1/2	cup Tamarind Sauce (see Basics)
2	cups catsup
1	tablespoon brown sugar
1/4	cup oyster sauce
1	tablespoon paprika
1/2	teaspoon ginger powder
1/2	teaspoon coarse ground black pepper
2	tablespoons dry sherry
1	small onion, finely chopped
2	pounds country-style spareribs

In large bowl combine all the ingredients. Cover and marinate 1/2 hour. Drain, reserving marinade. Grill spareribs over slow coals, frequently turn and brush with remaining sauce, until ribs are done, about 45 minutes. Yields 3 to 4 servings.

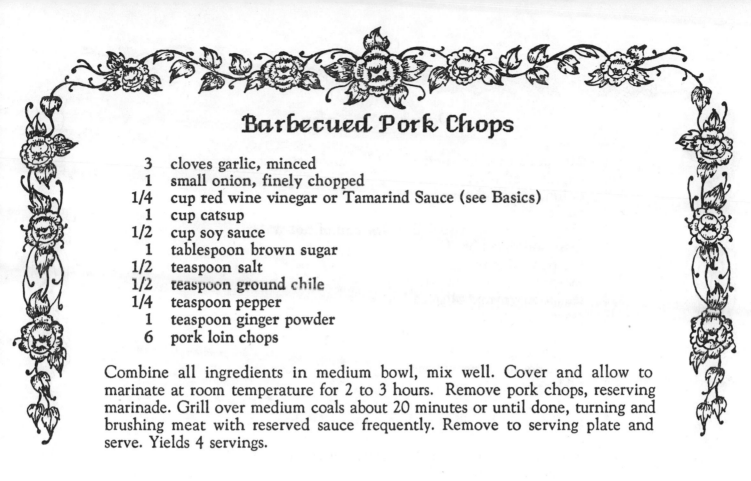

Barbecued Pork Chops

3	cloves garlic, minced
1	small onion, finely chopped
1/4	cup red wine vinegar or Tamarind Sauce (see Basics)
1	cup catsup
1/2	cup soy sauce
1	tablespoon brown sugar
1/2	teaspoon salt
1/2	teaspoon ground chile
1/4	teaspoon pepper
1	teaspoon ginger powder
6	pork loin chops

Combine all ingredients in medium bowl, mix well. Cover and allow to marinate at room temperature for 2 to 3 hours. Remove pork chops, reserving marinade. Grill over medium coals about 20 minutes or until done, turning and brushing meat with reserved sauce frequently. Remove to serving plate and serve. Yields 4 servings.

Palo Ham Hock
(Kha Moo Pa Lo)

3	tablespoons vegetable oil
1	small onion, sliced thin
3	cloves garlic, minced
1	thumb size-segment fresh ginger root, smashed
2	pounds raw ham hock, boned, cut in 2" x 2" pieces
6	hard boiled eggs, peeled
2	tablespoons pa lo powder
4	tablespoons soy sauce
1/2	teaspoon pepper
1/4	teaspoon coriander
4	cups water

Set 5-quart Dutch oven over high heat. Add oil and coat bottom of pot evenly. Add onion, garlic, and ginger, stir and cook, until light brown. Add ham hocks, stir and cook, until ham hocks are lightly browned. Add remaining ingredients, stir to blend. Cover and cook, until ham hocks are tender, about 45 minutes. Serve with steamed rice. Yields 6 servings.

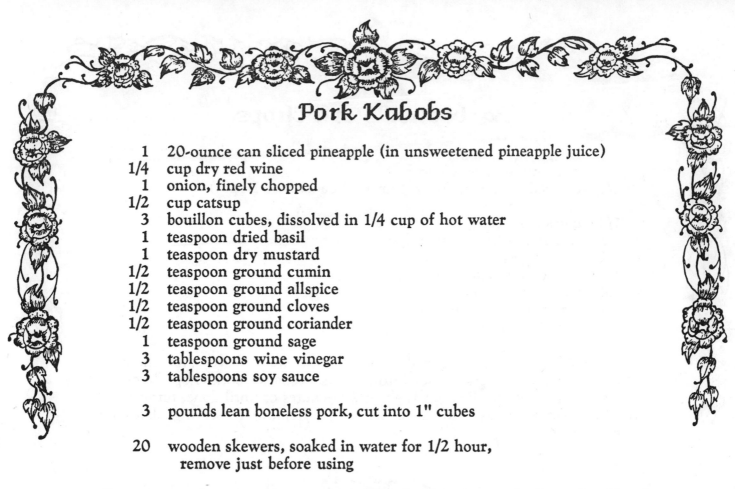

Pork Kabobs

1	20-ounce can sliced pineapple (in unsweetened pineapple juice)
1/4	cup dry red wine
1	onion, finely chopped
1/2	cup catsup
3	bouillon cubes, dissolved in 1/4 cup of hot water
1	teaspoon dried basil
1	teaspoon dry mustard
1/2	teaspoon ground cumin
1/2	teaspoon ground allspice
1/2	teaspoon ground cloves
1/2	teaspoon ground coriander
1	teaspoon ground sage
3	tablespoons wine vinegar
3	tablespoons soy sauce
3	pounds lean boneless pork, cut into 1" cubes
20	wooden skewers, soaked in water for 1/2 hour, remove just before using

Drain pineapple, reserve juice, cover and refrigerate pineapple. In medium bowl, combine pineapple juice and the next 13 ingredients. mix well. Add pork and coat evenly. Cover and allow to marinate at room temperature for 3 hours, or refrigerate overnight.

Drain pork, reserve marinade. Quarter each pineapple slice. Place 2 pieces together, thread pineapples on skewers alternatively with pork. Grill over medium coals about 15 minutes or until done, turning the kabobs often and brushing with reserved marinade. Transfer to serving platter and serve with Sweet Rice. Yields 6 servings.

Mu Shu Pork

2	large, dried black fungus (wood ear) mushrooms
2	tablespoons vegetable oil
1	tablespoon minced fresh ginger root
1	tablespoon minced garlic
1	pound pork or chicken breast, cut into 1" strips
2	cups thin sliced cabbage
1/4	cup shredded bamboo shoots
1/4	cup coarsely shredded carrots
1/4	teaspoon white pepper
2	tablespoons soy sauce
2	eggs, slightly beaten

Sauce:
- 3   tablespoons plum sauce
- 1   tablespoon soy sauce
- 1/4   teaspoon sugar
- 1/4   teaspoon light sesame oil

- 12   Chinese pancakes (see Basics)
- 3   stems green onion, sliced (white part only)

Soak mushrooms in hot water for 30 minutes. Drain and slice very thin. Set aside. Set wok over high heat, for 1 minute. Add oil and coat sides of wok evenly. Add ginger, and garlic and cook, until fragrant. Add meat, and mushrooms, stir and cook, until meat is done, about 2 minutes. Add the next 5 ingredients, stir and cook, until vegetable just begin to soften, about 1 minute. Add eggs, stir and cook, until eggs are firm. Remove to serving plate and set aside. Combine all sauce ingredients in a small bowl, mix well.

To serve: Open a pancake and spread 1 teaspoon of sauce over pancake. Sprinkle with a few pieces of green onion and spoon 2-3 heaping tablespoons of meat mixture into center. Roll up pancake, repeat with remaining pancakes and serve. Yields 4 to 6 servings.

Pork Chops with Tomato

- 2   stems fresh lemon grass, chopped (use bottom 2" of stems only)
- 2   tablespoons chopped fresh Laos root
- 2   tablespoons chopped fresh cilantro root
- 3   tablespoons chopped red onion
- 1   tablespoon chopped garlic
- 1/2   teaspoon coarse ground black pepper
- 1/2   teaspoon ground coriander
- 1   14-ounce can coconut milk

- 2   pounds pork chops (4 thick chops)
- 1   large tomato, cut into 1/4" wedges
- 2   tablespoons fish sauce (nam pla)
- 1/2   tablespoon brown sugar

- 3   fresh red jalapeno chiles for garnish

In blender combine first 7 ingredients, blend at medium speed until coarsely ground. Transfer to 5-quart Dutch oven, Add coconut milk and bring to boil, over high heat. Add the rest of ingredients, cover, cook until pork is done, about 5 minutes. Garnish with fresh red jalapeno chiles. Yields 4 servings.

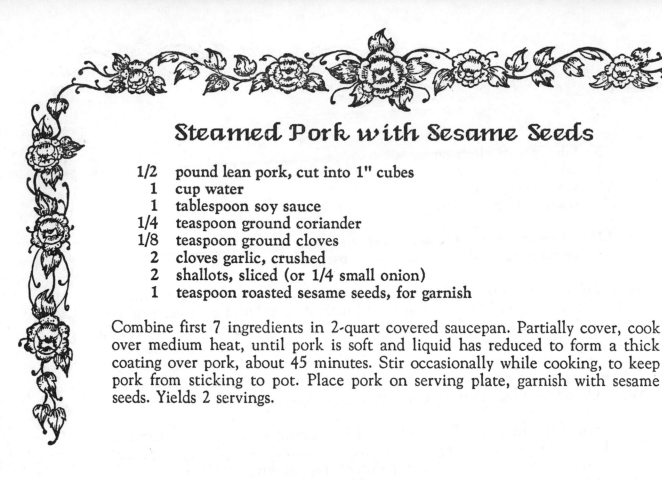

Steamed Pork with Sesame Seeds

1/2	pound lean pork, cut into 1" cubes
1	cup water
1	tablespoon soy sauce
1/4	teaspoon ground coriander
1/8	teaspoon ground cloves
2	cloves garlic, crushed
2	shallots, sliced (or 1/4 small onion)
1	teaspoon roasted sesame seeds, for garnish

Combine first 7 ingredients in 2-quart covered saucepan. Partially cover, cook over medium heat, until pork is soft and liquid has reduced to form a thick coating over pork, about 45 minutes. Stir occasionally while cooking, to keep pork from sticking to pot. Place pork on serving plate, garnish with sesame seeds. Yields 2 servings.

Pork with Zucchini

3	tablespoons vegetable oil
3	cloves garlic, crushed
1	pound pork, sliced thin, bite size
6	cups zucchini, (approximately), sliced into 1/2" thick pieces
3	tablespoons fish sauce (nam pla)
1/8	teaspoon pepper
2	eggs, beaten

Set wok over high heat for 1 minute. Add oil and coat sides of wok evenly. Add garlic and cook, until light brown. Add pork, stir and cook, until done, about 4 minutes. Add zucchini, stir and cook, until zucchini just begins to soften. Add remaining ingredients, stir and cook, until egg is firm. Remove from heat and serve with steamed rice. Yields 4 servings.

NOODLES

There are many different types of noodles. They come in small, medium, and large threads. Noodles come fresh or dried and are made with rice, bean, and wheat flours. They can be served with any meal, but are very popular for lunch. In Thailand, they can be purchased, from the street vendors or foods shops, in the form of Paht Thai, Mee Grob, and others.

Spring Rolls

8	medium, dried black fungus (wood ear mushrooms) or 1 cup thin-sliced mushrooms
2	12-ounce packages mung bean thread noodles
2	tablespoons vegetable oil
1	small onion, sliced very thin
1	pound ground pork
2	cups shredded bamboo shoots
1/4	cup fish sauce (nam pla)
1	12-ounce package frozen spring roll shells (leave at room temperature until soft)
3	tablespoons all-purpose flour mixed with 5 tablespoons of water
2	cups vegetable oil

Soak fungus mushroom in hot water for 30 minutes. Drain and slice into long, very thin strips. Soak bean thread in hot water for 10 minutes. Drain and cut into 2-inch lengths.

Heat oil in wok until sizzling hot and coat sides evenly. Add onion and stir fry until light brown. Add pork, stir and cook, until pork separates, about 1 minute. Add mushroom, bean thread, bamboo shoots, and fish sauce, stir to blend and remove from heat.

Place 3 heaping tablespoons of mixture diagonally across one corner of a spring roll shell. Using both hands, roll shell from corner, roll 2 turns and fold ends in toward center. Continue to roll up, securing loose end with flour and water mixture. Repeat with remaining shells and set aside.

Clean wok and set over medium heat, add 2 cups of oil and allow to heat until sizzling hot. Fry 3 to 4 spring rolls at a time, until golden brown. Remove spring rolls from oil and drain on paper towel. Repeat with remaining rolls, transfer to serving platter and serve with Sweet and Sour Sauce. Yields 6 servings.

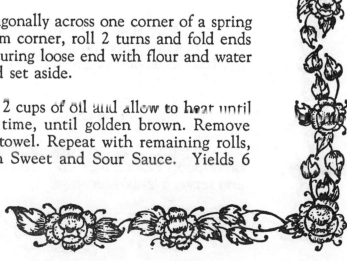

Bamee with Chicken or Pork
(Bamee Hang Gai Liew Moo)

This is a tasty and popular dish, and a good way to use some leftover meats. You can substitute any kind of leftover cooked meat, instead of the raw chicken or pork.

10	cups water
1	16-ounce package fresh thin Chinese egg noodles, cut in half and separated
1	tablespoon vegetable oil
2	tablespoons vegetable oil
3	cloves garlic, crushed
1	pound chicken or pork, sliced thin, bite size
4	cups sliced broccoli
3	tablespoons fish sauce (nam pla)
1	tablespoon soy sauce
1/2	cup coarse ground, roasted peanuts
1/2	cup chopped green onion
1/2	cup chopped cilantro
1	teaspoon crushed red chili

In 5-quart Dutch oven, bring water to boil, over high heat. Add noodles, stir and cook, until noodles are done, about 10 seconds (do not over cook noodles). Drain and mix noodles with 1 tablespoon of vegetable oil, set aside.

Set wok over high heat, for one minute. Add oil and coat sides of wok evenly. Add garlic and fry until light brown. Add chicken or pork, stir and cook, until meat is done, about 3 minutes. Add broccoli, stir and cook, until broccoli just starts to soften, about 1 minute. Add fish sauce and soy sauce, stir to blend. Remove from heat. In large bowl, combine noodles, meat, and broccoli. Add remaining ingredients and mix well. Transfer to serving plate and serve with Pickled Chili. Yields 4 servings.

Thai Egg Rolls

2	cups sliced, Red Roasted Pork (see Index)
2	cups bean sprouts
1/2	cup chopped green onion
1/2	cup chopped cilantro
1	cup Plum Sauce (see chapter on Basics)
8	Crepes (see chapter on Basics)

Toss together Roasted Pork, bean sprouts, green onion, and cilantro. Spread 1 tablespoon Plum Sauce on each crepe, then add 1/2 cup of pork mixture. Roll and serve. Yields 4 servings.

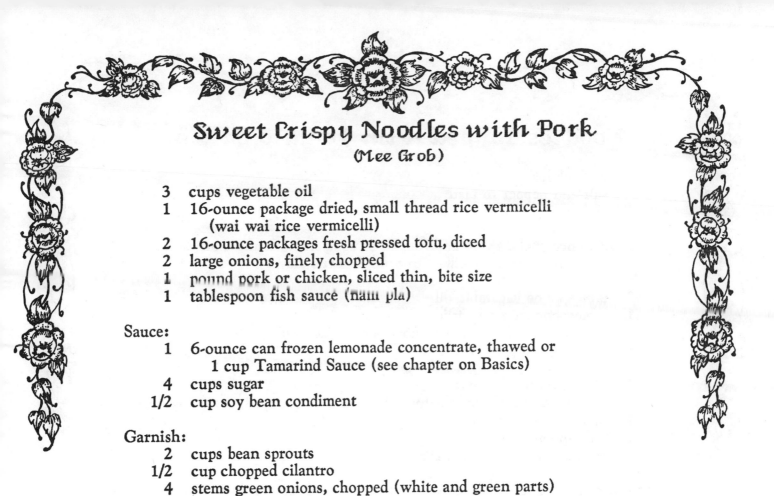

Sweet Crispy Noodles with Pork
(Mee Grob)

3   cups vegetable oil
1   16-ounce package dried, small thread rice vermicelli
       (wai wai rice vermicelli)
2   16-ounce packages fresh pressed tofu, diced
2   large onions, finely chopped
1   pound pork or chicken, sliced thin, bite size
1   tablespoon fish sauce (nam pla)

Sauce:
1   6-ounce can frozen lemonade concentrate, thawed or
       1 cup Tamarind Sauce (see chapter on Basics)
4   cups sugar
1/2   cup soy bean condiment

Garnish:
2   cups bean sprouts
1/2   cup chopped cilantro
4   stems green onions, chopped (white and green parts)

Heat oil in wok, over high heat, until sizzling hot. Deep fry a small handful of noodles at a time, until crisp and fluffy. Remove noodles from oil and drain. Repeat with remaining noodles. Deep fry tofu until crisp. Set aside.

Remove all but 1/4 cup of oil from wok and keep wok hot over high heat. Add onion and fry until light brown, remove onion from wok and set aside. Add pork to wok and stir fry, until pork is light brown. Add fish sauce and stir fry, until pork is dry and crisp. Remove from wok and set aside.

In 4 to 5-quart Dutch oven, combine lemonade concentrate or Tamarind Sauce, sugar, and soy bean. Cook over low heat, until sauce thickens, about 15 minutes, stirring occasionally. Add crispy tofu and browned onion, mix well. Remove from heat. In large bowl combine crispy noodles, crispy pork, and sauce mixture. Mix well. Transfer to serving plate. Garnish with bean sprouts, cilantro, and green onion. Yields 6 to 8 servings.

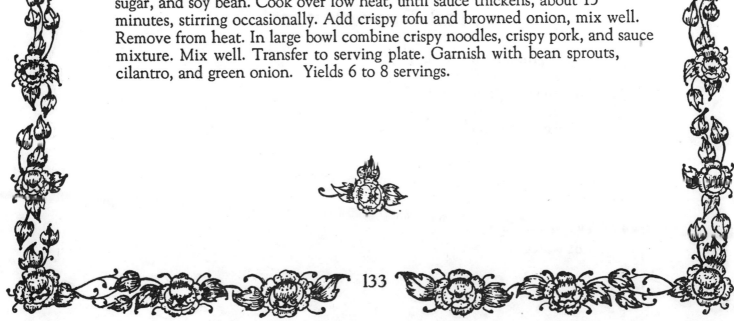

Noodles Topped with Tomato Sauce

2   pork chops
     salt and pepper to taste

4   cups water
2   3-ounce packages of Top Ramen or comparable brand Chinese or
         Japanese style noodles, in your favorite flavor

2   tablespoons vegetable oil
1   tablespoon minced garlic
1   bunch basil, chopped or 1 tablespoon dried basil
1   cup chopped parsley

1   cup sliced mushrooms
1   16-ounce can whole tomatoes, drained and chopped, reserving juice
1   tablespoon sugar
1   tablespoon dry sherry
1/2 teaspoon coarse ground pepper

Lightly salt and pepper pork chops on both sides and let stand for 10 minutes.
Bring water to boil in 3-quart saucepan, add noodles and cook until noodles are
soft, about 3 minutes. Drain and rinse with cold water, transfer to serving
plate. Set aside.

Set wok over high heat for about 1 minute. Add oil and coat sides of wok evenly.
Add pork chops and fry, until chops are done, about 3 minutes on each side.
Remove pork chops and lay on top of noodles. Quickly add garlic to wok, stir
and cook, until light brown. Add basil and parsley, toss and cook, until limp.
Add remaining ingredients, including flavor packs from noodles, and reserved
juice, stir and cook, until mushrooms are soft, about 5 minutes. Pour over pork
chops and serve with Parmesan cheese. Yields 2 servings.

Fried Dumplings

1/2 pound ground pork or beef
1   tablespoon soy sauce
1/2 tablespoon oyster sauce
1   tablespoon dry sherry
1/4 cup finely chopped water chestnuts
1   stem green onion, finely chopped (white and green parts)
1   teaspoon corn starch
1/8 teaspoon white pepper
1/4 teaspoon ground ginger

15   sheets square wonton skins
     hot water

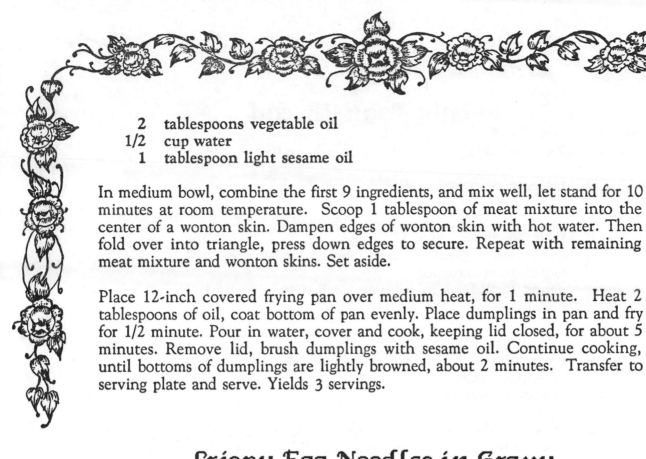

2	tablespoons vegetable oil
1/2	cup water
1	tablespoon light sesame oil

In medium bowl, combine the first 9 ingredients, and mix well, let stand for 10 minutes at room temperature. Scoop 1 tablespoon of meat mixture into the center of a wonton skin. Dampen edges of wonton skin with hot water. Then fold over into triangle, press down edges to secure. Repeat with remaining meat mixture and wonton skins. Set aside.

Place 12-inch covered frying pan over medium heat, for 1 minute. Heat 2 tablespoons of oil, coat bottom of pan evenly. Place dumplings in pan and fry for 1/2 minute. Pour in water, cover and cook, keeping lid closed, for about 5 minutes. Remove lid, brush dumplings with sesame oil. Continue cooking, until bottoms of dumplings are lightly browned, about 2 minutes. Transfer to serving plate and serve. Yields 3 servings.

Crispy Egg Noodles in Gravy
(Bamee Grop Laht Nah)

2	cups vegetable oil
1	16-ounce package medium thread, fresh Chinese egg noodles, cut in half and separated
4	cloves garlic, crushed
1	pound beef, sliced bite-sized
2	cups shredded bamboo shoots
3/4	cup soy sauce
4	stems green onions, cut into 1/2" pieces (white and green parts)
1/8	teaspoon pepper
1/2	cup all-purpose flour mixed with 3 cups of Chicken Stock (see chapter on Basics), until smooth

Heat oil in wok over high heat, until sizzling hot. Deep fry a small handful of noodles at a time, until crisp. Remove noodles from oil and drain. Be sure to keep oil sizzling hot. Repeat with remaining noodles and place noodles on a serving plate. Set aside.

Remove all but 2 tablespoons of oil from wok. Keep wok over high heat, add garlic and fry until light brown. Add beef, stir and cook, until beef is done, about 1 minute. Add remaining ingredients, stir and cook, until sauce thickens, about 2 minutes. Pour over crispy noodles and serve with Pickled Chili. Yields 6 servings.

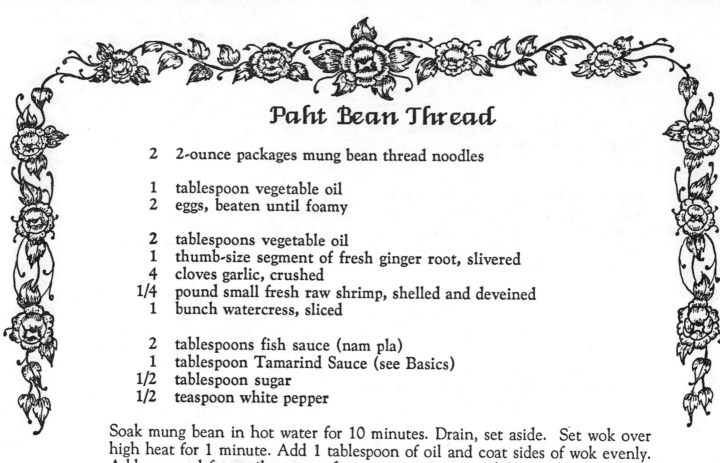

Paht Bean Thread

2   2-ounce packages mung bean thread noodles

1   tablespoon vegetable oil
2   eggs, beaten until foamy

2   tablespoons vegetable oil
1   thumb-size segment of fresh ginger root, slivered
4   cloves garlic, crushed
1/4 pound small fresh raw shrimp, shelled and deveined
1   bunch watercress, sliced

2   tablespoons fish sauce (nam pla)
1   tablespoon Tamarind Sauce (see Basics)
1/2 tablespoon sugar
1/2 teaspoon white pepper

Soak mung bean in hot water for 10 minutes. Drain, set aside. Set wok over high heat for 1 minute. Add 1 tablespoon of oil and coat sides of wok evenly. Add eggs and fry until eggs are firm, turn eggs over and fry until light brown. Remove eggs to cutting board and cut into thin strips. Set aside.

Keep wok on high heat and add 2 tablespoons of oil. Add ginger, and garlic, cook until light brown. Add shrimp, stir and cook, until shrimps turn pink, about 1 minute. Add watercress and cook, until watercress is limp. Add noodles, eggs, and the rest of ingredients, toss and cook until noodles are thoroughly heated, about 2 minutes. Yields 2 to 3 servings.

Yellow Noodles with Ham

4   medium, dried black mushrooms (shi-i-take)

10 cups water
1   16-ounce package fresh, thin Chinese style egg noodles,
      cut in half and separated

3/4 cup chopped bacon
1   tablespoon minced garlic
2   tablespoons minced onion
1   thumb size segment of fresh ginger root, minced
1   red bell pepper, minced
1   pound sliced ham, cut into strips
3   tablespoons fish sauce (nam pla)

2   stems green onions, cut into 1/2" pieces (white and green parts)

Soak mushrooms in hot water for 20 minutes, drain, remove bottom part of stem, slice thin and set aside.

Bring water to boil in 5-quart Dutch oven, add noodles and cook until done, about 10 seconds (do not overcook noodles). Drain, rinse with cold water and set aside.

Place wok over high heat for 1 minute. Add bacon and fry until light brown. Add garlic, onion, and ginger, stir and cook, until fragrant. Add bell pepper, ham, and mushrooms, stir and cook, until bell pepper is soft, about 2 minutes. Add noodles and fish sauce, toss and cook, until noodles are thoroughly heated. Transfer to serving plate, garnish with green onions and serve. Yields 4 to 6 servings.

Shrimp Noodles

4 medium, dried black mushrooms (shi-i-take)

2 2-ounce packages mung bean thread noodles

2 tablespoons vegetable oil
1 thumb-size segment of fresh ginger root, slivered

1/4 cup coarsely shredded carrots
2 tablespoons oyster sauce
1 tablespoon roasted sesame seeds, crushed
2 tablespoons dried shredded shrimp

Garnish:
8 steamed medium-size shrimp
1/4 cup cilantro (leaves only)

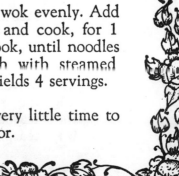

Soak mushrooms in hot water for 20 minutes. Drain, remove bottom part of stems, slice thin and set aside. Soak mung bean thread noodles in hot water for 10 minutes. Drain, cut in 2-inch pieces, and set aside.

Set wok over high heat for 1 minute. Add oil, coat sides of wok evenly. Add ginger, stir and cook, until fragrant. Add mushrooms, stir and cook, for 1 minute. Add noodles, and the rest of ingredients, stir and cook, until noodles are thoroughly heated. Transfer to serving plate, garnish with steamed shrimps and cilantro. Serve with Pickled Chiles, if desired. Yields 4 servings.

Note: This is great dish for an elegant supper and it takes very little time to prepare. The shrimp and cilantro add a beautiful touch of color.

Bean Thread Noodles with Shredded Vegetables

4	medium, dried black mushrooms (shi-i-take)
1/2	pound pork or chicken, cut into long slender strips, about 1/8" x 1/8" x 1"
2	teaspoons light sesame oil
1/8	teaspoon white pepper
1	tablespoon dry sherry
1	tablespoon oyster sauce
2	2-ounce packages mung bean thread noodles
2	tablespoons vegetable oil
1	thumb-size segment of fresh ginger root, slivered
2	cloves garlic, crushed
1/2	cup thin sliced celery
1/2	cup coarsely shredded carrots
2	teaspoons fish sauce (nam pla)
2	teaspoons dark soy sauce
1/2	cup Chicken Stock (see chapter on Basics)
1	tablespoon sesame seeds, roasted and crushed cilantro for garnish, optional

Soak mushrooms in hot water for 20 minutes. Drain, cut off bottom part of stems, slice thin and set aside. Combine the next 5 ingredients, set aside. Allow to marinate for 15 minutes, at room temperature. Soak bean thread noodles in hot water for 10 minutes. Drain, and cut into 2-inch lengths.

Set wok over high heat for 1 minute. Add oil, and coat sides of wok evenly. Stir in ginger, and garlic, cook until lightly browned. Add marinated meat, stir and cook, for 1 minute. Add mushrooms, and all remaining ingredients, except noodles, stir well. Cover and cook for 2 minutes. Add noodles, toss and cook, until noodles are thoroughly heated. Transfer to plate and garnish with cilantro if desired. Makes 2 to 4 servings.

Steamed Bean Thread Noodles

2	medium, dried black mushrooms (shi-i-take)
2	2-ounce packages mung bean thread noodles
2	strips bacon, chopped
3	cloves garlic, minced
1	tablespoon minced fresh ginger root
1/4	teaspoon pepper
1/4	teaspoon ground coriander

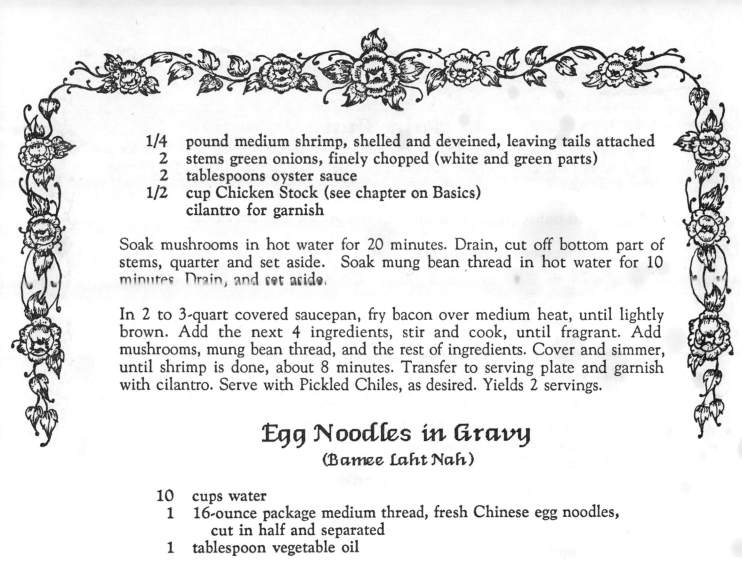

1/4   pound medium shrimp, shelled and deveined, leaving tails attached
2   stems green onions, finely chopped (white and green parts)
2   tablespoons oyster sauce
1/2   cup Chicken Stock (see chapter on Basics)
cilantro for garnish

Soak mushrooms in hot water for 20 minutes. Drain, cut off bottom part of stems, quarter and set aside. Soak mung bean thread in hot water for 10 minutes. Drain, and set aside.

In 2 to 3-quart covered saucepan, fry bacon over medium heat, until lightly brown. Add the next 4 ingredients, stir and cook, until fragrant. Add mushrooms, mung bean thread, and the rest of ingredients. Cover and simmer, until shrimp is done, about 8 minutes. Transfer to serving plate and garnish with cilantro. Serve with Pickled Chiles, as desired. Yields 2 servings.

Egg Noodles in Gravy
(Bamee Laht Nah)

10   cups water
1   16-ounce package medium thread, fresh Chinese egg noodles,
      cut in half and separated
1   tablespoon vegetable oil

2   tablespoons vegetable oil
4   cloves garlic, crushed
1 1/2   pounds chicken breasts, skinned, boned, sliced thin, bite-size

1   15-ounce can straw mushrooms, drained
1   cup very thin sliced carrots
3/4   cup soy sauce
4   stems green onions, cut into 1/2" pieces (white and green parts)

1/8   teaspoon pepper
1/2   cup all-purpose flour, mixed with 3 cups of Chicken Stock
      (see chapter on Basics), until smooth

Bring water to boil, in 5-quart Dutch oven, over high heat. Add noodles, and cook until noodles are done, about 3 minutes. Drain and mix with 1 tablespoon of vegetable oil, place on serving plate, set aside.

Heat oil in wok until sizzling hot. Coat sides of wok evenly. Add garlic and fry until light brown. Add chicken, stir fry until chicken is done, about 3 minutes. Add remaining ingredients, stir and cook, until sauce thickens, about 2 more minutes. Pour over noodles and serve with Pickled Chili. Yields 6 servings.

Paht Thai

This is a very representative Thai noodle dish. Most people familiar with Thai food are fond of Paht Thai. I hope you will prepare this dish for your family, for I know they will enjoy it.

- 1 16-ounce package chantaboon rice sticks, medium thread

- 1 tablespoon vegetable oil
- 6 eggs, beaten

- 1/4 cup vegetable oil
- 8 cloves garlic
- 1 pound pork, beef or chicken, sliced thin, bite-size, or shrimp, shelled and deveined
- 1/4 cup white vinegar

- 1/4 cup sugar
- 1 cup sliced salted radish (chai po)
- 1/4 cup fish sauce (nam pla)
- 1 cup coarse ground, roasted peanuts
- 2 tablespoons chile powder or paprika

- 2 cups bean sprouts
- 1 cup sliced green onion
- 1 cup sliced cilantro

Soak rice sticks in lukewarm water for 1 hour, drain and set aside. Set wok over high heat, for 1 minute. Heat wok with 1 tablespoon of oil until sizzling hot and coat sides of wok evenly. Add eggs and fry, until eggs set, turn over and fry, until light brown on both sides. Remove from wok and slice thin, bite-size. Set aside.

Heat 1/4 cup of oil in wok until sizzling hot. Add garlic and cook until fragrant. Add meat, stir and cook, until meat is done, about 1 to 2 minutes. Add rice sticks and vinegar, cook until rice sticks soften. Add eggs, and the next 5 ingredients, stir to blend. Remove to serving plate. Add bean sprouts to wok, toss and cook for 30 seconds over high heat. Pour over noodles and garnish with green onion and cilantro. Yields 6 servings.

Chop Suey in Gravy

- 4 medium, dried black mushrooms (shi-i-take)
- 10 cups water
- 1 16-ounce package fresh, thin Chinese-style egg noodles, cut in half and separated
- 1 tablespoon light sesame oil

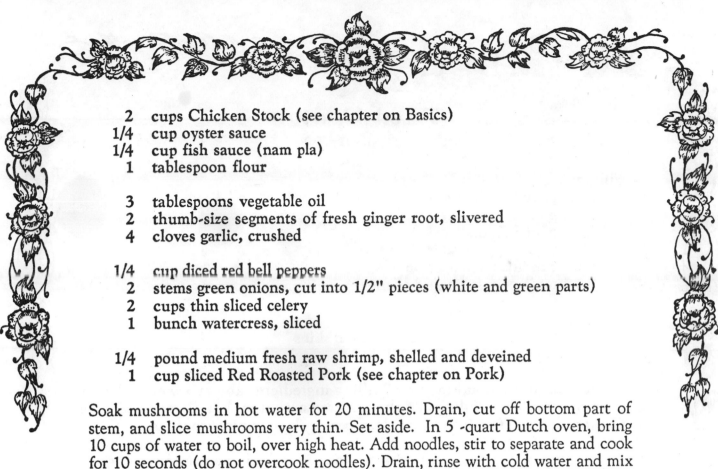

2	cups Chicken Stock (see chapter on Basics)
1/4	cup oyster sauce
1/4	cup fish sauce (nam pla)
1	tablespoon flour

3	tablespoons vegetable oil
2	thumb-size segments of fresh ginger root, slivered
4	cloves garlic, crushed

1/4	cup diced red bell peppers
2	stems green onions, cut into 1/2" pieces (white and green parts)
2	cups thin sliced celery
1	bunch watercress, sliced

| 1/4 | pound medium fresh raw shrimp, shelled and deveined |
| 1 | cup sliced Red Roasted Pork (see chapter on Pork) |

Soak mushrooms in hot water for 20 minutes. Drain, cut off bottom part of stem, and slice mushrooms very thin. Set aside. In 5-quart Dutch oven, bring 10 cups of water to boil, over high heat. Add noodles, stir to separate and cook for 10 seconds (do not overcook noodles). Drain, rinse with cold water and mix well with 1 tablespoon of sesame oil. Set aside. In medium bowl mix the next 4 ingredients, until smooth. Set aside.

Set wok over high heat about 1 minute. Add oil, and coat sides of wok evenly. Add ginger, and garlic, stir and cook, until lightly brown. Add mushrooms, and the next 4 ingredients, stir and cook, until watercress is limp, about 1 minute. Add stock mixture, stir and cook, until sauce thickens, about 1 minute. Add shrimp, and roasted pork, stir and cook, until shrimp turns pink, about 2 minutes. Add noodles, stir to blend and cook, until noodles are thoroughly heated. Remove from heat and serve. Yields 4 to 6 servings.

Thai Spaghetti

(Kanom Gean)

Kanom Gean is a must at Thai parties. This native Thai dish originally used home-made spaghetti noodles. To make the preparation easier, I have substituted the Japanese somen. If you would like to try the original Thai spaghetti, it is sometimes available in Thai grocery stores.

1	16-ounce package Japanese somen noodles
2 1/2	quarts water
1	teaspoon salt

In 5-quart Dutch oven, bring water to boil, over high heat. Add salt and somen, continue boiling for about 5 minutes or until noodles are soft. Drain and rinse with cold water. Serve with Chicken, Beef or Roasted Duck in Red or Green Curry Sauce. Yields 4 servings.

Fried Wonton
(Geiw Grob)

Filling:

1/4	pound fresh raw shrimp, shelled , deveined, and diced
1/4	pound crab meat
1/2	pound ground pork
1/2	cup chopped water chestnuts
1/2	cup finely chopped onions
2	tablespoons chopped cilantro
1 1/2	tablespoons soy sauce
1	8-ounce package square wonton skins
2	cups vegetable oil

In medium bowl, combine first 7 filling ingredients and mix well. Place 1 heaping teaspoon of filling into the center of a wonton skin. Dampen edges of wonton skin and fold into a triangle, repeat with remaining wontons.

Heat 2 cups of oil in wok until sizzling hot. Deep fry 5 to 6 wontons at a time, until golden brown and crisp. Remove wontons from oil and drain on paper towels. Repeat with remaining wontons. Transfer to serving platter and serve with Sweet and Sour Sauce. Yields about 20 wontons.

Paht Sen Me

1	12-ounce package dried rice sticks, small thread
3	tablespoons vegetable oil
1	thumb-size segment of fresh ginger root, slivered
2	tablespoons chili paste with bean oil (nam prig pao)
1/2	pound fresh raw small shrimp, shelled, deveined, tails attached
2	tablespoons rice vinegar (Seasoned Gourmet)
3	tablespoons fish sauce (nam pla)
1/4	cup soy sauce
1	cup coarsely shredded carrot
1	cup sliced green onions (white part only)

Soak rice sticks in lukewarm water for 1 hour. Drain and set aside. Heat oil in wok until sizzling hot and coat sides evenly. Add ginger, quickly toss and cook, until fragrant. Add chili paste, and shrimp, stir and cook, about 1/2 minute. Add rice sticks, toss. Add the rest of ingredients, stir and cook, until rice sticks are soft, about 5 minutes. Yields 6 to 8 servings.

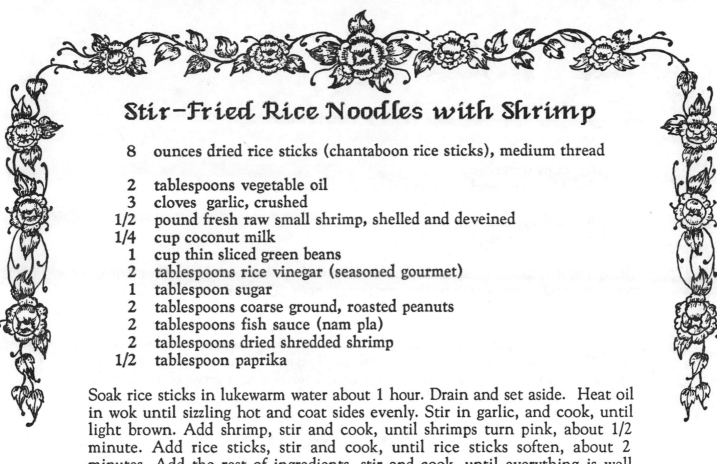

Stir-Fried Rice Noodles with Shrimp

8   ounces dried rice sticks (chantaboon rice sticks), medium thread

2   tablespoons vegetable oil
3   cloves garlic, crushed
1/2   pound fresh raw small shrimp, shelled and deveined
1/4   cup coconut milk
1   cup thin sliced green beans
2   tablespoons rice vinegar (seasoned gourmet)
1   tablespoon sugar
2   tablespoons coarse ground, roasted peanuts
2   tablespoons fish sauce (nam pla)
2   tablespoons dried shredded shrimp
1/2   tablespoon paprika

Soak rice sticks in lukewarm water about 1 hour. Drain and set aside. Heat oil in wok until sizzling hot and coat sides evenly. Stir in garlic, and cook, until light brown. Add shrimp, stir and cook, until shrimps turn pink, about 1/2 minute. Add rice sticks, stir and cook, until rice sticks soften, about 2 minutes. Add the rest of ingredients, stir and cook, until everything is well blended, about 1 minute. Yields 2 servings.

Ham Noodles

4   medium, dried black mushrooms (shi-i-take)
2   2-ounce packages mung bean thread noodles
1/4   cup chopped bacon
1/2   tablespoon minced garlic

1/2   pound cooked ham, diced
1/4   cup shredded carrots
1/4   cup diced celery

2   tablespoons fish sauce (nam pla)
1/2   tablespoon roasted sesame seeds, crushed

Soak mushrooms in hot water for 20 minutes. Drain, cut off bottom part of stems, slice very thin, and set aside. Soak bean threads in hot water for 10 minutes. Drain and cut into 2-inch long pieces. Set aside.

In wok, brown bacon over medium heat, until crisp. Add garlic and cook until fragrant. Add mushrooms and the next 3 ingredients, stir and cook, until ham is thoroughly heated, about 2 minutes. Add noodles, fish sauce, and sesame seeds, toss to blend, and serve. Yields 2 servings.

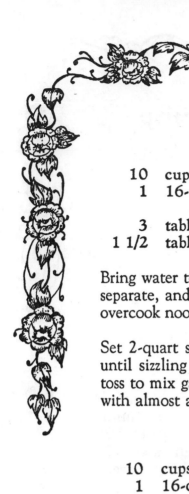

Garlic Noodles

    10   cups water
     1   16-ounce package fresh thin Chinese-style egg noodles,
                cut in half and separated
     3   tablespoons vegetable oil
 1 1/2   tablespoons pureed garlic

Bring water to boil in 5-quart Dutch oven, over high heat. Add noodles, stir to separate, and cook until noodles are done, about 30 to 45 seconds. (Do not overcook noodles.) Drain and set aside.

Set 2-quart saucepan over medium heat, add oil and coat pan evenly. Heat until sizzling hot. Add garlic and cook until light brown. Add noodles and toss to mix garlic into the noodles. Remove from heat and serve as a side dish with almost any entree. Yields about 4 servings.

Mandarin Noodles

    10   cups water
     1   16-ounce package fresh, thin Chinese-style egg noodles,
                cut in half and separated
     1   tablespoon light sesame oil

     3   tablespoons vegetable oil
     3   cloves garlic, minced
     1   thumb-size slice fresh ginger, chopped
   1/2   pound beef sirloin steak, sliced thin bite-size
     1   bunch spinach, (about 4 cups), chopped
     2   cups sliced mushrooms

   1/4   cup soy sauce
   1/4   cup rice vinegar (seasoned gourmet)
   1/4   cup fish sauce (nam pla)
     1   tablespoon ground fresh chile paste

In 5-quart Dutch oven, bring 10 cups of water to boil, over high heat. Add noodles, stir to separate and cook until noodles are done, about 10 seconds (do not overcook noodles). Drain, rinse with cold water, then add sesame oil. Mix well and set aside.

Set wok over high heat for 1 minute. Add oil, coat sides of wok evenly and heat until sizzling hot. Stir in garlic, and ginger, cook until fragrant. Add beef, stir and cook, until beef is done, about 1/2 minute. Add spinach and mushrooms, cook about 1 more minute. Return noodles to wok and add remaining ingredients. Stir and cook, until noodles are thoroughly heated, about 30 to 40 seconds. Serve while hot. Yields 4 to 6 servings.

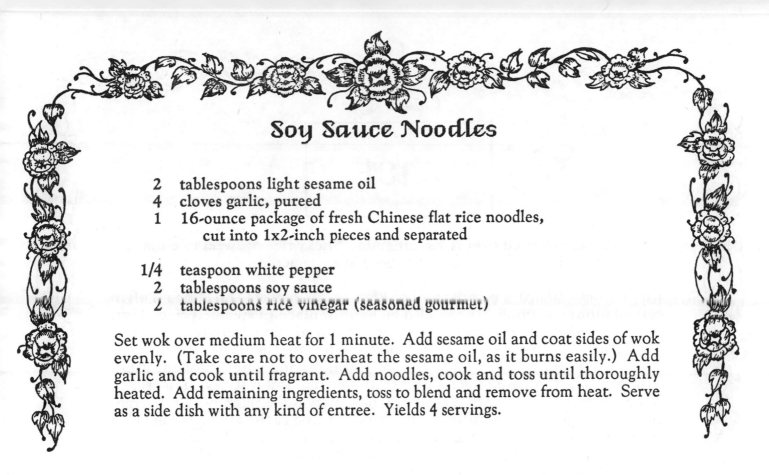

Soy Sauce Noodles

2 tablespoons light sesame oil
4 cloves garlic, pureed
1 16-ounce package of fresh Chinese flat rice noodles,
    cut into 1x2-inch pieces and separated

1/4 teaspoon white pepper
2 tablespoons soy sauce
2 tablespoons rice vinegar (seasoned gourmet)

Set wok over medium heat for 1 minute. Add sesame oil and coat sides of wok evenly. (Take care not to overheat the sesame oil, as it burns easily.) Add garlic and cook until fragrant. Add noodles, cook and toss until thoroughly heated. Add remaining ingredients, toss to blend and remove from heat. Serve as a side dish with any kind of entree. Yields 4 servings.

Fresh Chinese Flat Rice Noodles
with Pork Chops

1 pound pork chops (about 4 chops)
    salt to taste

2 tablespoons vegetable oil
1 16-ounce package fresh Chinese flat rice noodles,
    cut into 1x 2-inch pieces, separated
2 tablespoons soy sauce

2 tablespoons vegetable oil
2 tablespoons minced garlic
1 cup chopped parsley

Sprinkle salt on both sides of pork chops and let stand for 5 minutes at room temperature. Meanwhile, set wok over high heat for 1 minute. Add 2 tablespoons of oil and coat sides of wok evenly. Add noodles, stir and cook, until noodles are thoroughly heated. Add soy sauce, toss to blend. Transfer to platter and set aside.

Set 10-inch frying pan over high heat for 1 minute. Add oil and coat bottom of pan evenly. Add pork chops and fry, until chops are done, about 6 minutes. Remove pork chops and lay on top of noodles. Quickly add garlic, and parsley to frying pan, stir and cook, until parsley is soft. Spoon over pork chops and serve. Yields 2 to 3 servings.

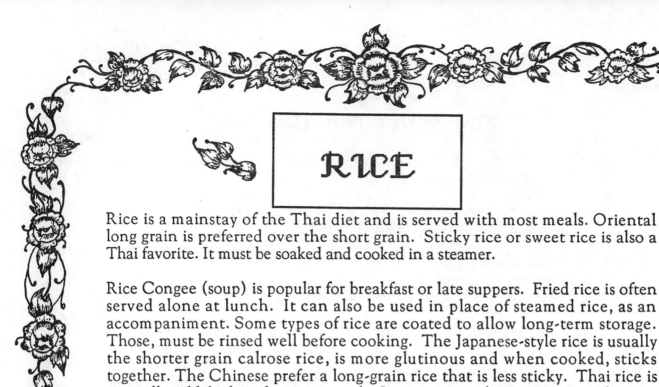

RICE

Rice is a mainstay of the Thai diet and is served with most meals. Oriental long grain is preferred over the short grain. Sticky rice or sweet rice is also a Thai favorite. It must be soaked and cooked in a steamer.

Rice Congee (soup) is popular for breakfast or late suppers. Fried rice is often served alone at lunch. It can also be used in place of steamed rice, as an accompaniment. Some types of rice are coated to allow long-term storage. Those, must be rinsed well before cooking. The Japanese-style rice is usually the shorter grain calrose rice, is more glutinous and when cooked, sticks together. The Chinese prefer a long-grain rice that is less sticky. Thai rice is normally sold fresh and is not coated. One variety is the "jasmine" or "fragrant rice." It has a wonderful aroma, while cooking, and at the table. When Thai rice is from a new crop, right after harvest, about 10 percent less water should be used when cooking. Otherwise, the rice will cook mushy. Most Oriental grocers carry these different kinds of rice.

Important Notes: -These recipes use Oriental long-grain rice. When cooking American rice, double the amount of broth or water.

-In planning quantities of rice, please consider the number of dishes you are serving. In general, 1/2 cup of cooked rice serves only as a small accompaniment.

Plain Steamed Rice

2   cups calrose or Oriental long-grain rice
2   cups water

Set 3-quart covered saucepan over high heat. Add rice and water, bring to boil. Allow to boil 1 minute. Do not stir. Cover, reduce heat and simmer for 20 minutes. Remove from heat, fluff with a fork and serve. Do not remove lid while cooking. Yields 4 cups.

Steamed Sweet Rice

Sweet rice, when steamed properly, sticks together, but is dry to the touch. It is usually eaten by hand and is a favorite with children.

4   cups sweet rice (at Thai markets)
10   cups water

Soak sweet rice in 5 cups water overnight, or in hot water for 3 hours. Drain and transfer sweet rice to steamer rack. Add 5 cups of water to steamer and set over high heat. Steam rice for 20 minutes, or until done. Remove from heat. Serve instead of Plain Steamed Rice. Excellent with barbecues. Yields 6 cups.

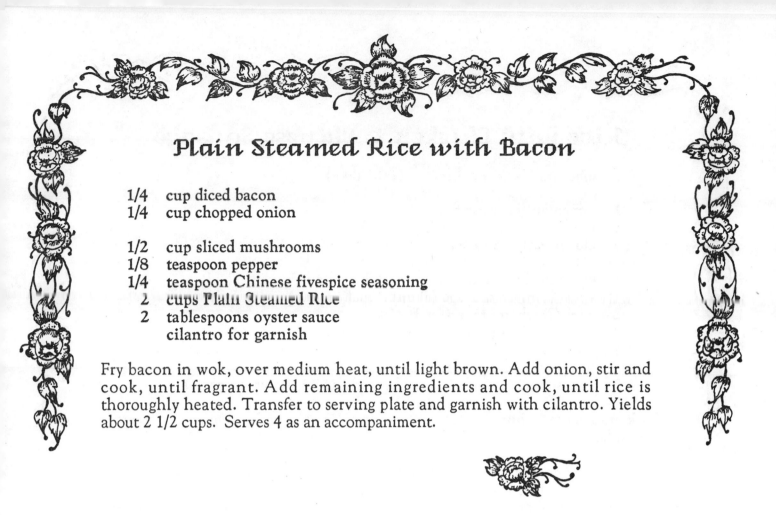

Plain Steamed Rice with Bacon

- 1/4 cup diced bacon
- 1/4 cup chopped onion

- 1/2 cup sliced mushrooms
- 1/8 teaspoon pepper
- 1/4 teaspoon Chinese fivespice seasoning
- 2 cups Plain Steamed Rice
- 2 tablespoons oyster sauce
  cilantro for garnish

Fry bacon in wok, over medium heat, until light brown. Add onion, stir and cook, until fragrant. Add remaining ingredients and cook, until rice is thoroughly heated. Transfer to serving plate and garnish with cilantro. Yields about 2 1/2 cups. Serves 4 as an accompaniment.

Rice with Onions & Peppers
(Kao Paht Nam Prig Pao)

Nam prig pao will light up your day, and also add some spice to it. For less spice reduce chile paste.

- 2 tablespoons vegetable oil
- 3 cloves garlic, crushed
- 1 tablespoon minced fresh ginger root

- 2 cups Plain Steamed Rice
- 1 stem green onion, finely chopped (white and green parts)
- 2 tablespoons minced red bell pepper
- 1 tablespoon fish sauce (nam pla)
- 2 teaspoons chile paste with bean oil (nam prig pao)
- 1/4 teaspoon pepper

- 1 small cucumber, sliced thin, on the diagonal
- 1 medium tomato, sliced

Set wok over medium heat for 1 minute. Add oil, coat sides of wok evenly. Stir in garlic, and ginger, cook until light brown. Add the next 6 ingredients, stir and cook, until rice is thoroughly heated. Transfer to serving plate and garnish with sliced cucumber and tomato. Yields 2 to 3 servings, as an accompaniment.

Rice with Chicken & Chinese Sausage

2   medium black mushrooms (shi-i-take)

1   ounce butter, unsalted
1   tablespoon minced fresh ginger root
3   cloves garlic, minced

1   chicken thigh, cut in half (with bone and skin attached)
1   stick Chinese sausage (about 5 inches long) cut in half
2   cups Chicken Stock (see Basics)
2   cups calrose or Oriental long-grain rice
1/4   teaspoon salt
1/4   teaspoon white pepper
2   stems green onions, finely chopped (white and green parts)

Soak mushroom in hot water, for 20 minutes. Drain, trim bottom part of stems. Set aside.

In 3-quart sauce pan, melt butter, over medium heat. Add ginger, and garlic. Stir and cook until fragrant. Add chicken and sausage, cook until lightly browned, about 2 minutes. Add remaining ingredients, stir to blend. Increase heat and bring to boil. Allow to boil for 1 minute. Cover and reduce heat, simmer for 20 minutes. Do not stir or remove lid during that time. Remove from heat, fluff with a fork, and serve. Yields 2 servings, as a main course.

Dill Rice

2   ounces butter or margarine, unsalted
6   tablespoons fresh dill (stems removed), finely chopped or
      2 tablespoons dried dill weed

2   cups water
2   cups calrose or Oriental long-grain rice
1   teaspoon garlic powder
1/2   teaspoon salt

In 3-quart covered saucepan, melt butter, over medium heat. Stir in dill, Then add the rest of ingredients, stir to blend, and cover. Increase heat, bring to boil, and allow to boil for 1 minute. Reduce heat and simmer for 20 minutes (do not remove lid during that time). Remove from heat and fluff with a fork. Yields 4 cups.

Note: Dill is commonly used throughout Thailand as a seasoning or as a vegetable.

Spicy Rice

Spices make this a superb side dish for serving with barbecues.

1/4	cup butter or margarine
6	cloves garlic, crushed
1	small onion, chopped
3	tablespoons grated fresh ginger root
3	cups calrose or Oriental long-grain rice
3	cups Chicken Stock (see Basics)
1/2	tablespoon salt
1/2	tablespoon coarsely ground black pepper

Set 4 to 5-quart Dutch oven over high heat for 1 minute. Add butter or margarine, coat bottom of pot evenly. Add the next 3 ingredients, stir and cook, until light brown. Add the remaining ingredients, stir and bring to boil. Allow to boil for 1 minute. Do not stir. Cover pot and reduce heat, simmer for 20 minutes. Remove from heat. Do not remove lid while cooking. Yields 6 cups and serves 6 to 8 as an accompaniment.

Chinese Fried Rice

2	tablespoons vegetable oil
1	thumb-size segment of fresh ginger root, minced
4	large shallots or 1/2 small red onion, chopped
4	cloves garlic, crushed
4	cups Plain Steamed Rice
1	cup diced Red Roasted Pork (see chapter on Pork)
1	cup shredded carrots
1/2	cup fresh or frozen peas
1/2	cup pecans, chopped
2	tablespoons raisins
1/4	pound medium, fresh raw shrimp, shelled and deveined
2	tablespoons fish sauce (nam pla)
3	stems green onions, finely chopped (white and green parts)

Set wok over medium heat for 1 minute. Add oil, and coat sides of wok evenly. Add ginger, shallots, and garlic, stir and cook, until lightly brown. Add remaining ingredients, stir and cook, until shrimp is done, about 5 minutes. Transfer to serving plate and serve. Yields 4 servings as a main course or 8 as an accompaniment.

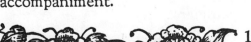

Fried Rice with
Shrimp, Chicken, Beef or Pork
(Kao Paht Goong, Gai, Nuah Liew Moo)

3	cloves garlic, crushed
1/4	cup vegetable oil
1/2	pound fresh raw shrimp, shelled and deveined, or chicken, beef or pork, sliced bite-size
6	cups Plain Steamed Rice
4	stems green onions, chopped (white and green parts)
1/2	cup chopped cilantro
1	medium tomato, chopped
2 1/2	tablespoons fish sauce (nam pla)
3	tablespoons catsup
1	tablespoon shrimp paste with bean oil
1	tablespoon chile paste with bean oil (nam prig pao)
1/8	teaspoon pepper
2	eggs, beaten
	parsley for garnish

Set wok over high heat until sizzling hot. Add oil and coat sides of wok evenly. Add garlic and stir fry until light brown. Add shrimp, or meat of your choice, stir and cook, until shrimp turns pink, or meat is done. Add next 9 ingredients, stir and cook, until rice mixture is thoroughly heated, about 3 minutes. Add eggs, stir and cook, until eggs are firm. Transfer to serving plate and garnish with parsley. Serve with raw vegetables of your choice or Cucumber Salad. Yields 4 servings.

Fried Rice with Corn (Japanese-Style)

1	ounce butter or margarine, unsalted
1/4	cup finely chopped onion
2	cups Plain Steamed Rice
1/2	cup canned, drained whole kernel corn
1	cup bean sprouts
2	stems green onions, finely chopped (white and green parts)
1 1/2	tablespoons soy sauce
1/4	teaspoon white pepper

Melt butter or margarine, in wok, over medium high heat. Add onion, stir and cook, until fragrant. Add steamed rice and toss to blend. Add the rest of ingredients, stir and cook, until bean sprouts just begin to soften, about 2 minutes. Yields 2 to 3 servings as an accompaniment.

Rice Congee
(Joak)

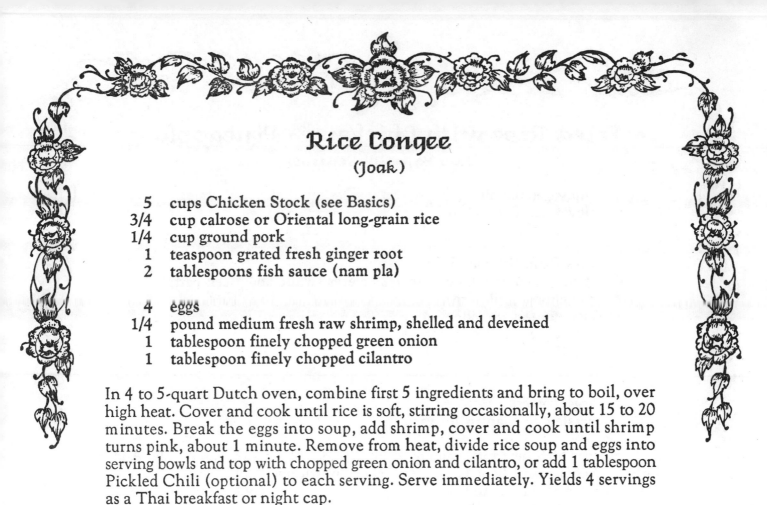

5	cups Chicken Stock (see Basics)
3/4	cup calrose or Oriental long-grain rice
1/4	cup ground pork
1	teaspoon grated fresh ginger root
2	tablespoons fish sauce (nam pla)
4	eggs
1/4	pound medium fresh raw shrimp, shelled and deveined
1	tablespoon finely chopped green onion
1	tablespoon finely chopped cilantro

In 4 to 5-quart Dutch oven, combine first 5 ingredients and bring to boil, over high heat. Cover and cook until rice is soft, stirring occasionally, about 15 to 20 minutes. Break the eggs into soup, add shrimp, cover and cook until shrimp turns pink, about 1 minute. Remove from heat, divide rice soup and eggs into serving bowls and top with chopped green onion and cilantro, or add 1 tablespoon Pickled Chili (optional) to each serving. Serve immediately. Yields 4 servings as a Thai breakfast or night cap.

Congee with Spinach

Cream of Wheat can be substituted for rice in preparing Congee.

4	cups Chicken Stock (see Basics)
1/4	pound fresh raw shrimp, shelled, deveined and minced
1/4	pound chicken breast, minced
1/4	cup cream of wheat
1	cup chopped spinach
3	tablespoons Maggi seasoning
1	stem green onion, finely chopped (white and green parts)
1/4	teaspoon white pepper
1	egg, beaten

Bring chicken stock to boil, over medium heat, in 5-quart Dutch oven. Add the next 7 ingredients and cook until cream of wheat is very soft, about 5 minutes. Add egg into mixture, gently stir and cook, until egg is cooked and firm, about 1 minute. Serve at once. Use as you would Rice Congee. Yields 4 servings.

Fried Rice with Chicken & Pineapple
(Kao Path Gai Separot)

1/4	cup vegetable oil
3	cloves garlic, crushed
1	pound chicken breasts, skinned and boned, sliced thin, bite size
6	cups Plain Steamed Rice
4	stems green onion, cut into 1/2" pieces (white and green parts)
1/2	cup chopped cilantro
1	medium tomato, chopped
2	cups chopped fresh pineapple
1/4	cup fish sauce (nam pla)
1/8	teaspoon pepper
2	eggs, beaten
	parsley or cilantro for garnish

Set wok over high heat for 1 minute. Add oil and coat sides of wok evenly. Add garlic and cook, until light brown. Add chicken, stir and cook, until chicken is done, about 3 minutes. Add next 7 ingredients, stir and cook, until mixture is thoroughly heated, about 3 minutes. Add eggs, stir and cook, until eggs are firm. Transfer to serving platter and garnish with parsley, or cilantro. Serve with Cucumber Salad. Yields 4 servings.

Chicken with Plain Steamed Rice
(Kao Mog Gai)

4	ounces butter, or margarine
4	cloves garlic, crushed
1	pound chicken breasts, skinned and boned, sliced thin, bite-size
8	cups Plain Steamed Rice
1	cup sliced mushrooms
1	cup chopped celery
1/2	cup chopped cilantro
1	cup chopped green onion
1/4	cup oyster sauce
1/4	cup fish sauce (nam pla)
1	small tomato, chopped
1/8	teaspoon pepper

Set wok over medium heat for 1 minute. Add butter, or margarine and allow to melt. Add garlic and cook until light brown. Add chicken, stir and cook, until chicken is done, about 3 minutes. Add remaining ingredients, stir and cook, until mixture is thoroughly heated, about 5 minutes. Remove from heat and serve with Cucumber Salad. Yields 4 servings.

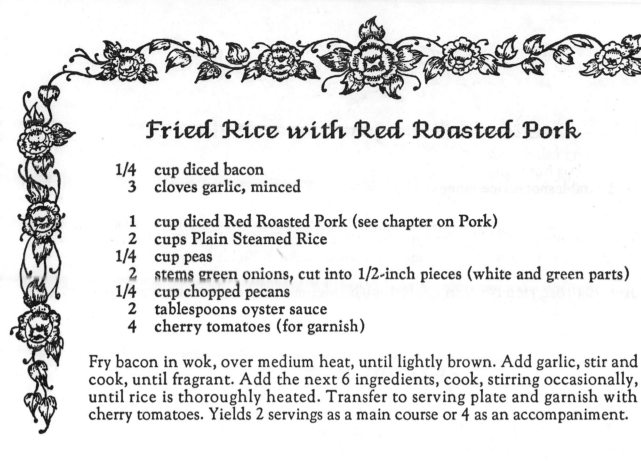

Fried Rice with Red Roasted Pork

1/4 cup diced bacon
3 cloves garlic, minced

1 cup diced Red Roasted Pork (see chapter on Pork)
2 cups Plain Steamed Rice
1/4 cup peas
2 stems green onions, cut into 1/2-inch pieces (white and green parts)
1/4 cup chopped pecans
2 tablespoons oyster sauce
4 cherry tomatoes (for garnish)

Fry bacon in wok, over medium heat, until lightly brown. Add garlic, stir and cook, until fragrant. Add the next 6 ingredients, cook, stirring occasionally, until rice is thoroughly heated. Transfer to serving plate and garnish with cherry tomatoes. Yields 2 servings as a main course or 4 as an accompaniment.

Thai Rice Stuffing

4 ounces butter, unsalted

1 small onion, diced
3 cloves garlic, minced
2 tablespoons minced fresh ginger root
1/2 teaspoon pepper

3 cups calrose or Oriental long grain rice
3 cups Chicken Stock (see Basics)
1/4 cup finely chopped parsley
1/2 cup raisins
1/4 cup peeled pine nuts
1 cup sliced mushrooms
1/4 cup diced bell pepper
1 teaspoon salt

Melt butter in 5-quart Dutch oven, over medium heat. Add next 4 ingredients. Stir and cook, until fragrant, but not brown. Add rice, toss to blend, add chicken stock, and cover. Increase heat, bring to boil and allow to boil for 1 minute. Reduce heat and simmer for 15 minutes. Do not remove lid while cooking. Remove from heat, add the rest of ingredients and toss to blend. Now you are ready to stuff a 12-pound turkey. For chicken or duck, use 1/2 the recipe. Rice is only partially cooked, so don't overstuff, allow plenty of room for expansion. Yields about 8 cups stuffing.

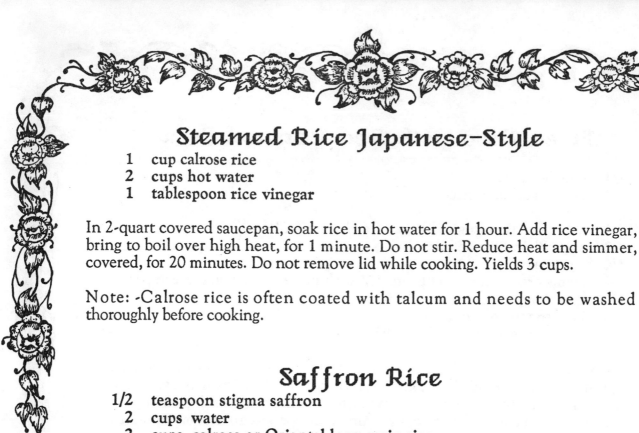

Steamed Rice Japanese-Style

1   cup calrose rice
2   cups hot water
1   tablespoon rice vinegar

In 2-quart covered saucepan, soak rice in hot water for 1 hour. Add rice vinegar, bring to boil over high heat, for 1 minute. Do not stir. Reduce heat and simmer, covered, for 20 minutes. Do not remove lid while cooking. Yields 3 cups.

Note: -Calrose rice is often coated with talcum and needs to be washed thoroughly before cooking.

Saffron Rice

1/2   teaspoon stigma saffron
2   cups water
2   cups calrose or Oriental long-grain rice
1/4   teaspoon, each, salt and garlic powder

1   ounce butter or margarine, unsalted
1/4   cup peeled, crushed pine nuts

In blender, blend saffron and water until saffron dissolves. In 5-quart Dutch oven, combine rice and saffron water and seasonings, bring to boil over high heat. Allow to boil for 1 minute. Cover, reduce heat and simmer for 20 minutes (do not remove cover during that time). Remove from heat, add butter and pine nuts, stir to blend and serve. Yields 6 servings as an accompaniment.

Fried Rice with Coconut Flakes

3   tablespoons vegetable oil
1/2   cup sweetened coconut flakes
1/4   cup minced onion
3   cloves garlic, minced

2   cups Plain Steamed Rice
1   cup thin-sliced Chinese long green beans or green beans
1   tablespoon anchovy paste

Set 3-quart sauce pan, over medium heat for 1 minute. Add oil and coat bottom of pan evenly. Add coconut, toss and cook, until light brown. Add onion, and garlic, stir and cook, until fragrant. Add remaining ingredients and cook, stirring occasionally, until rice mixture is thoroughly heated, about 3 minutes. Remove from heat and serve. Yields 4 servings as an accompaniment.

Steamed Whole Chicken & Spicy Sauce
(Kao Mun Gai)

1/2	cup butter or margarine

1/4	cup grated fresh ginger root
1	medium onion, chopped
1	whole garlic, minced
1/2	teaspoon ground coriander
1/2	teaspoon coarse ground black pepper

8	cups water
1	teaspoon salt
1	3 1/2 to 4 pound whole chicken, cleaned

5	cups rice, calrose or Oriental long-grain rice
	cilantro for garnish

Spicy Sauce:

6	serrano chiles, chopped
4	cloves garlic, minced
1	tablespoon grated fresh ginger root
1/3	cup soy sauce
2	tablespoons soy bean condiment
1	tablespoon white vinegar

Melt butter or margarine in 8 to 10-quart stock pot, over high heat. Add the next 5 ingredients and cook until light brown. Add water and salt, bring to boil. Add chicken, cover and cook about 30 minutes. Turn chicken over and cook 30 minutes more, or until chicken is done. Remove chicken, reserving stock. Carve the breast and cut remaining chicken into serving pieces. Set aside in warm oven.

In 5-quart Dutch oven, combine 5 cups of reserved stock and 5 cups of rice, bring to boil over high heat, allow to boil 1 minute. Do not stir. Cover and reduce heat, simmer for 20 minutes. Remove from heat. Do not remove lid while cooking.

In blender, combine all sauce ingredients, blend on medium speed until coarsely ground, set aside.

To serve: Scoop rice on serving plate. Arrange chicken over rice. Garnish with cilantro. Serve with Spicy Sauce, on the side, and Cucumber Salad. Yields 4 to 6 servings as a main course.

Fried Rice with Turkey Topping

1   tablespoon vegetable oil
2   eggs, beaten until foamy

4   cups Plain Steamed Rice
2   tablespoons soy sauce

Topping:
2   tablespoons vegetable oil
1   tablespoon minced fresh ginger root
3   cloves garlic, minced
1/4 cup chopped onion

1/4 cup carrots, diced
2   tablespoons raisins
2   tablespoons walnuts, chopped
2   cups cooked turkey meat, shredded
1   tablespoon rice vinegar (seasoned gourmet)
2   tablespoons soy sauce
1   tablespoon dry sherry
2   tablespoons corn starch mixed with 1/2 cup water until smooth
1/4 teaspoon white pepper

Set wok over high heat for 1 minute. Add 1 tablespoon of oil, coat sides of wok evenly. Pour in beaten eggs and fry until lightly brown about 1 minute. While cooking, break eggs into pieces with spatula. Add rice and soy sauce, stir and cook, until rice is thoroughly heated. Transfer rice mixture to serving plate and set aside.

Heat 2 tablespoons oil in 10" frying pan for 1 minute. Add ginger, garlic, and onion, stir and cook, until fragrant. Add the remaining ingredients, stir and cook, until mixture is thoroughly heated and sauce has thickened, about 2 minutes. Pour over rice mixture and serve. Yields 2 servings.

Note:-This is an excellent way to use leftover turkey.

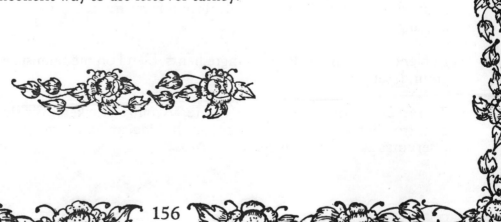

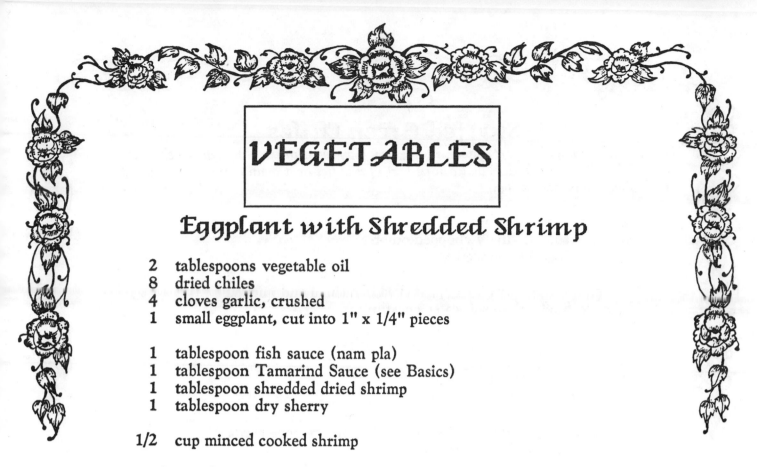

VEGETABLES

Eggplant with Shredded Shrimp

2	tablespoons vegetable oil
8	dried chiles
4	cloves garlic, crushed
1	small eggplant, cut into 1" x 1/4" pieces
1	tablespoon fish sauce (nam pla)
1	tablespoon Tamarind Sauce (see Basics)
1	tablespoon shredded dried shrimp
1	tablespoon dry sherry
1/2	cup minced cooked shrimp

Heat oil in wok over high heat until sizzling hot. Add chiles, quickly toss until dark brown. Remove chiles, set aside.

Add garlic to wok, stir and cook, until light brown. Add eggplant, cook about 5 minutes or until eggplant is soft. Add the next 4 ingredients, stir to blend. Transfer eggplant to serving plate, garnish with minced shrimp and chiles. Serve with fried rice. Yields 2 servings.

Mushrooms with Curry

2	tablespoons vegetable oil
1/2	small onion, finely chopped
2	cups sliced mushrooms
1/2	cup chopped walnuts
1/4	cup chopped parsley
1/2	cup coconut milk
1	tablespoon curry powder
1	tablespoon Maggi Seasoning
1	tablespoon all purpose flour, mixed with 3 tablespoons of water

Set 2-quart saucepan over high heat for one minute. Add oil and coat bottom of pan evenly. Add onion and cook until fragrant. Add next 3 ingredients, stir and cook, until mushrooms just begin to soften, about 1 minute. Add remaining ingredients, stir and cook, until sauce thickens. Remove from heat and serve. Yields 2 to 3 servings.

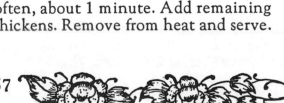

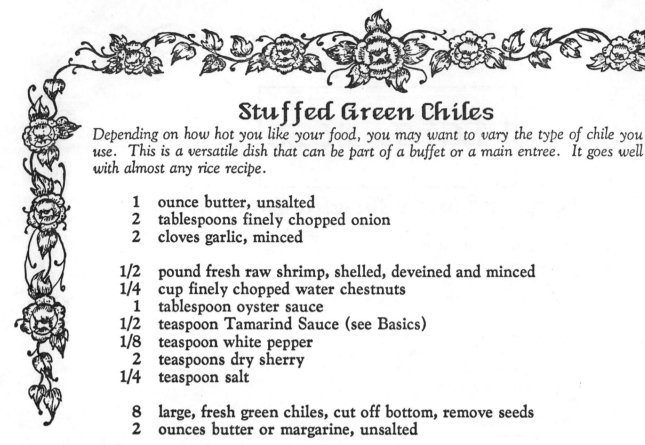

Stuffed Green Chiles

Depending on how hot you like your food, you may want to vary the type of chile you use. This is a versatile dish that can be part of a buffet or a main entree. It goes well with almost any rice recipe.

1	ounce butter, unsalted
2	tablespoons finely chopped onion
2	cloves garlic, minced

1/2	pound fresh raw shrimp, shelled, deveined and minced
1/4	cup finely chopped water chestnuts
1	tablespoon oyster sauce
1/2	teaspoon Tamarind Sauce (see Basics)
1/8	teaspoon white pepper
2	teaspoons dry sherry
1/4	teaspoon salt

8	large, fresh green chiles, cut off bottom, remove seeds
2	ounces butter or margarine, unsalted

Melt 1-ounce of butter, in 3-quart sauce pan, over medium heat. Add onion, and garlic, stir and cook, until fragrant. Add the next 7 ingredients, stir and cook, until shrimp is done, about 1 minute, remove from heat. Scoop about 1 1/2 tablespoons of shrimp mixture into each green chile. Repeat with remaining chiles, set aside.

In 12-inch covered frying pan, melt 2-ounces of butter, over medium heat. Place stuffed chiles in frying pan, cover and cook about 5 minutes on each side. Transfer chiles to damp cloth napkin, wrap and set aside for 10 minutes. Peel chiles and serve. Yields 2 servings.

Stir-Fried Tofu

Tofu is full of protein and is also, fat-free. It can be used as a meat substitute that is nutritious.

2	tablespoons vegetable oil
3	cloves garlic, crushed
1	thumb-size fresh ginger root, slivered
1	6-ounce package fresh pressed tofu, cut into about 1" x 1/2" pieces

2	stems green onions, cut into 1/2" pieces (white and green parts)
1	tablespoon oyster sauce
1	teaspoon chile paste with bean oil (nam prig pao)

Set wok over high heat for 1 minute. Add oil, and coat sides of wok evenly. Quickly stir in garlic, and ginger, cook until light brown. Add tofu, stir and cook, for 2 minutes. Add remaining ingredients, stir to blend, remove from heat and serve. Yields 2 servings.

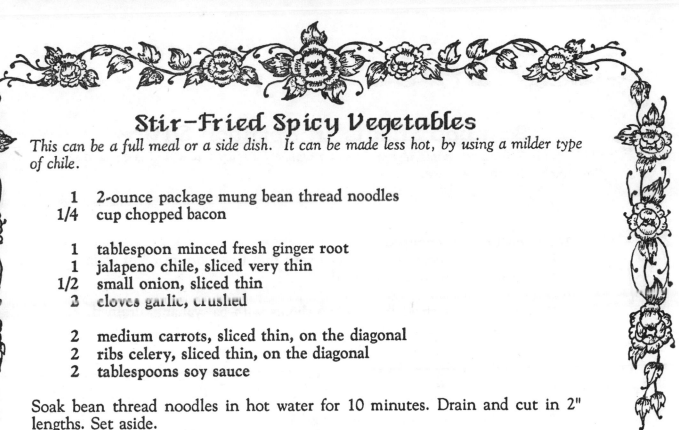

Stir-Fried Spicy Vegetables

This can be a full meal or a side dish. It can be made less hot, by using a milder type of chile.

1	2-ounce package mung bean thread noodles
1/4	cup chopped bacon
1	tablespoon minced fresh ginger root
1	jalapeno chile, sliced very thin
1/2	small onion, sliced thin
3	cloves garlic, crushed
2	medium carrots, sliced thin, on the diagonal
2	ribs celery, sliced thin, on the diagonal
2	tablespoons soy sauce

Soak bean thread noodles in hot water for 10 minutes. Drain and cut in 2" lengths. Set aside.

Set wok over high heat for 1 minute. Add bacon and fry, until brown. Add the next 4 ingredients, stir and cook, until fragrant. Add the next 3 ingredients, stir and cook, until celery just starts to soften, about 1 minute. Add noodles, stir and cook, until noodles are soft, about 1 minute. Remove to serving dish and serve. Yields 3 servings.

Eggplant with Black Mushrooms

4	medium black mushrooms (shi-i-take)
1	small eggplant
2	tablespoons vegetable oil
4	cloves garlic, crushed
1	tablespoon rice vinegar (seasoned gourmet)
1	tablespoon oyster sauce
1/2	tablespoon soy bean condiment
1	tablespoon chile paste with bean oil (nam prig pao)

Soak mushrooms in hot water for 20 minutes. Drain, remove bottom part of stems, slice thin, and set aside. Cut eggplant in half, lengthwise, then cut crosswise into 1/2 inch thick slices. Set aside.

Set wok over high heat for 1 minute. Add oil and coat sides of wok evenly. Quickly add garlic, and cook until light brown. Add mushrooms, eggplant, and the rest of ingredients. Stir and cook, until eggplant softens, about 5 minutes. Yields 4 servings.

Bamboo Shoots in Spinach Sauce

This recipe is from my home region. It has a wonderful spicy flavor and is good to serve for lunch with steamed rice.

- 2 cups water
- 2 cups chopped spinach
- 1/2 small onion, chopped
- 2 stems fresh lemon grass, sliced very thin (use bottom 2" of stems)
- 4 fresh serrano chiles, chopped

- 1 24-ounce jar shredded bamboo shoots with bai yanang, drained, and separated, reserve marinade
- 1/4 pound top sirloin beef, sliced thin
  kernels of one ear of corn
- 3 tablespoons fish sauce (nam pla)

- 3 stalks cilantro, cut in 1/2" lengths
- 2 stems green onion, cut into 1/2" pieces (white and green parts)

Combine the first 5 ingredients in blender and blend until coarsely ground. Pour into 6-quart Dutch oven, add the next 4 ingredients, including reserved marinade. Cover and cook, over high heat for about 6 minutes. Remove from heat, add cilantro and green onion, stir to blend, and serve. Yields 4 to 6 servings.

Vegetables & Tofu in Garlic Sauce
(Korean Style)

- 2 tablespoons vegetable oil
- 2 teaspoons garlic, minced
- 2 teaspoons sesame oil
- 1 6-ounce package fresh pressed tofu, sliced into 1/4" thick strips

- 1 bunch spinach
- 1 bunch watercress
- 2 cups bean sprouts
- 2 teaspoons roasted sesame seeds for garnish

Set wok over high heat for 1 minute. Add 1/2 tablespoon of vegetable oil and coat sides of wok evenly. Add 1/2 teaspoon of garlic, cook until fragrant. Add tofu, stir and cook about 1 minute. Add 1/2 teaspoon of sesame oil, stir to blend, and transfer to serving plate.

Wipe wok clean of food particles and repeat the above with each remaining vegetable. Garnish with sesame seeds, and serve. Goes well with barbecue. Yields 4 servings.

Vegetables in Sweet Sour Garlic Sauce

4	dried black mushrooms (shi-i-take)
2	cups Chicken Stock (see Basics)
3	tablespoons all-purpose flour
3	tablespoons soy sauce
1	tablespoon oyster sauce
1/2	tablespoon brown sugar
1	teaspoon vinegar
3	tablespoons vegetable oil
1	tablespoon minced fresh ginger root
3	cloves garlic, crushed
5	medium zucchinis, sliced 1/4" thick, on the diagonal
3	medium carrots, sliced very thin, on the diagonal
1	cup snow peas
1	cup water chestnuts or baby corn

Soak mushrooms in hot water for 20 minutes. Drain and slice very thin. Set aside. In 1 to 2 quart saucepan, combine next 6 ingredients. Blend until smooth, simmer until sauce thickens and set aside.

Set wok over high heat for 1 minute. Heat oil until sizzling hot and coat sides of wok evenly. Add ginger and garlic, stir and cook, until light brown. Add vegetables, stir and cook, until vegetables just begin to soften, about 2 minutes. Pour sauce over vegetables, mix well. Transfer to serving dish and serve. Yields 4 to 6 servings.

Steamed Asparagus & Black Mushrooms

4	medium, dried black mushrooms (shi-i-take)
1	pound asparagus, cut into 2" pieces
1 1/2	cups Chicken Stock (see Basics)
2	chicken-flavored bouillon cubes
1	tablespoon oyster sauce
1/2	tablespoon garlic, minced
1	teaspoon cornstarch, mixed with 2 tablespoons of water

Soak mushrooms in hot water for 20 minutes. Drain, remove bottom part of stems and slice very thin. Set aside. Combine mushrooms, and the next 5 ingredients, in a 2-quart covered saucepan. Cook over high heat, until the asparagus just begins to soften, about 6 minutes. Add the cornstarch mixture, and cook until sauce thickens, about 1/2 minute. Remove from heat and serve. Yields 4 servings.

Stuffed Cabbage

Stuffing:
1	pound ground pork or ground chicken
2	tablespoons oyster sauce
1	stem green onion, chopped (white and green parts)
3	tablespoons chopped cilantro
2	cloves garlic, minced
1/8	teaspoon pepper

In small bowl, combine all stuffing ingredients, mix well. Set aside.

8	large cabbage leaves, steamed until limp
3/4	cup water
2	ounces melted butter

Place 2 heaping tablespoons of stuffing in center of cabbage leaf, wrap leaf firmly around stuffing. Repeat with remaining leaves. Place cabbage rolls in 5-quart Dutch oven, add water, then brush with melted butter. Cover and cook over high heat, until meat stuffing is well done, about 15 minutes. Transfer rolls to serving place and serve with steamed rice. Yields 3 to 4 servings.

Cabbage or Spinach Quick Fry

3	tablespoons vegetable oil
4	cloves garlic, crushed
6	cups sliced cabbage or spinach
2	tablespoons oyster sauce

Set wok over high heat for one minute. Add oil and coat sides of wok evenly. Add garlic and cook until fragrant. Add remaining ingredients and cook until vegetables just start to turn limp. Yields 3 to 4 servings.

Sauteed Mushrooms & Zucchini

There are many ways to use Herbal Butter. When you make it, freeze it in small portions. Mushrooms and zucchini cooked this way, are simply delicious.

1/4	cup Herbal Butter (see Basics)
5	cups mushrooms
2	cups zucchini, sliced 1/2" thick (approximately)
1 1/2	tablespoons oyster sauce

In 4 to 5-quart Dutch oven, melt Herbal Butter over high heat. Add remaining ingredients, stir to blend. Cook until zucchini just begins to soften, about 3 minutes. Remove to serving dish and serve. Yields 4 to 6 servings.

Stuffed Bell Peppers

3	medium black mushrooms (shi-i-take)
3	bell peppers
1/2	pound ground pork, or ground chicken
1/4	pound fresh raw shrimp, shelled, deveined, and minced
1	tablespoon minced garlic
1	tablespoon minced fresh ginger root
2	tablespoons fish sauce (nam pla)
2	tablespoons oyster sauce
1	tablespoon dry sherry
1/4	cup chopped cilantro
2	teaspoons cornstarch
2	ounces of butter or margarine, unsalted

Soak mushrooms in hot water for 20 minutes. Drain, remove bottom part of stems, quarter, and set aside. Remove bottom and seeds from bell peppers. Cut each bell pepper lengthwise into 4 wedges. Set aside. In medium bowl, combine the next 9 ingredients, mix well. Set aside for 10 minutes to allow the flavors to blend.

Scoop 1 heaping tablespoon of meat mixture onto each pepper wedge. Top with one mushroom quarter. Melt butter or margarine, in 12-inch covered frying pan, over medium heat. Place pepper wedges into frying pan, cover and cook, until meat stuffing is done, about 10 minutes. Transfer to serving plate, and serve while hot. Yields 4 servings.

Asparagus with Cashews

2	ounces butter or margarine, unsalted
1/2	tablespoon minced garlic
1	pound fresh asparagus, cut into 2" pieces
1	tablespoon oyster sauce
2	tablespoons dry sherry
1/2	cup whole, roasted cashew nuts

Set wok over medium heat for 1 minute. Add butter or margarine and coat sides of wok evenly. Add garlic, stir and cook, until fragrant. Add remaining ingredients, including asparagus, stir and cook, until asparagus just begins to soften, about 5 minutes. Remove from heat and serve. Yields 4 servings.

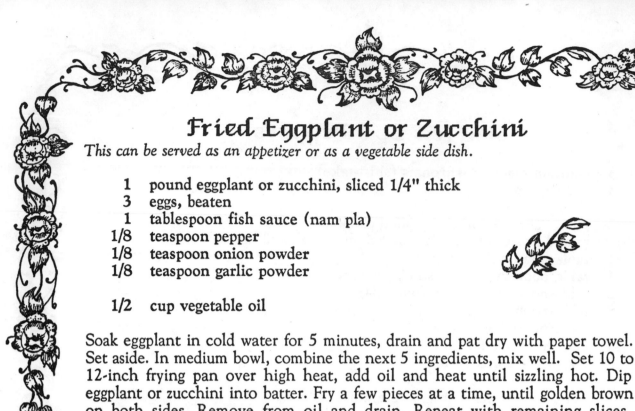

Fried Eggplant or Zucchini

This can be served as an appetizer or as a vegetable side dish.

1	pound eggplant or zucchini, sliced 1/4" thick
3	eggs, beaten
1	tablespoon fish sauce (nam pla)
1/8	teaspoon pepper
1/8	teaspoon onion powder
1/8	teaspoon garlic powder
1/2	cup vegetable oil

Soak eggplant in cold water for 5 minutes, drain and pat dry with paper towel. Set aside. In medium bowl, combine the next 5 ingredients, mix well. Set 10 to 12-inch frying pan over high heat, add oil and heat until sizzling hot. Dip eggplant or zucchini into batter. Fry a few pieces at a time, until golden brown on both sides. Remove from oil and drain. Repeat with remaining slices. Transfer to serving plate and serve. Yields 4 servings.

Watercress with Soy Beans

2	tablespoons vegetable oil
4	cloves garlic, crushed
2	bunches watercress
1 1/2	tablespoons soy bean condiment
1/4	cup whole roasted cashews

Set wok over high heat for 1 minute. Add oil and coat sides of wok evenly. Add garlic and fry until fragrant. Add remaining ingredients, stir and cook, until watercress is limp, about 1 minute. Remove from heat and serve. Yields 2 to 3 servings.

Spicy Vegetables

The chiles and garlic give the watercress a great new flavor. This can be a complete lunch, served with steamed rice.

3	tablespoons vegetable oil
5	jalapeno chiles, crushed
4	cloves garlic, crushed
1	bunch Oriental watercress or 2 bunches watercress, sliced
2	tablespoons soy bean condiment

Set wok over high heat for 1 minute. Add oil and coat sides of wok evenly. Add chiles and garlic, stir and cook, until light brown. Add remaining ingredients, stir and cook, until watercress is limp, about 2 minutes. Remove to serving dish and serve. Yields 3 to 4 servings.

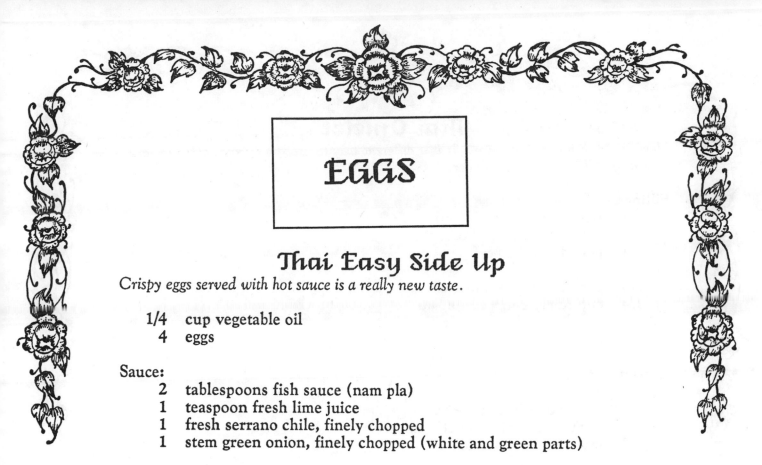

EGGS

Thai Easy Side Up

Crispy eggs served with hot sauce is a really new taste.

1/4	cup vegetable oil
4	eggs

Sauce:

2	tablespoons fish sauce (nam pla)
1	teaspoon fresh lime juice
1	fresh serrano chile, finely chopped
1	stem green onion, finely chopped (white and green parts)

In 10-inch frying pan, heat oil over high heat for 1 minute. Gently crack the eggs into the hot oil. Scoop oil over eggs frequently while cooking, cook until egg whites turn light brown and crisp, about 1 minute. Remove eggs to serving plate. Set aside.

In small bowl, combine sauce ingredients and mix well, pour over eggs and serve. Yields 2 servings.

Egg Foo Yung

5	eggs, beaten until foamy
1/2	teaspoon baking powder
1/2	teaspoon white pepper
1 1/2	tablespoons fish sauce (nam pla)
1	stem green onion, finely chopped (white and green parts)
3	tablespoons vegetable oil

Combine the first 5 ingredients in medium bowl, mix well. Set 12-inch frying pan over high heat for 1 minute. Add oil, coat pan evenly. Add egg mixture, fry until egg is firm and light brown on bottom, about 1/2 minute, turn eggs over and brown on the other side. Remove to serving place, and serve at once. Yields 2 servings.

Thai Omelet

Here is a dish for the egg lover. It is a different way to prepare an omelet. We serve it as a side dish at lunch or dinner.

Filling:
- 1 tablespoon vegetable oil
- 1/4 cup finely chopped onion
- 1 pound ground beef

- 1/4 cup chopped mushrooms
- 1/4 cup finely chopped tomato
- 1/4 cup finely chopped cilantro
- 1/8 teaspoon pepper

Omelet:
- 6 eggs
- 1 tablespoon fish sauce
- 1 stem green onion, finely chopped
- 2 tablespoons vegetable oil

Set 2-quart saucepan over high heat for 1 minute. Add 1 tablespoon of oil and coat bottom of pan evenly. Add onion and cook until light brown. Add ground beef, stir and cook, until beef is done, about 2 minutes. Add the rest of filling ingredients, stir and cook, until mushrooms soften, about 1 minute. Remove from pan and set aside.

In medium bowl combine the first 3 omelet ingredients, beat until foamy. Set 12-inch frying pan over high heat for 1 minute. Add 2 tablespoons of oil and coat bottom of pan evenly. Add egg mixture and fry until eggs are set. Turn omelet over and fry until golden brown. Spoon the meat mixture into the center of the omelet. Fold over and transfer to serving plate. Serve with Tomato Hot Sauce. Yields 3 servings.

Steamed Eggs
(Kai Toon)

- 4 eggs
- 1 tablespoon fish sauce (nam pla)
- 1 stem green onion, finely chopped (white and green parts)
- 1/4 cup water
- 1/8 teaspoon pepper

Preheat 4 cups of water in steamer over high heat. In medium bowl, combine all ingredients, beat with electric hand mixer, until foamy. Pour into small ceramic bowl. Place bowl on steamer rack and cover. Steam about 20 minutes or until egg mixture is firm. Remove from steamer and serve as a side dish. Yields 2 servings.

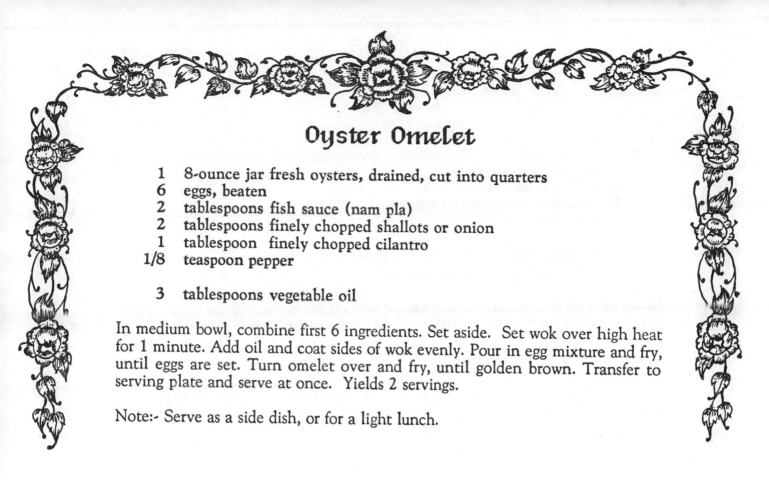

Oyster Omelet

1   8-ounce jar fresh oysters, drained, cut into quarters
6   eggs, beaten
2   tablespoons fish sauce (nam pla)
2   tablespoons finely chopped shallots or onion
1   tablespoon finely chopped cilantro
1/8 teaspoon pepper

3   tablespoons vegetable oil

In medium bowl, combine first 6 ingredients. Set aside. Set wok over high heat for 1 minute. Add oil and coat sides of wok evenly. Pour in egg mixture and fry, until eggs are set. Turn omelet over and fry, until golden brown. Transfer to serving plate and serve at once. Yields 2 servings.

Note:- Serve as a side dish, or for a light lunch.

Spicy Shrimp Omelet

5   eggs, beaten until foamy
1/4 cup diced cooked ham
1/4 pound fresh raw shrimp, cleaned, deveined and minced
1   tablespoon fish sauce (nam pla)
1/4 cup finely chopped parsley
1/4 cup shredded cheddar cheese
2   serrano chiles, finely chopped
1/4 teaspoon paprika

2   tablespoons vegetable oil

Combine first 8 ingredients in medium bowl, mix well. Set aside. Set 10" frying pan over high heat, for 1 minute. Add oil and coat bottom of pan evenly. Pour in the egg mixture, spread evenly and let the eggs cook until set, about 1/2 minute. Fold omelet in half, continue cooking, turning over omelet, until both sides are lightly brown. Yields 2 to 3 servings.

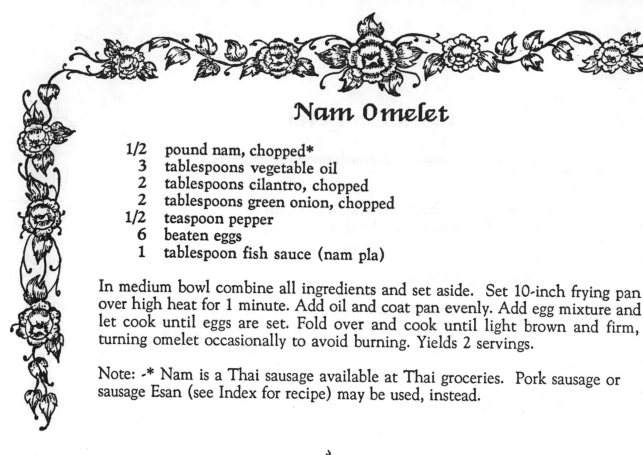

Nam Omelet

1/2   pound nam, chopped*
3   tablespoons vegetable oil
2   tablespoons cilantro, chopped
2   tablespoons green onion, chopped
1/2   teaspoon pepper
6   beaten eggs
1   tablespoon fish sauce (nam pla)

In medium bowl combine all ingredients and set aside. Set 10-inch frying pan over high heat for 1 minute. Add oil and coat pan evenly. Add egg mixture and let cook until eggs are set. Fold over and cook until light brown and firm, turning omelet occasionally to avoid burning. Yields 2 servings.

Note: -* Nam is a Thai sausage available at Thai groceries. Pork sausage or sausage Esan (see Index for recipe) may be used, instead.

Five Spice & Hard Boiled Eggs

4   medium, dried black mushrooms (shi-i-take)

1   cup Chicken Stock (see Basics)
4   hard boiled eggs (shelled)
1/4   teaspoon ground ginger
1/4   teaspoon five spice seasoning
1 1/2   tablespoons Maggi Seasoning
1   small carrot, sliced thin, on the diagonal

1   stem green onion, finely chopped (white and green parts)

Soak mushrooms in hot water for 20 minutes. Drain, remove bottom part of stems and quarter. Combine mushrooms and next 6 ingredients in 2-quart covered saucepan. Cover and boil over high heat, for about 5 minutes. Add green onion and serve. Yields 2 servings.

DESSERTS

Taro Root Pudding
(Kanom Mo Gaeng Puak)

1   pound taro root, peeled and diced
1   ounce butter or margarine
1   onion, sliced thin

1   14-ounce can coconut milk
1 1/4   cups palm sugar (or brown sugar)
6   eggs, beaten

In 5-quart Dutch oven, combine taro root and 3 cups of water. Boil over medium heat, until taro roots are soft. Drain and set aside. Melt butter or margarine, in 1 or 2-quart saucepan, over high heat. Add onion, stir and cook, until light brown. Set aside.

In medium bowl, mash taro root with a fork. Add remaining ingredients and blend with hand mixer until smooth. Lightly coat a 9" square baking pan with vegetable oil. Pour in the taro pudding.

Preheat oven to 350 degrees and bake the pudding for 30 minutes, or until light brown on top. Increase heat to 450 degrees and bake 15-20 minutes longer or until top is dark brown. Remove from heat and arrange browned onions on top. Set aside to cool. Refrigerate until chilled and serve.

Taro Root with Coconut Cream
(Gang Buoht Puak)

1   pound taro root, peeled and diced
1   14-ounce can coconut cream
1/2   cup sugar

In 2-quart covered saucepan, combine all ingredients. Cover and cook over high heat, until taro roots are soft, about 12 minutes, stirring occasionally. Remove from heat. Serve warm or cold. Yields 4 servings.

Note: - You may substitute bananas for the taro root. If you use bananas, cut each banana into 3 pieces. Cooking time will be about 5 minutes.

Coconut Cream

If you need a thick coconut cream for dishes such as curries, let this mixture stand until the thicker cream floats to the top, then spoon off some of the top cream and some of the juice below it. Use 2 parts of cream to 1 part juice.

Coconut cream separates when boiled. It should be separated, because when the cream and oil separate, you arrive at the true coconut flavor needed for curry sauces. To substitute coconut cream, use equal parts of half and half and milk. One whole coconut makes about 3 cups cream.

Fresh Coconut Cream

1   fresh coconut
    hot water

Use a fresh whole coconut. Crack shell and remove meat. Chop meat into small pieces. In blender combine 1 cup of hot water to every cup of coconut. Blend together at high speed, for 3 minutes. Strain through cheesecloth, squeeze by hand until all liquid is removed. Discard pulp, use liquid right away.

Note: -Coconut cream or milk can be purchased in cans.

Fresh Fruit with Coconut Cream

1/2   honeydew melon (or 1 cantaloupe)
  1   cup coconut cream
1/4   cup sugar
1/2   cup crushed ice

Scoop out melon into balls, place in serving bowl. Combine coconut cream and sugar in small bowl, mix well. Pour mixture over melon balls, add crushed ice and serve. Yields 2 servings.

Thai Custard

1   cup coconut cream
1/2   cup sugar
4   eggs

Combine all ingredients in medium bowl. Beat with hand mixer until foamy. Pour into 1-quart metal or porcelain (heat-proof) mold. Place the mold onto steamer rack, add 5 cups of water to steamer. Cover and cook over high heat, for 45 minutes or until a knife inserted in the center of the custard comes out clean. Remove the mold from the steamer and set aside to cool. Then refrigerate the custard until it is thoroughly chilled. Yields 2 to 3 servings.

Sweet Rice with Coconut
(Kao Knew Geiw)

1   cup Steamed Sweet Rice
1   cup coconut milk
1   cup sweetened coconut flakes
1   cup ground peanuts
1/2 cup brown sugar
1/4 teaspoon salt
1   teaspoon vanilla extract

Combine all ingredients in 3-quart saucepan. Cook over medium heat for 15 minutes, stirring occasionally to prevent sticking to pot. Pour into mold, smooth the top and set aside to cool. Yields 4 servings.

Sweet Rice with Corn
(Kao Knew Kao Poad)

2   cups Steamed Sweet Rice
1/2 cup coconut milk
1   cup sweetened coconut flakes
1/4 cup sugar
1/2 cup roasted cashew nuts, crushed
1   cup drained, canned corn, whole kernel
1/4 teaspoon salt

In medium bowl, combine all ingredients, mix well and serve. Yields 4 servings.

Pineapple Jam

This is great on top of your favorite ice cream. It also is nice to spread on bread.

1   medium pineapple, very ripe, peeled and finely chopped
1   14-ounce can coconut milk
1 1/2 cups brown sugar
2   cups water
1/2 teaspoon salt
1/4 cup roasted peanuts, crushed

Combine all ingredients in 5-quart Dutch oven, bring to boil over high heat. Reduce heat and simmer, until mixture thickens, about 2 hours, stirring occasionally during that time. Remove from heat and set aside to cool. Transfer to jar and store in refrigerator. Yields about 3 cups.

Golden Fried Sesame Cakes

2	cups rice flour
1/4	cup sesame seeds, crushed
3/4	cup coconut milk
1/2	cup brown sugar
1	cup sweetened coconut flakes
1	teaspoon light sesame oil
1	tablespoon sesame seeds
1 1/2	cups vegetable oil

Knead the first 6 ingredients together, until they are well mixed. Separate dough into 12 equal pieces, roll each into a 1" ball. Spread sesame seed on working surface, roll each ball over sesame seeds and flatten to make patty. Set aside.

Heat oil in wok, over medium heat until sizzling hot. Add 1 patty at the time and deep fry about 3 minutes, or until golden brown on both sides. Remove from oil, drain on paper towel. Repeat with remaining patties. Yields 12 cakes.

Coconut Wonton Wrapper

1	cup sweetened coconut flakes
1/2	cup coarse ground cashew nuts
1/4	cup brown sugar
1/8	teaspoon salt
1	egg plus 1 egg yolk
1	8-ounce package square wonton skins
1	egg white, beaten
1	cup vegetable oil

In medium bowl combine first 5 ingredients, mix well. Add 1 teaspoon of mixture into center of each wonton skin. Dampen edges of wonton with beaten egg white and fold into triangles. Repeat with remaining wontons, set aside.

Place wok over high heat for 1 minute. Add oil, reduce heat to medium. Drop a small piece of wonton skin into hot oil. If piece rises to the top immediately, the oil is ready. Deep fry 4 pieces at the time, until golden brown on both sides, remove from oil and drain. Repeat with remaining wrappers. Transfer to serving plate. Yields 25 wrappers.

Note: -These wrappers can be prepared one day ahead and stored in airtight container.

Banana Bread

As American as this may appear, it is a favorite in my sister's bakery in Thailand.

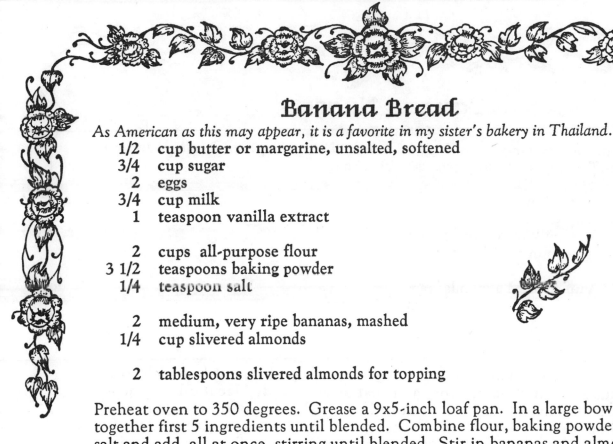

1/2	cup butter or margarine, unsalted, softened
3/4	cup sugar
2	eggs
3/4	cup milk
1	teaspoon vanilla extract
2	cups all-purpose flour
3 1/2	teaspoons baking powder
1/4	teaspoon salt
2	medium, very ripe bananas, mashed
1/4	cup slivered almonds
2	tablespoons slivered almonds for topping

Preheat oven to 350 degrees. Grease a 9x5-inch loaf pan. In a large bowl, stir together first 5 ingredients until blended. Combine flour, baking powder and salt and add, all at once, stirring until blended. Stir in bananas and almonds. Do not overmix, the less, the better. Spread batter evenly into prepared pan, sprinkle top with 2 tablespoons of almonds and bake for about 1 hour, or until a cake tester, inserted in center, comes out clean. Yields a 9x5-inch loaf.

Crispy Pan Cake with Rambutons

Rambuton is a sweet Asian fruit, much like "lychees." Crunchy and sweet even when canned, it complements pancakes nicely. This is nice for breakfast or dessert.

1/2	cup rice flour
2	tablespoons all purpose flour
1/3	cup milk
1	egg
2	tablespoons sugar
2	tablespoons vegetable oil
2	egg yolks
1	cup canned rambuton, sliced thin (available at Oriental groceries)

In 2 to 3-quart bowl, blend first 5 ingredients until smooth. Place 12" frying pan over high heat for 1 minute. Add 1 tablespoon of oil and coat bottom of frying pan evenly. Pour in half of flour mixture, spread to make thin pancake, and fry until lightly brown, about 1/2 minute. Turn pancake over and spread 1 egg yolk over top of pancake, continue cooking until egg yolk is firm. Gently remove pancake to serving plate, and top with 1/2 cup sliced rambutons. Repeat with second pancake and serve. Yields 2 servings.

Banana Nuggets
(Goui Taud)

There are many recipes for fried bananas. I have included 2 which are my favorites. This one is especially good with ice cream.

1	cup all-purpose flour
1/2	cup sugar
1	cup milk (or coconut cream)
1	teaspoon vanilla
1/4	cup slivered almonds
3	ripe bananas, peeled, cut into 2" pieces
2	cups vegetable oil
1	tablespoon rum

In medium bowl, blend the first 4 ingredients together, until smooth. Add almonds and stir. Add bananas and coat pieces evenly. Heat oil in 2-quart saucepan, over medium heat, until sizzling hot. With spoon, scoop a banana piece and some batter into the hot oil, about 3 to 4 pieces at a time. Deep fry until golden brown and crisp on both sides. Remove from oil and drain on paper towel. Repeat with remaining bananas. Place bananas on serving plate, sprinkle with rum just before serving. Yields 4 servings.

Fried Bananas-Thai Style
(Goui Taud Bab Thai)

3/4	cup sugar
1	cup tapioca flour (Paeng Tao Yai Mom)*
1	cup rice flour
1/4	cup sesame seed
1	cup sweetened flaked coconut
3	cups coconut milk
6	ripe bananas, peeled, cut in half and split
2	cups vegetable oil

In medium bowl, blend the first 6 ingredients together, until smooth. Add bananas and coat pieces evenly.

Heat oil in wok, over medium heat until sizzling hot. Using a serving spoon, scoop banana and some batter into the hot oil, about 3 to 4 pieces at a time. Deep fry, until golden brown and crisp on both sides. Remove from oil and drain on paper towels. Repeat with remaining bananas. Transfer to serving plate and serve. Yields 6 servings.

Note: -*May be purchased at Thai grocery stores.

Thai Iced Tea
(Char Yen)

      2   quarts water
   1 1/2   cups Thai tea
      1   cup sugar
      1   cup sweetened condensed milk
             half and half
             crushed ice

Bring water to boil, in 4 to 5-quart Dutch oven, over high heat. Add tea, reduce heat and simmer 10 minutes. Strain tea through cheesecloth, add sugar and condensed milk, stir to blend. Set aside to cool.

To serve: Fill 12-ounce glass with crushed ice, add 1 cup of tea mixture, float 2 tablespoons of half and half on top.

Iced Tea
(Char Dum Yen)

      4   quarts water
   1 1/2   cups Thai tea
      1   cup sugar
      1   whole lemon, sliced thin
             crushed ice

Bring water to boil, in 4 to 5-quart Dutch oven, over high heat. Add tea, reduce heat and simmer 10 minutes. Strain tea through cheesecloth, add sugar and stir to blend. Set aside to cool.

To serve: Fill 12-ounce glass with crushed ice. Add 1 cup of tea mixture, float sliced lemon on top.

Iced Coffee
(O 'Lieng)

      2   quarts water
   1 1/2   cups Thai coffee
      1   cup sugar
             crushed ice

Bring water to boil, in 4 to 5-quart Dutch oven, over high heat. Add coffee, reduce heat and simmer 10 minutes. Strain coffee through cheesecloth, add sugar and stir to blend. Set aside to cool.

To serve: Fill 12 ounce glass with crushed ice, add 1 cup of coffee mixture.

Thai Coffee
(Garfair Yen)

Like the Thai Iced Tea, this is rich and smooth. Add a couple of tablespoons of dark rum...delicious.

2 quarts water
1 1/2 cups Thai coffee
1 cup sugar
1 cup sweetened condensed milk
half and half
crushed ice

Bring water to boil, in 4 to 5-quart Dutch oven, over high heat. Add coffee, reduce heat and simmer 10 minutes. Strain coffee through cheesecloth, add sugar and condensed milk, stir to blend. Set aside to cool.

To serve: Fill 12 ounce glass with crushed ice. Add 1 cup coffee mixture, float 2 tablespoons of half and half on top.

Mango with Sweet Rice

My family asks often for this wonderful dessert. The blend of the exotic flavors of mango and coconut makes this an experience. Other types of fresh or canned fruit can be substituted.

2 cups sweet rice
1 14-ounce can coconut milk
1/2 cup sugar
2 tablespoons roasted sesame seed
1/8 teaspoon salt

1 tablespoon peeled mung bean, roasted over low
heat until golden brown (or chopped pecans)
4 ripe mangos, peeled, seeds removed and sliced

Soak sweet rice in hot water for 3 hours or overnight. Drain water and pour sweet rice into steamer rack. Add 5 cups of water to steamer, steam over high heat for 20 minutes or until rice is soft.

In medium bowl, combine steamed sweet rice, 1 cup of coconut milk, and the next 3 ingredients, mix well. Cover and let stand for 10 minutes.

To serve: Scoop steamed sweet rice mixture onto serving plate. Sprinkle with remaining coconut milk, and roasted mung beans or pecans. Arrange mangos over top and serve. Yields 4 servings.

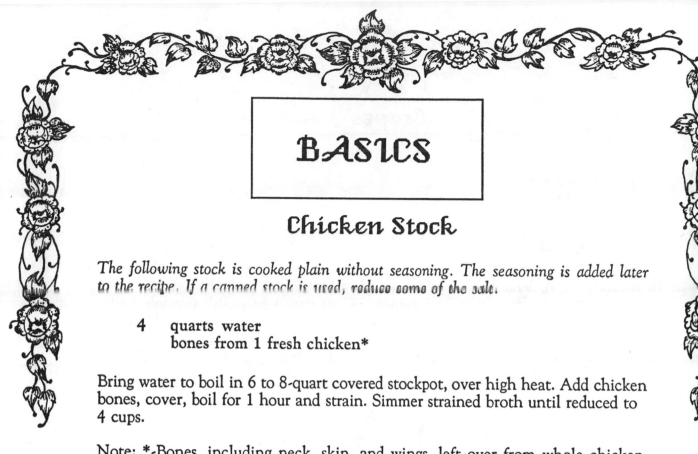

BASICS

Chicken Stock

The following stock is cooked plain without seasoning. The seasoning is added later to the recipe. If a canned stock is used, reduce some of the salt.

```
4    quarts water
     bones from 1 fresh chicken*
```

Bring water to boil in 6 to 8-quart covered stockpot, over high heat. Add chicken bones, cover, boil for 1 hour and strain. Simmer strained broth until reduced to 4 cups.

Note: *-Bones, including neck, skin, and wings, left over from whole chicken, which has been deboned and the meat used for other purposes.

Sweet & Sour Chile Sauce

```
2    whole pickled garlics, finely chopped
1    cup water
1/4  cup sugar
2    tablespoons ground fresh chile paste
2    tablespoons white vinegar

1    tablespoon cornstarch mixed with
        3 tablespoons pickled garlic juice, until smooth
1/2  teaspoon salt
```

In 2-quart saucepan, combine all ingredients. Bring to boil over high heat. Reduce heat and simmer until sauce thickens, stirring occasionally. Serve with barbecued chicken, etc. Store in refrigerator, keeps well for 1 month.

Pickled Ground Fresh Chile Sauce

```
1/4  cup ground fresh chile paste
1/4  cup white vinegar
1    clove garlic, minced
```

Combine all ingredients in jar, close tightly and shake well. Store in refrigerator, keeps well for 1 month. Serve as condiment with noodle dishes or soups.

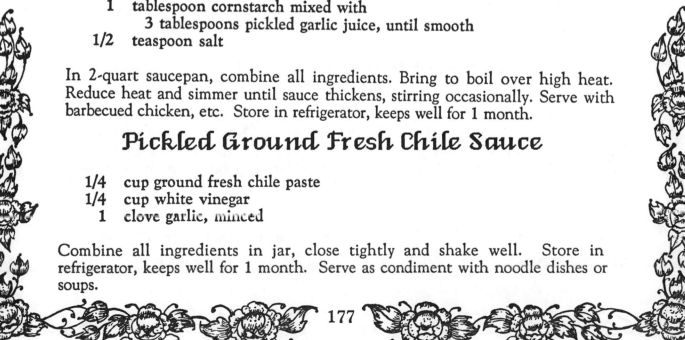

Crepes

         2   eggs
     1 1/4   cups milk
     1 1/4   cups flour
       1/4   teaspoon salt

             vegetable oil

In medium bowl, beat together first 4 ingredients, until smooth. Set 10-inch frying pan over medium heat for 1 minute. Coat pan lightly with vegetable oil and heat until sizzling hot. Add 1/4 cup of batter and spread evenly over bottom of pan, cook until bottom side is lightly browned. Turn pancake over and lightly brown other side. Set aside. Repeat with remaining batter, coating pan with oil as needed. Yields 8 crepes.

Basic Chinese Pancake

       2   cups all-purpose flour
     3/4   cup hot water
            vegetable oil

In medium bowl combine flour and hot water, mix with fork. Let cool for 2 to 3 minutes, then knead for about 5 minutes. Roll dough into long 1 1/2" diameter roll. Cover with damp cloth, and allow to stand for about 10 minutes.

Cut dough into 12 equal pieces. Roll out each piece, on a lightly floured surface, to form thin pancakes, about 6" in diameter. Set aside.

Lightly coat 8-inch skillet with oil, and place over medium-high heat until sizzling hot. Fry each pancake until lightly browned, about 20 seconds on each side. Fold in half, place on plate and cover with cloth napkin to keep warm. Repeat with remaining pancakes, recoating skillet with oil for each pancake. Pancakes can be cooked ahead and frozen. Yields 12 pancakes

To use:
Defrost pancakes and reheat by wrapping pancakes in damp cloth. Place on a steamer rack, over 2 cups of water and steam over high heat, until pancakes are thoroughly heated, about 5 minutes.

Red or Green Curry Paste

Curry Paste can be purchased in Thai markets, but here's how to make it at home.

- 1 teaspoon caraway seed
- 1 teaspoon coriander seed
- 1 teaspoon chopped dried makrood rind
- 1 teaspoon ground dried laos root
- 2 tablespoons chopped fresh lemon grass (use bottom 2" of stems only)
- 2 tablespoons chopped red onion
- 10 cloves garlic, peeled

- 2 tablespoons red chile powder*
- 1/2 teaspoon salt
- 1/2 teaspoon shrimp paste

Red Curry Paste: Combine first 7 ingredients in blender. Blend on medium speed until coarse ground. Set aside. In mortar, combine chile and salt, add the spice mixture and pound to paste with pestle. Add shrimp paste, pound until paste is thoroughly mixed. Keeps well in refrigerator for several months.
Green Curry Paste: Prepare as above, but substitute fresh green serrano chiles for the chile powder, fresh makrood rind for the dried, and fresh laos root for the dried.

Note: -*To prepare in authentic Thai manner, cut open 6 dried chile pods and remove seeds. Soak pods in warm water for 1/2 hour. Drain and squeeze out excess water. Use instead of chile powder.

Bean Dip
(Nam Prig Tua Dang)

- 1 8-3/4 ounce can kidney beans, drained
- 1/2 cup roasted chile paste with bean oil (nam prig pao)
- 2 tablespoons fish sauce (nam pla)
- 2 tablespoons brown sugar
- 2 tablespoons Tamarind Sauce (see Basics) or white vinegar

- 3 tablespoons vegetable oil
- 1/2 small onion, finely chopped

Combine first 5 ingredients in small bowl. Mash together with fork, set aside. Set 2-quart saucepan over medium heat for one minute. Add oil and coat bottom of pan evenly. Add onion and cook until light brown. Add bean mixture, stir and cook, until mixture is thoroughly heated, about 3 minutes. Remove from heat and serve as a dip, with fresh raw vegetables or chips of your choice. Keeps for several weeks when refrigerated. Yields about 2 cups.

Roasted Serrano Chile Sauce

15   fresh serrano chiles, roasted
1/4   cup chopped cilantro
1/4   cup fish sauce (nam pla)
1/4   cup Tamarind Sauce (see Basics)
1   teaspoon anchovy paste
1   small tomato, roasted
4   cloves garlic, roasted
4   shallots, roasted

Combine all ingredients in blender, blend at medium speed, until coarse ground. Store in refrigerator, keeps well for 2 weeks. Serve as condiment with any steamed or raw vegetables or barbecue.

Pickled Chile

10   fresh serrano chiles, sliced thin
1/2   cup white vinegar
1   clove garlic, minced

Combine all ingredients in jar, close tightly and shake well. Store in refrigerator, keeps well for 1 month. Serve as condiment with noodle dishes or soups.

Orange Curry Paste

2   tablespoons red chile powder or 8 red fresh serrano chiles
1/2   teaspoon salt
3   tablespoons chopped red onion
1/2   tablespoon shrimp paste

Combine all ingredients in mortar, pound with pestle to paste. Keeps well in refrigerator for several months.

Sweet & Sour Sauce

1   cup honey
1/4   cup white vinegar
2   teaspoons ground fresh chile paste

Combine all ingredients in 1 quart saucepan. Stir and cook over low heat, until sauce is hot. Remove from heat and serve while hot, with Thai barbecued chicken.

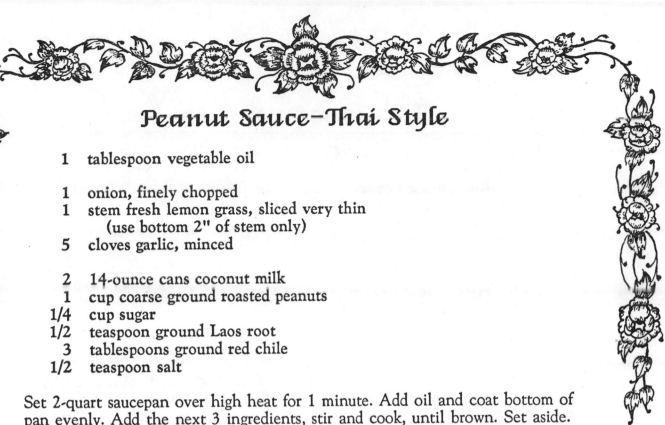

Peanut Sauce-Thai Style

- 1 tablespoon vegetable oil

- 1 onion, finely chopped
- 1 stem fresh lemon grass, sliced very thin
    (use bottom 2" of stem only)
- 5 cloves garlic, minced

- 2 14-ounce cans coconut milk
- 1 cup coarse ground roasted peanuts
- 1/4 cup sugar
- 1/2 teaspoon ground Laos root
- 3 tablespoons ground red chile
- 1/2 teaspoon salt

Set 2-quart saucepan over high heat for 1 minute. Add oil and coat bottom of pan evenly. Add the next 3 ingredients, stir and cook, until brown. Set aside. Heat 3/4 cup of the coconut milk in 4-5 quart Dutch oven, over high heat. Cook until coconut milk separates, about 5 minutes, stirring frequently. Add the onion mixture, stir, add remaining ingredients, bring to boil. Reduce heat and simmer, until sauce thickens, about 45 minutes, stirring occasionally.

Peanut Sauce

- 1 14-ounce can coconut milk
- 1 cup peanut butter
- 1/2 tablespoon Red Curry Paste
- 1 tablespoon chile paste with bean oil (nam prig pao)
- 2 tablespoons sugar
- 1/4 teaspoon salt

In 2-quart saucepan, heat coconut milk over medium heat until boiling. Add red curry paste and chile paste, stir to blend. Bring to a boil, add the rest of ingredients, stir and cook, until sauce is thoroughly heated, about 3 minutes. Remove from heat and serve with sate.

Plum Sauce

- 3/4 cup water
- 1/2 cup plum sauce
- 1/2 tablespoon cornstarch
- 2 tablespoons sweet soy sauce
- 2 tablespoons brown sugar
- 1 tablespoon white vinegar

Combine all ingredients in 2-quart saucepan. Cook over medium heat until sauce thickens, about 5 minutes, stirring occasionally.

Thai Guacamole Dip

3 avocados
1 small onion, minced
1 small tomato, chopped
1 tablespoon ground fresh chile paste
1/2 teaspoon salt
1/4 teaspoon pepper
4 cloves garlic, minced
1/2 cup sour cream
1 tablespoon fresh lime juice
1 tablespoon Worcestershire sauce

6 lettuce leaves for garnish

Skin avocados and remove pits. Place in small bowl and mash with fork. Add remaining ingredients and mix well. Garnish with lettuce leaves. Allow to stand at room temperature for at least 30 minutes before serving. Serve with your favorite chips.

Tomato Hot Sauce

1 large tomato, roasted, peeled, chopped fine
4 fresh jalapeno chiles, roasted, peeled, and finely chopped
1 small onion, finely chopped
2 stems green onions, finely chopped (white and green parts)
1/4 cup chopped cilantro
3 cloves garlic, minced
1 teaspoon salt
2 tablespoons fresh lime juice

Combine all ingredients in blender, blend on medium speed until coarse ground. Cover and store in refrigerator. Serve as condiment with meats or vegetables of your choice.

Tamarind Sauce
(Nam Makarm)

1 8-ounce package wet, seedless tamarind, cut into small pieces
3 cups water

Combine tamarind and water in blender, blend until smooth. Keeps well in refrigerator for several weeks.

Note: -Tamarind Sauce can be substituted for vinegar, lime or lemon juice in some dishes. Some Thai grocery stores carry prepared Tamarind Sauce.

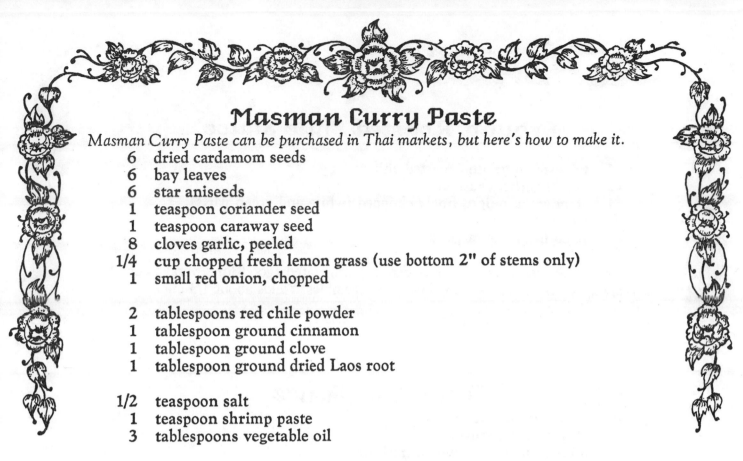

Masman Curry Paste

Masman Curry Paste can be purchased in Thai markets, but here's how to make it.

- 6 dried cardamom seeds
- 6 bay leaves
- 6 star aniseeds
- 1 teaspoon coriander seed
- 1 teaspoon caraway seed
- 8 cloves garlic, peeled
- 1/4 cup chopped fresh lemon grass (use bottom 2" of stems only)
- 1 small red onion, chopped

- 2 tablespoons red chile powder
- 1 tablespoon ground cinnamon
- 1 tablespoon ground clove
- 1 tablespoon ground dried Laos root

- 1/2 teaspoon salt
- 1 teaspoon shrimp paste
- 3 tablespoons vegetable oil

In a 1-quart saucepan, cook and stir first 8 spices together until brown, grind until smooth in food processor or blender, set aside. In mortar, combine next 4 ingredients, add spice mixture and pound to paste with pestle. Add salt and shrimp paste, pound until thoroughly mixed. Brown this mixture in oil, over low heat, for 2 minutes. Keeps well in refrigerator for several months.

Herbal Butter

- 8 ounces (1 cup) unsalted butter or margarine
- 1/4 cup grated shallots
- 1/4 cup grated onion
- 1/2 cup finely chopped parsley
- 5 cloves garlic, grated
- 1/2 teaspoon paprika
- 1/2 teaspoon white pepper
- 1/2 teaspoon tarragon
- 1/4 teaspoon ground coriander
- 4 cubes instant beef flavor bouillon, dissolved in 2 tablespoons of hot water

Keep butter or margarine at room temperature until soft. In medium bowl, combine all ingredients. Beat with hand mixer until creamy. Use to saute mushrooms, shrimp, etc.

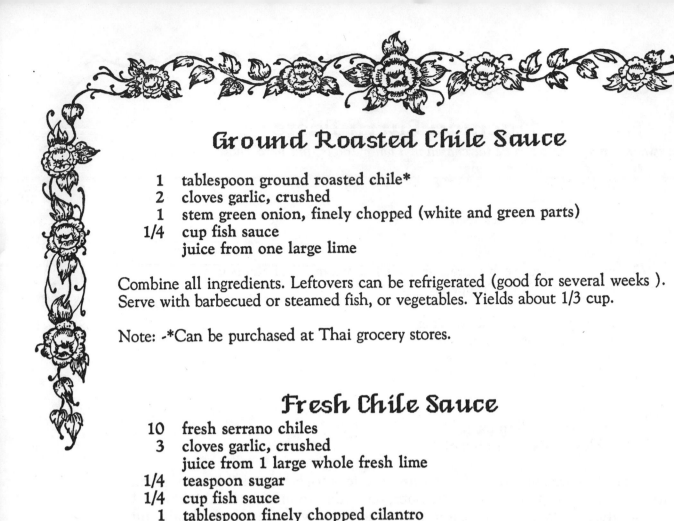

Ground Roasted Chile Sauce

1 tablespoon ground roasted chile*
2 cloves garlic, crushed
1 stem green onion, finely chopped (white and green parts)
1/4 cup fish sauce
    juice from one large lime

Combine all ingredients. Leftovers can be refrigerated (good for several weeks). Serve with barbecued or steamed fish, or vegetables. Yields about 1/3 cup.

Note: -*Can be purchased at Thai grocery stores.

Fresh Chile Sauce

10 fresh serrano chiles
3 cloves garlic, crushed
    juice from 1 large whole fresh lime
1/4 teaspoon sugar
1/4 cup fish sauce
1 tablespoon finely chopped cilantro

Combine all ingredients in blender, blend at medium speed, until coarse ground. Use right away or store in refrigerator (will keep up to one week). Serve as a dip for steamed or grilled seafood. Yields about 1/3 cup.

Tamarind Barbecue Sauce

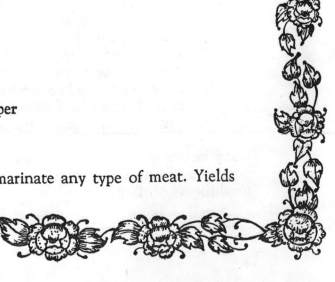

1/4 cup Tamarind Sauce (see Basics)
2 cups catsup
1/2 cup Maggi seasoning
1 tablespoon brown sugar
3 tablespoons oyster sauce
4 cloves garlic, minced
1 tablespoon paprika
2 tablespoons grated ginger powder
1/2 tablespoon coarse ground black pepper
1 small onion, chopped
1 tablespoon ground fresh chile paste

Combine all ingredients, mix well. Use to marinate any type of meat. Yields about 3 cups.

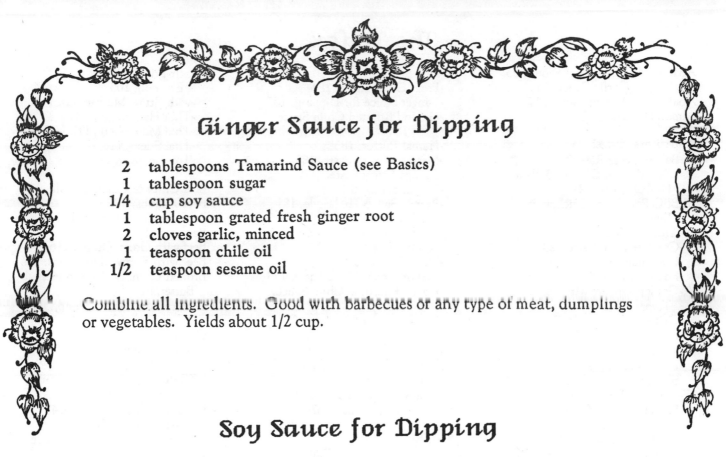

Ginger Sauce for Dipping

2 tablespoons Tamarind Sauce (see Basics)
1 tablespoon sugar
1/4 cup soy sauce
1 tablespoon grated fresh ginger root
2 cloves garlic, minced
1 teaspoon chile oil
1/2 teaspoon sesame oil

Combine all ingredients. Good with barbecues or any type of meat, dumplings or vegetables. Yields about 1/2 cup.

Soy Sauce for Dipping

4 fresh serrano chiles, minced
1/4 cup soy sauce
2 cloves garlic, minced
1 large shallot, minced
1 tablespoon fresh lime juice

Combine all ingredients. Good with barbecues or any type of meat, dumplings or vegetables. Yields about 1/2 cup.

Barbecue Sauce

1 quart catsup
1/2 cup soy sauce
1/4 cup oyster sauce
1 tablespoon onion powder
1 tablespoon garlic powder
1 tablespoon coarse ground black pepper
1 tablespoon ground ginger
1 teaspoon paprika
1 small onion, finely chopped
4 cloves garlic, crushed

Combine all ingredients. Now you are ready to marinate any type of meat. Yields about 5 cups.

The Index

The Index (Cont.)

The Index (Cont.)